University Professor

JOHN M. DORSEY

None of me can be bygone. . . .
I am *only. I* am *my life.*
All of my living is
now-living.

Books by John M. Dorsey, M.D.

The Foundations of Human Nature, 1935
Living Consciously: The Science of Self, with Walter H. Seegers, 1959
Illness or Allness: Conversations of a Psychiatrist, 1965
American Government: Conscious Self Sovereignty, 1969
Psychology of Emotion, 1971
Psychology of Language: A Local Habitation and a Name, 1971
Psychology of Political Science: With Special Consideration for the Political Acumen of Destutt de Tracy, 1973
Psychology of Ethics, 1974
An American Psychiatrist in Vienna, 1935–1937, and His Sigmund Freud, 1976
Selected Essays, 1976
The Psychic Nature of Physiology, 1977

Edited Volumes
The Jefferson-Dunglison Letters, 1960
The Growth of Self-Insight, 1962

University Professor
JOHN M. DORSEY

⇢⟫ ⟪⇠

by

John M. Dorsey, M.D.

University Professor Emeritus
Wayne State University

WAYNE STATE UNIVERSITY PRESS

Detroit, 1980

Grateful acknowledgment is made to the Center for Health Education
and to the John M. Dorsey Publishing Fund for assistance in
the publication of this volume.

Except where indicated, photographs were made by George R. Booth, Jr.,
producer and director of the Production Department,
Wayne State University Center for Instructional Technology.

Library of Congress Cataloging in Publication Data

Dorsey, John Morris, 1900–1978
  University professor John M. Dorsey.

  Includes index.
  1. Dorsey, John Morris, 1900–1978   2. Psy-
chiatrists—United States—Biography.   I.   Title.
RC339.52.D67A38   001.2′092′4   [B]   79-25046
  ISBN 0-8143-1645-X

Contents

Foreword
by Harlan L. Hagman   7

Preface   9

1   Introduction   17
2   Perspective   29
3   My Education   65
4   My Psychology   87
5   My Science   122
6   My Religion   142
7   My Health   171
8   Summary   187

Glossary   210

Appendix   217

Epilogue
by George E. Gullen, Jr., President Emeritus,
Wayne State University   267

Index   277

Illustrations
*Illustrations are grouped following pages 33, 91, 149, and
191.*

Publisher's Note

→>> <<←

University Professor Emeritus John M. Dorsey died August 6, 1978. He had completed and submitted the manuscript of this book to the Wayne State University Press, together with a group of photographs. The editor has arranged the photographs chronologically and has provided explanatory captions, where it seemed appropriate, to suggest the range of Dr. Dorsey's personal, professional, university, and community interests. This could not have been done without the assistance, here gratefully acknowledged, of Mrs. Mary Louise Carson Dorsey; Michael R. Sibille, assistant director, Information Services, University Relations; Dr. Walter H. Seegers, professor and chairman of the Department of Physiology; and the staff of the Wayne State University Archives.

The Foreword by Professor Harlan L. Hagman accompanied the manuscript when Dr. Dorsey submitted it for publication. The Epilogue is drawn from President Emeritus George E. Gullen, Jr.,'s remarks at the Wayne State University memorial service for Dr. Dorsey, August 23, 1978. President Gullen's permission to include it here is gratefully acknowledged.

Foreword

The designating of a distinguished professor as *University Professor,* or in better style *Professor of the University,* is not a new idea but it is still uncommon. What is usually intended is the creating of a professorship attached to the university as a whole and to no one department or other unit. It requires of its holder unusual capacity to range over many disciplines and fields of interest as well as the ability to meet on common ground with individuals of diverse intellectual persuasions and occupations.

The present age does not permit of the ideal of Renaissance Man but the University Professor may be expected to approach that ideal, given the limitation of having only a single life of learning and an exploding universe of knowledge and speculation. The University Professor ought to be fellow of all faculties, with understanding of numerous fields and greatly different scholarly investigations. Perhaps the center is necessarily in philosophy, the grounding of all learning however disparate the several disciplines may appear to be. Philosopher, poet, and scholarly observer combine in Emerson's *Man Thinking.* Such a man would seem to be the ideal University Professor.

But it is as a person that the University Professor comes into the special role expected of him. He, or she, needs to be an exceptional person, of broader intellectual gauge than most other persons, of greater philosophical insight, of unique capacity to command many disciplines, of more than ordinary depth of scholarship. In all this, for such a professor, the major resource must be the Self. The professor must have internal reserves in order to have unendingly something to profess.

7

As Wayne State University's first, and for the many years of his tenure its only, University Professor, Dr. John M. Dorsey was as near as anyone could be to the university's universal professor. He ranged comfortably from medicine and psychiatry to literature and the arts. He was exemplar of the many-faceted intellectual, author, lecturer, host to distinguished visitors, commentator, inspirer of other faculty, and good-humored observer of university life. His was a positive influence, leaving the University better for having him as its chosen Professor of the University.

In many ways, he charted his own course, choosing what he would do to meet the charge that then-President Clarence B. Hilberry gave him. The role of University Professor suited him, and his assignment as the first holder of the chair was a fortunate one. He was comfortable in it and happy in the work which he performed with distinction.

In accordance with his life philosophy, his account of his University Professorship years does not chronicle "past" events but rather records his conscious self-growth in the continuing present of those years. Dr. Dorsey's living of his University Professorship as constantly in the making has enriched the lives of colleagues, students, good friends, and all others who have come to know him.

Harlan L. Hagman

Preface

The following chapters reflect edification I have grown and made conscious for my intentional guiding of the wholeness that I call my life. They are the result of disciplined, responsible, and formative living of my consciously imagined allness. Each idea in them is an integral force of my organic being, ordered into the systematic identity that I name my self. In scientific terms, I have recorded an ontology of my existence as University Professor, wittingly describing my subjectivity *as if* it might be objectivity. However, in no way, except by using my imagination to fancy it, can I separate myself from whatever I may observe.

The seeming privation of subjectivity is ever the cost of apparent objectivity so-called. As a pseudoscientist I may try to make my theory of "objectivity" a more realistic existent than its prior subjectivity that engendered that theory. In scientific work, above all else, *existence* must not be taken for granted or otherwise denied its true force. My only possible authenticity must be personal. My ability to *imagine* myself to be "one of many" is of lifesaving value, hence it is essential for my health and welfare that I diligently cultivate such imagining as acknowledged imagining.

The concept of my so-called school, society, or whatever imagined collectivity, regularly depends upon my ignoring, overlooking, or otherwise disallowing the law of necessary succession obtaining in the history of every "organization." Thus I may tend to imagine an unverifiable founder whom I endow with the dominant wish to be an insightless leader and whom I then equip with insightless followers. Meanwhile, the only omnipresent fact is that I, alone, constitute the entirety of all of

9

these formulations. I may pay little or no attention to the enormous consequence of my illusional "objectivity." My practice of it tends to deprive the use of my senses of their value for revealing the functioning of my subjectivity. Then I may try to reduce my difficultly maintained personal practice of self-consciousness to easy generalizations attributable to an impersonal "school of existentialism." *Each of my insightless "collectivity" illusions becomes normative for my directing the conduct of my own life.* Little wonder if I become prey to depreciating my own wonderful nature, even to questioning my own existence or the existence of my own mind.

In the interest of my health, my well-ordered wholeness, I have disciplined my mind to renounce kindly my wishes to be an insightless follower or a leader of anyone but my own original conscious self. To this end my teaching has become understandable by me as self-education only. With my student I speak and write of myself to myself, featuring the truth that I can morally justify only this self-continent meaning of growth of learning. To illustrate, as a rule an author writes (as if) for an imaginary readership other than the author. I imagine that I write for one reader only, myself.

It is readily understandable that I, as a pupil, tend to live my teacher as I did my parent before my mind was strong enough to assume responsibility for being all that I could possibly mean by my parent. Therefore, instead of conscious self-identity, I might feel only a very deep "kinship" with the founder of my religion, science, philosophy, or whatever life-interest, whose own authentic life devotion may have been faithfully directed to appreciation for the wonderfulness, just divinity, of his very own completely original being.

Only my growing clearly *conscious self-helpfulness* can ever aid me to appreciate my wholeness-allness-oneness identity. My practice of this self-insight is the wellspring of my ideology idealizing my solipsistic or mystic nature. It is true of my solipsism as it is true of my selfishness itself: my problem cannot be that I am "too selfish," only that I am not sufficiently selfish about all of me (including my "you"). I alone must discover how I originate the consequence of honoring or dishonoring any of my whole nature. Thus my Søren Kierkegaard (1813–1855) saw his identity in his unity, declaring that his ethical life really chooses the whole of itself steadfastly. And my Ralph Waldo Emerson (1803–1882) observed nothing at last to be sacred but the integrity of his own mind. My sense of wonderful wholeness grows only from my fascination for every bit of it duly recognized as such.

I am my only "we" because all of the meaning that I live named "you," "us," "they," etc., exists only in the ontogenetic unity I name "myself." My understanding is attained by consciousness for my own unity acknowledged as such. All of my so-called worldly experience consists of meaningful growth of my individuality, another name for my indivisible life. Everyone either consciously or unconsciously is a specialist, a special one, a mystic or solipsist. Thus my every meaning for plurality, such as a collective or disjunctive of any kind, is really the same as any other meaning I create, namely, a manifestation of my own self-generating unity.

Only I, the very spirit or soul of me, can be found anywhere in my life. My Sir Thomas Browne (1605–1682) declared he preferred William Harvey's finding of the circulation of the blood to Columbus's discovery of America. My discovered circulation of my self only in the world of my creation provides me with my most luminous enlightenment. I find *there is no "cure" for living but its conscious justification revealed by the lamp of self-consciousness.* My every word is a synonym for *I*, but it seems easier "common sense" to write pages of futility traceable to pluralities of no possible responsibility.

How to discipline myself to honor the truth of my individuality, how to teach myself to use all of my mental power, including sensation and perception, in the spirit of the individuality that is necessarily mine, is of lifesaving health significance. Yet it can seem easiest for me to live as if some collective or other could be the consummate unit of mankind rather than the individual. How to maintain finest sensibility in identifying with myself, in actually feeling equal to my ever innovating constitution, is at once my philosophical realism and medical hygiene. It is in my activated self-consciousness and lull of any other functioning such as perception or passion, that I can best study the truth of the wonder of my being. *From my experience I know that I alone discover, when I find my proof in my own living of it.* I write nothing that I do not observe entirely in myself.

In my consciously solipsistic life orientation I do not in any way lose or depreciate my earlier opinions and precepts identifying me with my colleagues and teachers. Indeed I esteem my earlier stages of mental development all the more, knowing that they are the indispensable roots of my present and future educational growth. I do not call in question, but rather honor, the doctrines of Hippocrates, Galen, Harvey, Osler, or of any other physician ancient or modern.

I regularly exercise life-revering insights. Thus, biologically adequate veneration for my wholeness requires that I understand that I owe my ability to appreciate my present view to my appreciation for each one that preceded it, including its opposite. My consciousness for mental wholeness (health) cannot be the consequence of my repudiating *any* previous mental activity of mine as "faulty" or whatever. Rather, it results from my enlightening discovery that I owe my life itself to *whatever* I have already succeeded in living. As did many a scientific forebear for fear of the loss of his/her peace of mind, I would comfortably restrain publication of my "unpopular" idea were it not for my physicianary ideal warning me of the enormous health risk involved in self-repudiation.

My linguistic habit of entifying my "materialistic otherness," *at the cost of seeming to make that much of a non-entity of my ideal self,* is of the driving force of addiction. Therefore my awareness of living as being entirely awareness of my creating myself, is a spiritual insight that I resist growing as much as I can. Yet conscious self-possession is the only possible source of joyous appreciation for the unique dignity of individual life. An assumed meaning of sheer reality without life must be an arbitrary creation of life itself. My vital existence is all that is, or can be, real or meaningful for me in any sense. A strong sense of possession of total self-existence is the product only of disciplined conscious functioning of that specific life appreciation. I find such cosmic consciousness a perfectly natural process to the extent that I am willing to take the trouble to attain it. It makes my very own divinely-human greatness and glory my solemn truth to behold.

Essentially what I mean by religion is wonderful worship of godliness such as truth, piety, goodness, love, justice, helpfulness, wholeness, allness, joy, desirability, perfection. *Whatever* I live, my every possible experience, is a fact of my life that can be *scientifically demonstrated repeatably* to be perfectly true, good, just, helpful, and desirable in every respect.

I observe that the wonderfulness of my existence beggars all, including verbal, description. I cannot verbalize the meaningfulness of my life itself. A word, as all else, is only and all about itself and cannot consist of any other meaning. However, my every spoken or written word is a true individuation of my own individuality and, as such, is revealing of the nature of my wholeness. Nevertheless, the seeming objectification in wordage can be deceptive, so that I must freely acknowledge that I, alone, can know what I mean by my every word, regardless of popular parlance, dictionary consultation, or whatever futile effort to achieve a common language. Such "common" words can seem cheap, but they do achieve enormous worth for concealing myself from myself. Furthermore, it is just when my self-consciousness for my wholeness is clearest that I become aware of the extent to which my "words fail me" so that I cannot compose an articulate account of my mental condition.

For me the terms *individual, mystic,* and *solipsist* are synonymous. It is healthful to dispel the illusion that a mystic or solipsist is a rare occurrence. The fact is that there is no other kind of person. Every individual is entirely and only a unique one consisting of his/her individuality only. What is a rarity is an individual who is conscious for the singular truth of his whole individuality. Becoming aware of that stupendous truth is the awakening mystic or solipsistic experience that creates the *conscious* mystic.

The only criterion for awakening to the truth of my mystic nature is my realization that my every meaning for reality or unreality is my own mental experience, my own subjective ideality. I am my only certainty. Doubt is always my painful feeling that my faith is my wholeness is being jeopardized.

As a consciously mystic scientist I willingly grow my recognizable mind in the direction of creating its sensory experience in order to discover that much further personal unity (including harmony) in the sensory dimension of my wholeness-being. All that I can ever do is be; and all that I can ever consciously be is whatever I am willing to discover of me. My life consists of growing continuous self-unification.

By *mystic* I refer to more than occasional spells of subjectivity convincing me of my ideality at the time. I refer specifically to my repeatably, continuously validatable discovery of the vital truth of my absolute self-continence that makes me consciously whole. It is the biological adequacy of adhering to this law of my life that provides me with conscious self-helpfulness (including my pulling myself up by my own bootstraps) that nourishes my will to live. My life *creates* all of its being, the biological source of my joy of living.

In my field of psychic research I find that a *conscious* mystic is a rarity. He understands the necessity for his colleague's fierce resistance to going all the way in his acknowledgment of his whole individuality since he too had to struggle all of that way.

As an *unconscious* mystic I must discontinue the enlargement of my self-consciousness involved in conscious living of my others and, instead, rely upon my reasonings to account for them. Then I advance reasons instead of conscious self-

observations to support my time-honored source of security
in *seeming* accessibility of so-called otherness, externality, alien
control. Unable to observe the truth of my absolute self-
continence I cannot impute such mystical accomplishments to
my colleague.

My reader asks, "Please illustrate precisely what you mean
by your considering that you help yourself by recognizing that
your reasoning is of limited helpfulness, whereas your self-
consciousness is wholly helpful. It seems to me that my capacity for reasoning is compatible with my feeling that I can communicate with my fellowman, whereas my self-consciousness
makes myself the subject of my attention, thus ruling out communication. Not being a conscious mystic myself I have to
accept your word, or what seems to be your word, for your
statement that you cannot communicate. Does not this negation of communication itself constitute unconscious affirmation of your ability to converse?"

I conceive my you as imagining that you can communicate.
Certainly this is not the same as communication itself. I can
also imagine that I can communicate and I do not deny that I
can imagine it.

Again, my reader asks, "Not being a conscious mystic or
solipsist, I have to reason some explanation of your seeming to
be able to communicate even though you know that you are
not performing that act. In your respecting all of your self-
hood, as a conscious mystic must, it seems to me that you are
ruling me out of your mind. In fact I have some of the feeling
of being overlooked by you. I am more comfortable if you, as
a conscious mystic, allow yourself to use your reasoning as I
use mine, and I ask you not to bring your self-consciousness
into all of your living of your conversation that seems to me to
be with me."

As I live my you earnestly addressing yourself on this all-
important subject of the necessity for absolute self-continence,
I appreciate each observation that (my) you makes. Dispute,
argument, is based upon reasoning, never upon self-con-

sciousness. The plea, "Be reasonable," happens often; the declaration, "I am self-conscious," occurs rarely.

Without ceasing I try to write (or speak, read, and hear) with special purpose of acknowledging only my own self-identity in all of my linguistic functioning. Thus I can enjoy imagining my rare reader's authoring her/his Dorsey writings with the chief benefit of experiencing an author who feels responsibly aware that he can write only to, for, and of his own self. My health ideal is that of cultivating my conscious love of my life to include all of the meaning of my world that my mind creates.

1
Introduction

This little book met with but a small sale,
five hundred copies being sold only after
twelve years; yet it attracted the attention
and the warmest enthusiasm of a few persons.
Moncure Daniel Conway, on Emerson's Nature *(1836)*

After I assumed my post as Wayne's first University Professor my medical colleagues asked me to write a description of my concept of my new assignment. As best I can I renounce the indulgence of the illusion of stock writing. The following solipsistic statement sent to the society's president, William H. Kelly, M.D., appeared in the September, 1964, "Newsletter" of the Michigan Society of Neurology and Psychiatry, Michigan District Branch, American Psychiatric Association. It describes just how I was working my mind at the time and, therefore, I present it fully and freely:

The University Professorship plan was proposed to the members of Wayne State University faculty in President Clarence B. Hilberry's "Informal Notes" of March 9, 1960. Subsequently both the Council of Deans and the University Council endorsed the program April 5 and June 2, 1960, respectively. This new concept in higher education and the man selected by President Hilberry to accept the office, myself, were approved by Wayne State University's Board of Governors, December,

1960. In recommending the appointment President Hilberry said:

I believe this venture will pay enormous rewards and will be watched with keen interest across the nation.

A few other universities have experimented with this general concept of freeing individuals to work in the broad fields of concern to them. None, so far as I know, has named a man with responsibility to be and to represent the "generalist" for the whole academic community.

The University Professor is a man with the creative gift of knowledge, not in pieces but whole—as nearly whole as is possible in these days.

Perhaps none of Wayne's problems is more urgent or more difficult than the job of wisely controlling the constantly increasing emphasis on specialization. This specialization in universities is a direct response to the needs of our campus society. And it tends to produce not only students who become more and more narrow in their interests as they advance through the upper division and graduate work, but also professors who become increasingly high specialists.

I believe it is clearly both impossible and undesirable to try to reverse the trend in higher education. What is necessary at all times is to lay particular emphasis upon the opposite approach to human life and knowledge and to do so in a wide variety of new ways.

Upon taking office, I made two statements: "I am going to be spending my time for quite a while just educating myself," and, "At present all I can do is to consider it my office to appreciate the full importance of the complete individuality of everyone associated with Wayne State University." I cannot improve upon this job description right now, except to add that my day's work provides me with the finest imaginable opportunity for self-fulfillment.

Looking backward, I see my profession of psychiatry had ever required my extending the range and depth of my identifications, and thus prepared me for university-wide responsibilities. As director of the Children's Center and Child Guidance Division of the Children's Fund of Michigan, I worked up a most practical community-wide general health and welfare orientation. Every psychiatrist tends to educate himself broadly in his so-called humanities, as well as in his *equally humane* scientific way of life. I kept my pre-medic interests up with my medical development—particularly education, literature, aesthetics, epistemology, psychology, linguistics, history, religion and ethics, philosophy, foreign language, sociology, and most notably, "the gay science," poetry. Wayne State University being uniquely an urban educational development favored consistently my comprehending my greater community in my concept of my medical school office. Two campus-wide appointments seemed to top off my preparation for my new duties: the Leo M. Franklin Memorial Lectureship in Human Relations for 1960, and the University Social Committee.

My psychiatric teaching orientation ideally furthered my spreading my serviceableness. It consisted essentially of always presenting myself as being the patient as well as the physician. I defined my sanity not as the absence of insanities, but as my mind's conscious tolerance for, and control over, its insanities. I described my delimiting of my sense of personal identity, that is, my circumscription of my conscious mental functioning, as my specific source of every so-called mental disorder; and my extension of my *conscious* living as my every specific psychotherapeutic. I consider "subjectivity," "individuality," "reality," "truth," "meaning" and "allness," to be synonyms. I note "objectivity" can mean only: subjectivity which is denied the living process of existence. I observe that denial of subjectivity is the creation of the negation, "objectivity." My idealistic view of reality attributes true fullness of being only to subjectivity and thus tends to respect the morally free spiritual interests of man. On this ethical principle of reverence for individual human life, the disciple of every belief may stand. My only in-service educational project was also most elementary: research upon the individual's cultivation of his capacity for peacemaking self-sovereignty, through his gradually discovering *his* world to be his own.

On several occasions President Hilberry spoke with me of his cherished wish to establish the office of University Professor on the administrative level of the University in order to promote ongoing realization of the wholeness of university living. Sensitive to any evidence of the "splintering" effect occurring in his academic living, the president upholds the organic completeness of his beloved University. He would like to provide opportunity for each faculty member in one college to be able to see his identity in his university colleague from every other college. Not only science but every interest of man is a well-made language for describing its particular culture of meanings. Wayne's president wishes to resolve the problem of seeming alienation inherent in the necessity that the educator of every discipline build up a vocabulary specific for his particular interest.

As is true of the human body one may wisely conceive every part of the university economy as integrally vital for its every other part. However, as the poet says, it is "the most difficult of tasks to keep Heights which the soul is competent to gain." *Consciousness for this truth of my University's intact oneness is necessary for the due accrual of its benefits.* As his Wayne has grown in every dimension, President Hilberry has recognized the desirability of its reaping the enormous advantage of its duly heeded integration. Such arousal and continuation of ongoing consciousness for his University's oneness and wholeness is indispensable for the most careful and caring view of its educational potential.

To illustrate, on one end of the campus it is possible for the educator to live his educational discipline with limited regard for its *hygienic* force. Thus, he may overlook the important fact that education must be recognized as self-experience in order to be hygienic. On another end of the campus it is possible for the medical educator to be living his medical discipline with limited regard for its educational force. Every medical experience of a physician or a patient is essentially an educational experience and it is hygienic for each physician and patient to open his mind's eye to see every kind of medical experience thus as self-experience.

Education is potentially the most dangerous of all of the "professions" of man, for it is specifically through his way of living his process of learning that each person's appreciation for his life itself is decided. If he learns with the realization that his education is entirely his own personal development of his own self-knowledge, he upholds his due realization of the wonderful worth of his life, and prizes life accordingly. On the contrary, to the extent that he conceives his learning to be the acquisition of impersonal information, he practices a systematic impairment of his appreciation of his wholeness, suffers associated signs of self-disesteem, and misprizes the conscious self-helpfulness in self-insight.

When a student "goes to college," it is only too easy for him to displace upon his institution his proper sense of self-worth as the creator of his knowledge, and thereby lose access to his sense of his own personal greatness. He can overwhelm himself with temptations to learn "objective lessons," to acquire "external data," to try to get "out of himself," to "lose himself" in his studies, and so on and on. What he is not ready to live consciously as his own self-growth, he may be tempted to ascribe to "the world of phenomena."

He may or may not realize his giving birth to his being in two ways, not merely in the conventional sense of being born, but mind-formingly in his creating his personal meaning for *his* world of reality. His ego is the result of the latter nativity. His observing the real unity (sameness) underlying his mind's apparent plurality, is his hold of sanity. *Often he urgently needs help himself to see his real unity in his apparent diversity.* It is always vitalizing for him to realize that his great campus structures exist in him—not he in them. His Alma Mater can be wonderful only as it achieves wonderfulness from his spirited living of his various learning disciplines. Every person is great, but it is the rare one who has cultivated consciousness for the true extent of his greatness.

By every avenue available, I live openly my campus and off-campus presence. Yesterday, I spoke of my cherishing the comprehensiveness of my mind over radio. Tomorrow, I conduct a seminar consisting of earnest religious educators. Next day I prepare lists on self-helpfulness and arrange privileged faculty access to a rare private library. I am ever witnessing the allness and excellence of man, of every man of my world, in speeches, articles, "books," conversations, meetings, television and newspaper opportunities, official "communications" with campus and off-campus officials, and the like.

Through a five-year McGregor Fund grant I have been able to bring to Wayne individuals of demonstrated devotion to the principle of conscious self-knowledge. Each of these self-knowing ones meets informally with faculty members and students and usually offers a lecture open to a University audience, including interested community persons. This specially planned program has provided integrating experience for audiences representing widely diverging interests.

In summary, I am a generalist in my living of my whole academic community. A circumnavigator of my own being, I must renounce living as my fellowman if that entails a negation of myself. I am available for living as self-insightfully as I can in each college. My day is entirely my own,—a very full one consisting of privileged and freely structured work, such as special appointments, lectures, committee meetings, press conferences, University Press assignments, continuing McGregor Center research and other medical and civic duties. I have imagined a suitable emblem on my office to be a flag of Self-Sovereignty bearing both the University Seal and my motto: "The Individual is the Universal."

* * *

At this present writing I am unable to acknowledge how I aided myself with each of my colleagues as I did. One freely gave continuously of his fine helpfulness, Charles E. Feinberg, famous bibliophile and friend of many an individual personally unknown to me that I wanted to bring to the campus. I feel sure that access to the literary treasures at the beautiful home of Charles and Lenore Feinberg added rare satisfaction to the visit of each of my guests, quite as it did to similar hospitality extended by Charles to each student and faculty member as a function of my University Professorship.

Early in the development of this unique office I conceived the plan of forming an ideal organization consisting of so-designated professors of universities. I felt that very much understanding of the cognitive process and of conscious self-sovereignty might be derived from examining the unique actuality of each university professor's being able to practice his privileged insight, while creating his organizational experience. Thus he might observe and record that all of his organization really belonged to him, owing all of its activity to his very own creating of it; that each so-called member must grow nothing but his own identity in all of his so-called social experience, and so on.

My own living of myself as a circulating medium cultivating identity in each college of my university has been performed under as many shapes as I have been able to devise methods of working my solipsistic nature. Inured to a kind of chameleonic and adventurous mentality I thrived upon what amount of soul nourishment seemed my portion. My ever practical Emerson helped,

> The hero is not fed on sweets,
> Daily his own heart he eats.

Daily, hourly, seeking my own level by ever realizing that I am never absent from, always present in, whatever meaning my mind enlivens, enlarges my perception of the boundless resources of a consciously living soul.

John Henry Newman (1801–1890) recorded his classic statement, *Idea of a University*, describing knowledge as being its own end, its purpose being to enter into the making of the mind of the student.

In a speech delivered before the Detroit Economic Club, May 12, 1947, eminent educator Robert Maynard Hutchins (1899–1977) stated that Americans do not take education very seriously, "And, in the past there has been no particular reason why they should," in view of reduced fear of hostility. He went on to stress the immediate need for education presently as most urgent and effective prevention against atomic warfare: "What education can do, and about all it can do, is to produce a trained mind. . . . Now, getting a trained mind is hard work. As Aristotle remarked, 'Learning is accompanied by pain.' . . . The fact is that the best practical education is the most theoretical one. . . . A boy may be a brilliant mathematician, or a musician . . . but I never knew of a child . . . who had much to say about the ends of human life, the purpose of organized society, and the means of reconciling freedom and order."

William Torrey Harris (1935–1909), most insightful United States Commissioner of Education for sixteen years, in "What the Universities can do for the People" stated plainly, "The most practical of all instruction is that which finds the unity of all branches of knowledge, and teaches their human application. Ethics is certainly the most practical of all branches of human learning."[1]

Of the many conscious life orientations that I have purposefully cultivated, my solipsistic stand is unquestionably the most objectionable one of all. That important fact is freely acknowledged. Of course it must be most unpopular, denounced, and defamed, since it discovers the most personal resistances. Its only defense against reproach is to remain concealed. My democracy itself has been described as the most intolerable of all governments with but this single exception, namely every other kind of government. And so it is with my truth of conscious self-continence. It is the whole truth and nothing but the truth about the inviolable integrity of my indi-

---

[1] Kurt F. Leidecker, *Yankee Teacher: The Life of William Torrey Harris* (New York: The Philosophical Library, 1946), p. 555.

vidual mind. But, since the solipsist arduously includes all that he can mean by society, government, and every other abstraction of collectivity in his own mind (and renounces the illusion that he is merely one of the many), he necessarily forfeits every claim to popularity and rather expects to encounter resistance in his well-meaning fellowman who has not yet worked up full responsibility for being all of his self.

I actually wrote the idea of uniting forces to several of my fellow university professors of other great academic centers, there being a greatly limited number of such colleagues at the time. The response and lack of response were not encouraging. I am glad to note some gradual increase in number of this kind of university office. The educational service thus provided is potentially mighty. I would like to see established for every college at least one university professor responsible for working up within and outside his college growing appreciation for the beneficial *wholeness* of educational self-development. Dean Harlan L. Hagman favored this idea, too.

A most satisfying recent event has been the establishment in 1976 of the Wayne State University first Clarence B. Hilberry University Professorship, including the excellent choice of Executive Vice President and Treasurer Edward L. Cushman for this important chair. Here and now is borne fruit of Dr. Hilberry's ideal, a worthy educational expansion, an enlivening university self-growth.

Either to revere or to reject life honoring self-insight needs a mind boldly consecrated to self-responsibility. Discipline with self-consciousness is my mind's attainment of salvation. Believe what I will, it is first necessary for me to believe in my own life, the valid and verifiable source of all of my understanding. I am my life. I am the meaning of the history of my growth. *Whole-life appreciation for one's own living is the moral law governing the just conduct of life.* To dare to pioneer my vital meaning *consciously* to its perfect freedom of functioning constantly tests the growth of my moral heroism. I deem conscious self-insight to be the most fitting apparatus for all scientific research. A man is either the pilot or prisoner of the way he grows to use his mental power, enjoying the adventure of being all of his self, or suffering the helpful elephantiasis from accretions of so-called otherness warning him of his self-neglect.

Revealing of the nature of my own moral courage (including cowardice) during my University Professorship epoch, I have included a partial list of names and a few pictures of consciously insightful ones I brought to the Wayne campus.[2] For the record I wish to state clearly my purpose in providing visiting speakers, as furthering my University Professorship program devoted to promoting conscious self-education. Certainly it is not that of simply continuing my traditional illusion of a knowing educator's "imparting" his knowledge or understanding to an unknowing student or colleague. I am able to renounce lovingly this helpful illusion upon which my so-called formal education not only began but continues helpfully to this day as a mostly unrecognized kind of diluted autohypnosis. The realistic meaning of speaking and listening is illustrated by the studious one who practices it at home or at school as his way of making sure he knows his lesson. I chose each speaker for the extent of his ability to honor the wholeness and allness of his own absolute individuality; to soliloquize so that anyone present might then possibly discover how and why he, the would-be listener, must feel and voice his life discontent just to the degree that he presently repudiates any of his mental content as being his own.

Because of their vital meaning for my rapidly developing interest in the office of the University Professor, I include in the Appendix essential contents of letters of President Hilberry to Mr. William J. Norton, president of McGregor Fund, and of mine to President Hilberry and to Harlan L. Hagman, dean of administration.

Throughout my writing I like to find myself observing unity in my personalistic and absolutistic perspective; desirability of

[2]See Appendix.

renouncing customary and conventional aims to favor a cultivation of consciously spiritual ideals; love of life itself besides of the possessions it creates for me; consciousness for my wholeness rather than dedication to my mere intellectualism; growth of new creation, beyond seeming appropriation of ready-made experience; appreciation for all unpleasure as inhibited pleasure; nothing but my own identity in whatever I experience.

To be conscious for my history is to be freed from any authority seeming to be other than my own will. Warner Fite (1867–1955), Princeton University professor, asks as he answers the vital truth, "For what, for the most part, is our boasted historical method but the reduction of spiritual movement to time-series of events?" Historian Carl Becker (1873–1945) self-continently asserted, "Every Man His Own Historian." As in my other writings, this book has served as a kind of integrative connective tissue for my organic mind. I have tried to approximate the description of the intelligent author who encloses the most of reality in the least possible compass (Gottfried Wilhelm Leibniz, 1646–1716).

The accompanying biographical statement of my views and ventures as University Professor is all and only about itself; hence whatever boldness, native childishness, and mere mindedness it may claim. It does not knowingly represent any intention to try to prove or disprove anything at all, for I recognize that whatever is must be its own and only proof. On the other hand, it does not even question the equal value of every other definition of proof. All of my mind is equally life-worthy, equally reverend.

It does amount to a self-helpful, diaristic elaboration of what I call the self principle, or soul principle, which affirms ownness, absolute self-possession, and self-continence to be the indispensable essence of whatever exists in my living experience. I am my own whatever I am. I cannot transcend the limit of my life.

As is my speaking, so my writing is purposefully autodidactic, the top form of educational force that exists for me. My every word, read or heard, can be only an extemporaneous signet of my life's meaning. As a position statement it is as decisive, searching, and otherwise considerate, especially of its collegial reader, as I can make it at present. Its logic is the product of the growth of my self-consciousness, rather than reasoning, and therefore often seems absent. It does approximate my free associating to myself about the discharge of my moral duty to myself, helping me to draw a deeper breath, as it were, of the fresh world of my innovative being. Thus maintaining production from my unconscious vitality yields enthusiastic energy to "keep going." The practice of conscious self-functioning is itself the well-spring of hygienic education.

2

Perspective

What happens to a part of the whole is, in clear-cut cases,
determined by the laws of the inner structure of its whole.
Max Wertheimer (1880–1943), Gestalt theorist

President Hilberry's fulfillment of his magnificent lifework
(January 11, 1966) left a wide opening most difficult to heal
without scarring. As did his intrepid predecessor, President
David D. Henry, he distinguished clamor or glamour from
responsible self-counsel. He had arranged for me to secure
whatever academic cooperation I might need through Winfred A. Harbison, vice president for academic administration
who, in turn, relegated this indispensable resource to Harlan
L. Hagman, dean of administration. These provisions resulted
in greatest advantage to me for furthering the concept of
University Professor as ably defined by President Hilberry.

The temporal successor to Dr. Hilberry's executive leader-
ship must be another paragon of independence. Even though,
as Virgil put it, not all of us can do all things, to vigorous
President William R. Keast must go immense credit for con-
fronting with head erect the sea of troubles of his great urban
university, as a unique learning opportunity he would not
choose to miss.

Briefly stated, during Dr. Keast's incumbency (1965–1971)
it soon appeared clear that, although the University Professorship originally was not his own idea, he generously allowed it

to exist alongside the trend of his many immediate academic interests. I found him gracious personally, indicating his understanding of the nature of my commission. As did President Hilberry, he left to Vice President Harbison and Dean of Administration Hagman the administrative collaboration for the conduct of my office.

June 30, 1971, diligent Dr. Keast relinquished his university duties to his most able associates originally of his own choosing. From each one, President George E. Gullen, Jr., and Executive Vice-President Edward L. Cushman, continuing into my active status as University Professor Emeritus, beginning in 1971, I have experienced insightful understanding, as well as ideal and correspondingly spirited collaboration of the most desirable kind. Each was aroused to his only life in his self, enjoying active affirmation of intact self-wholeness. I have benefited from such self support for my campus-wide academic experience that would frequently test my ability to discern Universal Man only in individual man, Divinity only in Dick and Dora, my own intuition in all of my mentality.

When President Hilberry renewed his proposal in 1960 that I consider "coming up to the main campus to practice my living self consciously" as University Professor, my main reluctance to seize this most attractive offer continued to be my feeling of obligation to further my privileged opportunity to represent the nourishing and healing power of conscious self-helpfulness with my fellow medic, graduate as well as undergraduate. With the indispensable support of my wife, Mary Louise Carson Dorsey, I finally accepted the challenging and rewarding new university development with the understanding that it would include my devotion to my medical student. This it did to a considerable extent. Arthur Neef, dean of the Law School (also vice-president and provost of the university), was especially helpful in setting up my new official situation.

During those stressful years I helped myself immeasurably by the rare philanthropic understanding of (my) each McGregor Fund trustee.[1] How rarely "rare" it is to be able to honor the absolute necessity for complete self-responsibility in the conduct of life that is always *individual* life! Only the individual can be unethical or ethical, ignorant or self-knowing, ungoverned or self-disciplined, "reformed" or further formed. My weekly visiting with William J. Norton and Douglas Dow continued to serve me well. Cleveland Thurber proved to be a steady friend as ever.

Each trustee of McGregor Center, the Hospital for Health Education and Rehabilitation, continued to function as trustee of the Center for Health Education; the issue of the hospital itself, devoted to furthering my work of conscious self-growth for conscious life-appreciation, was now extended to the whole university.[2] My regular monthly sessions and in-between meetings with individual trustees are systematically intended to be conscious self-elucidating opportunities. My weekly visits with Dr. Walter H. Seegers, professor and chairman of physiology, methodically feature the indispensable benefit of conscious self-discovery.

This mind-consciousness is of special importance for the student. As Benjamin Franklin wrote his brother John, a man cannot be said to be fully born until he be dead. Living is being born anew. All of my behavior is traceable to my growing it. Thus all of my understanding is intuitive. Intuition is constant, continuous, as mental life. However, intuition that is consciously recognized as such does not seem to be constant, and hence the benefit derivable from experiencing a consciously whole person, a poem seeming to be instinct with its poet's intuition, a book reflecting its author's conscious self-appreciation. Appearance or traditional opinion to the contrary, nothing but mind can act on mind. I must metabolize all of my so-called physical or mental pabulum before it can become my nourishment.

I cannot revere too much the truth of my innateness. My

[1]See Appendix.
[2]See Appendix.

self never acquires, but creates all that it can originate. Everyone is great. Consciously honored self-greatness is necessary for the direct spirited perception of truth. My every theory of self-experience features the distinction: "Is it just so, or is it consciously just so." Consciousness acknowledges the necessary psychic self-identity in all meaning. Along with it goes a conscious subjectivity which honors the intact organic unity of the individual. It is my powerful habit of taking myself for granted, hardened by exercise, that vies with my need to develop biologically adequate appreciation for my life itself.

Obviously I could not expect my academic colleague to have worked up his self-insight just as I did. Especially my necessity to see naught but my own identity in my unconsciousness-ridden psychiatric patient required my developing extraordinary mind awareness. My theory of knowing then and now consists of being, being myself of course, and observing accurately what I find that I am. I cannot appropriate whatever I am not. All of my help or hindrance involves my own being only. Seeing my fellowman in need is to feel that much of my self in need. *Only the ideal can be practical.* Such is the spirited truth, the heroic necessity, in consciously united individuality.

While remaining with complete appreciation for every other systematized or unsystematized academic method of self help, I wished nothing to interfere with my concentrating upon my growing health ideal, my luminous moral discovery. In order to avoid health trouble, I must willingly and wittingly *teach myself:* 1) the wonderful health power that is ever already mine and 2) the necessity to grow my hygienic constitution according to the law of identity implicit in my unique living of my nature only. This self-growth ideal is the same for attaining my religious, scientific, and civic reaches. My arduous life discipline, i.e., practice of consciousness as being always and only *self* consciousness, my honoring conscious self-education as being the absolute truth of all education, is indispensable for my developing recuperative clarity about the inviolable wholeness of my nature.

Above all, it is my vocation lovingly to renounce appearances of extraneity and to observe and heed the natural history of my growing mind. All seeming alien energy that I can observe is really integral meaning of my mind connate with all other meaning of my life. When I see the lifesaving consequence in studying my consciousness as much as I see that worth in studying the air I breathe, I shall be able to consider myself a liberated scientist.

My senses properly report my being just *as if* it is not inside me at all, but rather something or someone "outside" me. Thus they seem capable of withdrawing my attention from my ever ideal self. "Properly" because in my early mental development, which seemed to repeat the mental powers of my animal and plant fellow creations, I could not assume responsibility for being all of my own experience. I soon grew the habit of believing such *as if* reporting of my senses. Renouncing this habit is most trying, hence seldom considered as a biological requirement for attaining conscious self-continence, the *summun bonum* of human life.

I can care duly for my life merely to the extent of my cultivating my realization that it constitutes my any and every experience, meaning, interest. My life's indescribable greatness necessitates that making self-consciousness be my choice life vocation, if I would raise my full worth to just appreciation.

I must revere the absolute identity in *any* of my becoming-conscious with my becoming-conscious-of-myself, if I would grow up judiciously crediting my individuality with its ever functioning wholeness, allness, integrity, truthfulness, —its perfect helpfulness of every kind and degree. By overlooking the necessary perfection of whatever exists, I relax the awesome appreciation for my conduct of my life and resort to so-called value judgments for deciding the worth of my living (moral relativism).[3]

---

[3]See my *Psychology of Ethics* (Detroit: Center for Health Education, 1974), pp. 139–63.

*Dr. Dorsey's work with the Children's Fund of Michigan was the begin-
ning of a long association with William J. Norton, executive vice-
president of the fund from 1929 until 1954. A trustee of the McGregor
Fund from 1925 to 1968, Norton served as its president from 1955
until 1968, when he became chairman of the board. (For Dr. Dorsey's
personal account see the Appendix to this volume, "Teaching, Training
and Research, 1938–1961.")*

Dr. Dorsey administers the Declaration of Geneva at Detroit Receiving Hospital, 1961, to Wayne State University senior medical student Sylvester Gilbert, Jr., unable to attend commencement exercises. Dean Gordon H. Scott, Wayne State University School of Medicine, stands at Dr. Dorsey's right.

Dr. Dorsey and Dean Broadus N. Butler, Wayne State University, invest Vice-President of the United States Lyndon Baines Johnson with the L.L.D. degree at the Honors Convocation, January 6, 1963, celebrating the centennial of the Emancipation Proclamation. President Clarence B. Hilberry of Wayne State University holds the citation.

Harlan L. Hagman (left), dean of administration, Wayne State University, and Dr. Dorsey talk with Mark Van Doren and examine his writings during Miles Modern Poetry Week, April 29, 1963.

Poet Mark Van Doren with William D. Snodgrass, professor of English at Wayne State University, engaged in conversation during Miles Modern Poetry Week, April 29, 1963.

Archibald MacLeish, poet, lectured at Wayne State University under the auspices of the University Professor, October 24, 1963. Photo by Tom Venaleck, Detroit Free Press.

Author and editor Louis Untermeyer presents Dr. Dorsey with a copy of his collected poems, Long Feud, on the occasion of his lecture, "The Writing and Reading of Poetry," February 27, 1964.

Four associates of Dr. Dorsey in Detroit's Prismatic Club are (left to right) John J. Danhof, James S. Holden, Clarence B. Hilberry, and Ralph J. Burton. Dr. Dorsey had lectured to the club April 25, 1964, on "Shakespeare, the Poet." Photo courtesy of the Prismatic Club of Detroit.

Dr. Dorsey greeted an old acquaintance when Marquis Childs, veteran Washington correspondent, public affairs columnist, and author visited Wayne State University to be main speaker at its Sixteenth Annual Journalism Day, October 16, 1964. They were classmates at the University of Iowa in the 1920s.

United States Senator Frank Church of Idaho is greeted by Dr. Dorsey. The senator's address to the International Relations Club of Wayne State University, February 22, 1965, was sponsored by the Department of Political Science and the University Professor.

Novelist Isaac Bashevis Singer (left) talks with Dr. Max Kapustin, director of B'nai B'rith Hillel Foundation at Wayne State University. Singer's lecture, February 23, 1965, "The Kabbalah and the Modern Mind," was sponsored by the foundation and the University Professor.

Poet Wilbert Snow, pictured here with his son Gregory, presents a volume of his Collected Poems to Dr. Dorsey, April 2, 1955, at a reading-lecture sponsored by the University Professor. Snow visited Wayne State University on several occasions, perhaps most notably as a Franklin Memorial lecturer in 1960. His "Individuality in the Work of Ralph Waldo Emerson" appears in The Growth of Self-Insight *(1962), edited by Dr. Dorsey, holder of the Franklin Memorial Chair in Human Relations, 1959–1960.*

Professor Ross Stagner (left), chairman of the Psychology Department, Wayne State University, talks with Dr. Dorsey and Dr. Lee Edward Travis, dean of graduate psychology at Fuller Theological Seminary, on the occasion of Dr. Travis' lecture, June 25, 1965, sponsored by the University Professor.

Robert St. John, author and foreign correspondent, shows a copy of his latest book, Roll Jordan Roll, to Dr. Dorsey on the occasion of his lecture, September 30, 1965, sponsored by the University Professor.

John Ciardi, poetry editor of the Saturday Review, discusses one of his own poems with Dr. Dorsey. His lecture, "Poetry Is for People," March 11, 1966, was sponsored by the University Professor, the Detroit Association of Phi Beta Kappa, and the Friends of the Detroit Public Library.

Dr. Harold A. Basilius, director of the Wayne State University Press, is awarded honorary membership in Phi Beta Kappa, December, 1966, for his many contributions to its scholarship goals. Presenting the key is Victor A. Rapport, dean for international studies at Wayne State University and former president of Wayne's Phi Beta Kappa chapter. Looking on are Liberal Arts Dean Martin Stearns, chapter president, and Professor Thelma G. James, member of the honorary award committee. Dr. Dorsey served on the Wayne State University Press Editorial Board during Dr. Basilius' tenure as director.

The deepest need of humanity must be the deepest need of every human being. I find that depth of desire in my fervent wish to be justifiable to my self. In operant practice my self-responsibility, made possible by my self-acknowledgment, achieves for me that omnific life-satisfaction of consciously experiencing my innate goodness. To the feeling of loss of this virtue I trace all doubt, misgiving, fear, anxiety, guilt, shame, and similar symptoms of impeded love of life, my life.

All of the meaning of my life occurs as an already accomplished event, a mental position implying the outcome of psychic growth. I can observe the finished product, but I can only speculate as to its previous being. The study of the natural history of my growing mind can contribute richly to my cherishable appreciation for my marvelous nature. The fact that I cannot in any way teach, train, discipline, or otherwise communicate any of these precious facts of wonderful existence to another soul frustrated me until I finally grew the insight to realize what an indescribable loss such a successful invasion of another individual would necessarily entail, namely, having one person do some of another person's living for him. My highest educational ideal is to live so that my student may observe his (her) teacher who understands that his only possible learning must be entirely self-grown by him and of him. All studying must be a reading of my own thoughts which I have not yet acknowledged as such. Any crowd or mob may terrify me and paralyze my will if I cannot recognize it as naught but mental content of my own creating.

To become wise to the intact totality of my being, authorizing the greatest growth of my life appreciation, I must consistently apply my devotion to recognizing my self-identity *only* in any and all of my living. All of *my* so-called materiality is nothing but my applied subjectivity. Ralph Waldo Emerson saw his life distinctly, "Every material organization exists to a moral end, which makes the reason of its existence."[4] So far as

[4]See *The Massachusetts Quarterly Review*, no. 1, December, 1847.

I know that I am whatever I mind, I can be consciously free. By neglecting this fundamental exercise of biologically wholesome self-esteem, I force my growing mind to substitute the hardy truth of its augmenting integrity with the strengthening illusion that it (my mind) can consist of varying degrees of worth in conflict with each other. Therefore I must acknowledge so-called loathsome, shameful, disgusting, dreadful, awesome, or whatever unpleasing or pleasing self-experience as wholly, helpfully, and desirably my own in order to be true to my natural growth, just as my Emerson of strongest sanity did,

> Forging through swart arms of Offense,
> The silver seat of Innocence.

My continuous experience with university living for almost sixty years may justify my need to describe my concept of my university growth unless, as my light-hearted skeptic may object, I have merely lived one year of it sixty times.

To begin with, I have to honor the truth that there must be as many universities to describe as there are students, educators, and all other individuals attending them. Furthermore I honor my fellowman's description of his university as I do my own. This adequately generous concession spares me no end of trouble. What I name my university has all of its meaning only about me. Its only real "place" is within my mind although, of course, I can imagine (my) its independent existence in itself, quite as I exist entirely in myself. My motivation for reporting that self-understanding in this writing is to record how I have helped myself by growing the insight to appreciate the wonderfulness of my life by proceeding from viewing my self as one student almost indistinguishable in a great institution of learning to augment my view of my self as one student creating in and of his own marvelous mind all that he can possibly mean by university.

My unexpected discovery that nothing can happen in my

life unless and until all of the truth necessary to make it happen is present resolved completely all of the confusion I created for myself by arbitrarily dividing my knowledge into two categories, sacred and secular. This dissociation had substituted my awareness of my mental integrity with the appearance of mental duplicity. By recognizing in the scientific law of sufficient reason a restatement of the ethical law implicit in the justice of truth, I enjoyed a mighty access of unity that has conferred its economic efficacy ever since. No longer need I keep my morality and devotion to my science in separate mental compartments. No longer might I repress my morality on the basis of its being unscientific. Rather must I extend my conscious moral obligation to include all of my living—physiological, biochemical, environmental, or whatever.

As I grew further self-understanding to reveal my every duality (good-bad, right-wrong, God-devil, just-unjust, etc.) as my convenient device for solving my current inability to observe ever prevailing unity, my realization of the health importance of revering the truth of oneness or the oneness of truth became strong, strong enough to teach me to love devotion to it and to fear neglecting it on any count.

Once this life orientation of my perfect wholeness became mine, my next self-felt necessity was to do all possible to see to it that *my* fellowman might find opportunity to grow similar self-helpfulness as his very own. How he might plant the seeds of conscious self-reliance in his own self-educational living, is already the issue of first priority in the mental development of my every fellow student by necessity. However, how he is to make this lifesaving educational principle *his keenly conscious one,* remains to him to be worked out.

To this *acknowledged* ideal, of understanding learning as each student's knowledgeable living only, I have addressed my educational force as University Professor. My method of operation has been to practice conscious self-continence to the best of my ability. Strengthening my mind to be able to sense the same identity of perfection in all of my life's meaning has proved to be an enormous economy. Renunciation of helpful pejorative or meliorative (each "faultfinding") value judgment has enhanced my fact-finding (perfection-finding) propensity correspondingly. My demand of the consequence of ideal "quality" education is that it be biologically adequate, creating self meaning that is completely worth living. *Whatever* happens or can happen, is always as helpful then as it can be, and certainly is therefore best lived with that realistic appreciation.

The free and complete function of the fully developed mind is that of being able to observe, consider soberly, and justly reconcile whatever it experiences for what that living of itself may mean in terms of the best interests of self-wholeness. For purpose of self-preservation it is advantageous for me to be able to discipline my mind gradually to conscious self-control so that I may grow the mental strength, i.e., amount of conscious self-identity, to distinctify my every experience, however distressing, as really being subject to me as I identify my whole self, rather than as my seemingly being subject to it.

To be consciously self-possessed consistently requires my recognizing not only that my imagined fellowman (in whose real existence I have complete faith) cannot oppose any idea or opinion of mine but also that any one idea or opinion of mine cannot even oppose any other, either of my fellowman's or of my acknowledgeable own. Hence I may consider my need to defend any of my own ideas implies that I do not respect its capability to enforce its own worth and importance. Whatever is, is all that can prove or vindicate itself.

Dispute implies that neither disputant can understand that each one cannot in any way have meaning for the other; that each one can only present his views about himself and to himself. Only the truth about each debater can *appear* to "out." Really all truth is entirely and wholly *indwelling*, being all about itself and *in* itself. To be consciously self-continent, as an inviolably whole individual, I cannot but observe the impossibility of my influencing, or being influenced by, another inviolably whole individual.

When I first grew this mind-freeing degree of acknowledge-able self-consciousness I experienced it as a display of power which, before that generation of conscious self-love happened, would have had to seem miraculous. My life satisfaction in my developing the realization that any and all of my rejection, repudiation, denial, negation, or any kind or degree of resis-tance, merely indicates my mind's present limitation in honor-ing some of my own justifiable existence, is an access of joy of living that is indescribable. What a glorious freedom: to be able to renounce lovingly my every need to condemn any of my living ever, past, present, or yet to be, since it is always necessarily my own acknowledgeable or unacknowledgeable goodness, capable of demonstration only as goodness.

I can imagine my reader, who is unrelieved by his idea that he has no choice other than to author whatever he reads, saying to himself, "All of that 'I can do no wrong because I am perfect' leaves me cold. At best I can only say, 'It is too good to be true.' " Yet, study of the facts involved, repeatably and without exception, reveals that nothing can happen until suffi-cient truth is present to make it happen. And that evidence is too true not to be good. However, even this life affirmation is the outgrowth of the life denial preceding it. Each new mental experience must first undergo the rigor of rejection before it can find lovable room for itself in my mind that constantly tends to preserve its *status quo.*

My colleague wonders how his Dorsey can experience what appears to be passionate or deadly opposition with complete calm, only because my good fellowman cannot yet recognize that each mind can and must only give expression to the way it has thus far experienced its own development. To be able to formulate what I consider to be a correct diagnosis is always accompanied by a feeling of relief, as in the solving of a puzzle, and also my patient may experience some satisfaction through observing his doctor's subsequent contentment.

My colleague too may help himself by diagnosing his Dorsey as unorthodox, mystic, unconventional, ingrown, pantheistic, or whatever. And to such, similar, or any, appellation (which, by the way, becomes wholly created by me in my growing my hearing or seeing it) I must invest kind self-identity, enabled by my already having grown the self-insights that I am my dislikes precisely as I am my likes, and that my liking or disliking is all and only about itself. I love my mind too well to be upset by, or otherwise reject, names petrifying self-unkindness. It is such desirable self-understanding that enables me to entertain any so-called bad name as being a repressed good name.

Of course, this self-understanding is the outgrowth of all of the limited self-understanding preceding it which also continues to function ably in my being. Hence I can appreciate how my colleague may need to help himself temporarily by giving his very own Dorsey an unpleasant name, and yet be unaware of hurting himself thereby. Living my fellow creature wittingly as myself, whether hard-favored or no, I discipline my diagnostic power to begin and end with one truth. Thus my initial and final diagnoses assert: It is I. With the practical sensitiveness that this conscious self-orientation provides, I can conduct my life generally, as well as professionally, with the greatest help and least trouble to myself, including necessarily my fellow being. Experience teaches me consistently that it is unsafe to go without laboring the point that this conscious growth of self-contained individuality has all of its roots in the (equally helpful and desirable) unconscious individuality preceding and accompanying it.

My habit of mind had been to construct all of my notions of materiality out of the negations of my spirit or ideality. I had been prone to use my illusion of materiality as the object of my belief in reality, thereby neglecting the truth that *of necessity* all that I can mean by the term "spiritual" is the subject of my only possible conscious reality. I secured faith in my illusional materiality from being unfaithful to my spirituality.

Anew, once the life orientation of my fidelity to my perfect wholeness became mine, my next self-felt necessity was to do all possible to see to it that *my* fellowman might possibly find opportunity to grow similarly revealing self-helpfulness as his very own.[5]

A most promising characteristic of my contemporary schoolman is his revival of interest in a kind of education with which I can help myself to learn how to behave myself in a way that need not interfere with my fellowman's similarly behaving. Surely such self-responsibility must enter into wholesome learning.

No doubt there would be so-called universal agreement that *all* public school work is intended to promote, or at least not prevent, moral rather than immoral education. Present evidence witnessing the sanity of this aspect of the work is gradually increasing. Much is already made of school spirit, and some specifically of self-spirit.

There is a distinct place for featuring the basic ethical character of any and all education, in every training course for teachership. However, I record the following supreme conviction with experienced appreciation for the difficulty involved in my own cultivation of it. Wholesome awareness for the necessity that every teacher or pupil is always his one and only subject requires self-discipline. Ignoring or rejecting this responsibility is unhealthy. I speak and write about the specific way to the health educational goal of conscious self-possession.

As Wayne's professor of psychiatry, I repeatedly honored my American government because, more than any other, its Declaration of Independence and Constitution honor the dignity of the individual citizen. Specifically, they free each citizen to try to grow equal to recognizing the magnificence of his own human being and to develop the self-control essential for his acknowledging the privileges and responsibility of declared self-sovereignty.[6] For the Bicentennial Convocation at Thomas

---

[5] My William Alanson White (1870–1937) promoted the "organism-as-a-whole" perspective with great self-understanding.

[6] See *American Government: Conscious Self Sovereignty* (Detroit: Center for Health Education, 1969), and *Psychology of Political Science: With Special Consideration for the Political Acumen of Destutt de Tracy* (Detroit: Center for Health Education, 1973).

Jefferson University, celebrating Thomas Jefferson's birthday, held April 14, 1976, the focus of my speech was on the making of the American citizen through his cultivating his awareness for the comprehensiveness of his individuality, quite as did Mr. Jefferson and his personal physician, Robley Dunglison.[7]

In my medical classes I taught both "orthodox" medical psychology and my own method featuring self-insight. Thus I pointed out the healthful consequence of growing conscious self-knowledge (a guaranteed right of American citizenship), for cultivating the self-understanding essential to sanity. My writing also featured the identity of 1) psychogenesis creating the strong insightful mind and 2) adequate growth of American citizenship. Receiving federal financial aid for my psychiatric department, of course I regularly reported my training orientation to the proper officials who naturally wondered what I was "up to." One site visit cleared up any questions of understanding.

With my medical student, especially the married one, the idea that conscious self-identity can be extended, and must be extended in the interest of mental health, gradually took hold, following initial resistance. Temporary lack of understanding is hardly a refutation of the lifesaving helpfulness of a new self-view. Most repudiated was the feelingful thought that I can measure how much I am needing to make my peace with any consideration, whatsoever, by how much I must now live that consideration with dislike. My living with my newly created appreciation that it *is* mine, is what I mean by discovering the new man ever-existing in my self.

In my research on psychogenesis I am often sensing the necessity for my new development as being the requirement of my own growth. To possess my mind in infanthood and childhood seems like being given my heart to play with. All of

---

[7]See *Freedom Record,* ed. Kurt F. Leidecker (Fredericksburg, Va.: Thomas Jefferson Institute for the Study of Religious Freedom, Inc., 1977), no. 1.

my living is sacred before I am able to know the meaning of the word. I find great life satisfaction in readily enjoying my identity in the recorded writings of my Baruch Spinoza (1632–1677). He claimed that to attain full human happiness, man must attain knowledge of his union with the whole of nature, "But above everything a means of healing the mind must be sought out, and of purifying it as much as possible at the outset so that it may happily understand things without error and as completely as possible."

The incomparably wonderful, ever constant, yet obscurely indispensable wholeness of my life, itself, is the sole source of whatever power is mine. This unity of my nature is not susceptible of simple observation but is imaginably conceived as constituting the whole subjectivity or spirit of my organismic integrity. It is all that lives, individuating the all of me, converting my real spirit into its apparent objectivity.

Only my wholeness is alive and growing, accounting for the genesis of my self-world. It is the force of my *living* that generates my every meaning and constitutes the identity of all of my individuality. The greater my obedience to this law of my unique being the more I honor my own nature in my every reality, in my growing of my each experience. My sensation or perception is all and only my fresh creation of that much of my own existence, made accurate and faithful by the functioning of my conscious wholeness in its production.

Equipped with functioning of sufficient self-consciousness I can appreciate all of my so-called environment, which I can sense, as manifesting my own vitality. My interest in my surroundings, my love of nature, is entirely an extension of my self-interest, including my self-love. My glory of my heavens, as my horror of my hell, is wholly a production of my protean psychicality. My reverence for the Creator of All is a believable extrapolation of my evidence for my own divinity.

Whatever is, mystically is. The opposite of mystic must be magic, conscious or unconscious. Mystic refers to absolute self-continence that duly respects the truth of growing solipsistic individuality. Magic refers to the illusion that anything can happen without a history explicating it. I must cultivate the kind of personality or character that the conduct of my life necessitates. The greatness of my nature requires that I study it assiduously in order to be able to know how it works itself. This study is hardest of all; hence every other kind of study seems more alluring. The longer I persevere in my *conscious* self-study, the fuller my conscious self-identity grows, the stronger my mind becomes, and the more my appreciation for my life is developed.

Thus, my spirited reader: "How can I fervently devote myself to the difficult task of deeply understanding how my mind works itself. I can scarcely grasp the subtlety of the true meaning of self-insight, much less conceive that insight as providing the totality of my realization that all of my mind is my own. Furthermore all of this kind of thinking reminds me of imagination, and I learned early to beware of that along with too much curiosity. I cannot admit that I generate *my* all. I cannot stand for the complete man."

I honor resistance to learning how to use my mind just as I affirm any other mental functioning. I have discovered, much against my expectation, that my so-called common sense is nothing but my unconscious idealism. All of my creating self-conscious ideas is accompanied by the birth pain of resistance to seeing my identity in it.

My rare reader goes on: "You describe numerous obstacles to renouncing your habits of unconscious minding of your conduct, of giving up observing it *as if* it were not unconscious. First I have to find for myself my large enough perception, the one and only private way, my method of living consciously, I mean. Then I have to mobilize sufficient free devotion to be able to discipline myself in persevering practice of acknowledging I *am* living whatever experience I am living.

"Certainly I cannot become a mind-conscious practitioner from reading or hearing about it. Each of my other studies is much easier to master. I can find no zeal for such hard work as you describe, but when I consider the alternative, an anonymous existence, I cannot be satisfied with that, either.

"It is the blaze of my self-consciousness that liberates me from the burning heat of my emotionality. I do observe that I can acknowledge my own original greatness, the worth of my life, to the same extent that I can recognize my identity in all of my mental activity. Too, I agree, although grudgingly thus far, that I can feel responsible only for whatever living of mine I can own up to being. Also I can *imagine* that I must live all of my disowned experience with some form of distress. Without fully understanding the consequence I think I would rather go on impairing my health (conscious wholeness) than take the trouble, and I mean trouble, to restore it. I can imagine, though, the deeper cheer and the awareness of personal strength to be derived only from conscious self-functioning."

To all of this helpful resistance to becoming enlightened with life consciousness I say, yes. Becoming a conscious mental athlete requires the same kind and degree of intense interest, unfaltering diligence, and unswerving loyalty to that one effort as does becoming an accomplished gymnast. Training of my body is unconscious mental hygiene. My body meaning is the nucleus of all of my further meaning of my life experience. I must experience insight in terms of my wholeness only. Thus I *feel* insightful living throughout my being as profound, as self-identity, as my living of me.

Dependent upon reasoning and habit far more than upon self-consciousness and originality, I tend to reject whatever potential self-insight might seem "unreasonable," such as that one idea cannot rule out another; contradictory ideas may coexist without conflict; developing a new self-orientation does not mean riddance of the former one (because it is an outgrowth of what preceded it); an idea is just as substantial as connective tissue; physical exercise *is* mental hygiene; when I am not self-conscious I am living a degree of autohypnosis; I cannot repudiate any of my mind's nature without its assuming obsessive force and illusional meaning; nothing that I ex-

perience can be alien to me; what seems alien control is unconscious self-control; every man is all of his own experience
of his femininity; every woman is all of her own experience of
her own masculinity; all I can be or do is my own growing of
my individuality; my commonsense vocabulary is my built-in
self-belittlement.

For making my peace with any of my difficult life experience, only whole life is large enough. It is indispensable that I
gradually grow to realize: the exact wherewithal of that "difficult" occurrence is totally my creation and I have succeeded in
saving my life by providing it. Such is the *happy* "scheme of
things entire."

I discover my world cannot be a mighty maze without a
plan. Indeed I can make no complete discovery without including *its* own universal scheme of self-sufficiency. How
much is made of this reliable requirement of existence in the
great order of the universe I can but remotely imagine. How
much is made of this self-continence in the great order of my
own living I can but nearly imagine. During my University
Professorship I have made myself as ingenious as possible to
set this strongest self-insight of all to work for me in many
ways, otherwise feeling "idly busy" (my Goldsmith).

In Sanskrit literature, about 600 B.C., appeared the earliest
recorded treatise on the Vedic religion, considered the most
coherent and illuminating of all the Upanishads. It is not
known whether its author, Yajnavalkya, was a historical person or whether this name applied to a group of thinkers and
teachers. Concerning the self, the following excerpts reflect its
solipsistic orientation:

> In sooth, a husband is dear,—not because you love the husband;
> but a husband is dear because you love the Self. In sooth, a wife is
> dear,—not because you love the wife; but a wife is dear because you
> love the Self. . . . In sooth, the gods are dear,—not because you love
> the gods; but gods are dear because you love the Self. In sooth,
> beings are dear,—not because you love beings; but beings are dear
> because you love the Self. In sooth, the whole world is dear,—not

because you love the whole world; but the whole world is dear because you love the Self.

It is your self which is in all things. . . . You could not see the seer in seeing, you could not hear the hearer in hearing, you could not think the thinker in thinking, you could not discern the discerner in discerning. It is your self that is in everything. Anything else [means] woe.

That which [though] dwelling in all being, beings do not know, whose body all beings are, governs all beings from within,—that is your Self, the inner controller, the immortal one.[8]

Review

All appreciation, including realization of the truth of wholeness, is naturally a product of the mind creating it. Mind only is capable of growing understanding of the necessity for the indivisible unity of individuality. My conception of my solipsistic self is most simple but must seem difficult, or even impossible, if I have practiced necessary self-disregard traceable to any kind of self-education to which I have seemed to subject myself, rather than practiced my *conscious* self-education which I find subjected to me.

Anew, my consciously reeducating myself, "working through" my self-insight in terms of revering my wholeness, grows out of my previous way of educating myself in terms of my overlooking my intact wholeness. Therefore this most desirable *conscious* self-cultivation *cannot* emerge at the cost of my ridding myself of its roots in unconscious-self living. Rather, all of my previous living indicates the direction along which my mind has coursed in following its necessary self-interest. For example, out of the seeming physical concepts of cause and effect, that is, out of "determinism," the helpful illusion of the nineteenth century scientist, has grown the solipsistic reality that whatever exists is its own cause, its own effect, its own all.

[8]Dagobert D. Runes, ed., "The Self," *Treasury of Philosophy* (New York: Philosophical Library, Inc., 1955), pp. 1245–47.

All of my writing and formal lecturing is as technical, specialized, and exhaustive as I can make it for sketching, explaining, and justifying in myself the scientific truth that my life, all of it, is naturally and wholly all about itself only. My teaching myself how to conduct my life in the clear light of this blazing truth is my only possible way to mind my nature with biological adequacy.

Fortunately, my straying from this straight and narrow path of conscious responsibility for living whatever I live is signalized by symptoms of health trouble. I am doubly fortunate if I can teach myself to honor my every sign or symptom of health difficulty (so-called pathology of any and every description) as the effort of my whole organic nature to warn me about such perilous straying.

My wholeness is my only real. Such imaginative insight regarding my conscious integrity is the consequence of 1) imagination that is appreciated with insight and 2) insight that is appreciated with imagination. I need all of my imagination free to conceive that what I name "abstract" is all that I can mean by what I name "concrete." I need all of my free imagination to realize that my only possible solid or sharp scientific landmark is nothing but meaning created entirely by my own mind, nothing but a fixed concept or counter of my feelingful thought.

Conscious self-understanding is not communicable at all, any more than any other self-development can be. It is my wholeness alone that does *all* of my innate growing. My hand or foot, or whatever else I can possibly mean, grows only as an individuation of my wholeness. Only my wholeness has any so-called history as far as all of my living is concerned.

To this acknowledged integrity of my living I owe all of my meaning of freedom. Without it the freedom of freedom is unimaginable. It is my natural need to live the unity of my wholeness that enables me gradually to observe and learn to appreciate the unity that I name my self. Obviously, it is the singular power of my wholeness that enables me to distinctify any individuation of my self as being completely whatever it may be.

My emotionality, expressing my likes and dislikes, accounts for my setting up many life values instead of observing the just value, perfection. For example, when I feel angry I seem to be made up of anger only, when I feel guilty I seem to be all guilt, and so on. Thus the cloud of my feeling can appear to vie with or even eclipse the sun of my self-consciousness, which alone can illuminate my self-wholeness.

Freedom with regard to my emotionality is secured only by my realizing that each emotion really is all and only about itself, rather than what it otherwise may appear to be about. Guilt is all and only about guilt. With this insight I liberate my whole self from the obligation to slavishly obey guilt, or whatever emotion, without regard for my wholeness. William Penn (1644–1718) declared: "Liberty without obedience is confusion, and obedience without liberty is slavery."

Each emotion is a sign indicating my feeling associated only with my own living. Thus, when I am angry, my anger warns me of my disregarding the pacifying truth of my intact wholeness. Each unhappy feeling is an indicator of a similar shortcoming. Each happy feeling signifies that my behavior is compatible with my respect for my wholeness.[9]

---

[9]See my *Psychology of Emotion* (Detroit: Center for Health Education, 1971), pp. 85–137.

3

My Education

When a man mistakes his thoughts for persons and
things, he is mad. A madman is properly so defined.
Samuel Taylor Coleridge

Needed most of all by myself as a formal educator, as a
teacher seeking to understand what is most worth learning, is
an explanation of the necessity for the existence of the numerous educational perspectives preferred by my several fellow
educators through the ages. Why must there be such an enormous lack of unanimity about the basic nature of education
itself? And above all, why must one protect one's own view of
the learning process as if defending one's very life thereby?
Surely my way of accounting for the nature of my learning
process must enter into the meaning that I ascribe to it.
Therefore I must realize that all I can know of my religion,
philosophy, psychology, science, or whatever egotizing experience, is the product of my particular kind of educational experience (growth).

Nothing can merely happen by chance. There must always
be present each necessity required to make happen whatever
can ever occur. What must be going on therefore in order to
sufficiently justify the methodology of each unique educational orientation that obtains? What if any insightful understanding about becoming knowledgeable is it that honors all of
the others, that fully accounts for the helpfulness of each
pedagogical choice?

My experience has taught me that I never do anything until I have to. Thus I never require my mind to work up a new way of learning as long as I can feel safe in continuing my present way. Nevertheless, my discovering just *how* I learn has led to my benefiting from my knowledge that I could not attain from discovering just *what* I learn. Now then, what does what I learn have to do with how I learn?

It is this kind of inquiry that has sometimes preceded and sometimes succeeded the following expositions of the cognitive process. Viewed from the only accurate perspective, namely that of consciously responsible mentality, the only true educational psychology must be that of each unique educational psychologist; one's learning process *is* nothing but his life of his mind; all that can be "going on" in my mind is its growing of its meaning; only consciously responsible mentality (conscious solipsism) can honor its meaning for each and every system of psychology; only my arduously developed and cultivated understanding of how I learn can enable me to grow my mind with acknowledgeable responsibility for its being all mine (conscious solipsism). My conscious solipsism can emerge out of my unconscious solipsism only, there being no other source possible. I shall always need my self-unconscious way of living quite as I shall need my self-conscious way of living.

I can see clearly in my own educative history how I resisted developing a new way of learning out of my then present way by blindly fearing that the latter must exclude the former, whereas any new way must depend basically upon the present way, being entirely an outgrowth of it. *What* I learn is most helpfully conceivable from the viewpoint of how it can contribute to my cultivating a new way of learning. It is this insight, about how I become knowing, that enables me to recognize identical self-helpfulness in each of the various so-called systems of educational psychology.

My young, relatively inexperienced, and seemingly irresponsible mind uses the least burdensome kind of psychical functioning available, that of ignoring responsibility for the fact that mentality exists at all. My first recognition of the existence of so-called mental functioning concerns psychical responsibility other than my acknowledged own. To begin with I can attribute responsible mindfulness to somebody else more easily than to myself. Biologically adequate conscientiousness for being all of my marvelous mentality is avoided as long as possible because it demands most careful self-accounting.

Hence it is that my conscious self-identity, however restricted it may be, can be required to "make do" for the truth of my whole (solipsistic) identity. It does not irresponsibly happen that I choose to use one form of religion or philosophy or science or whatever. I choose to regulate my conduct on the basis of how prepared I am to live my mind responsibly as wholly my own. All my mental strength consists of the relative mental weakness which entered into its creation. All so-called mental weakness constituted my only mental strength in its time.

In the preface of his *Psychology*[1] my esteemed colleague John B. Watson, professor of psychology, the Johns Hopkins University, recorded, "The key which will unlock the door of any other scientific structure will unlock the door of psychology." My experience has taught me that I cannot understand any mentality except in terms of my understanding my own. In fact I have found that my ability to "unlock the door of psychology" has depended *specifically* upon how much hard work I have done of one particular kind, namely, in arduously developing my capacity for sprouting, extending shoots of, my *self* consciousness. By *self* consciousness I mean precisely: awareness for my germinating mental activity as being entirely and only my own.

Without my taking the trouble to create my self-consciousness further I can "unlock the door of psychology" only as far as I have already grown my conscious self-understanding, no

---

[1](Philadelphia: J. B. Lippincott Co., 1919), p. vii.

further. I mislead myself dangerously insofar as I imagine that I can become an insightful psychologist without being willing to discipline my mind steadily with full responsibility for germinating itself. I must choose either to recognize my conscious *responsibility* for being all of my burgeoning mentality, or to ignore my necessitating unconscious guilt for denying my being all of my ever waxing mentality.

Clear understanding of the difference between my strong and my weak mind can be attained only by realizing the hard work required for a weak mind to develop itself into a strong one. Self-insight, that is, willing self consciousness, is the unit of mental strength. In other words, my mind is strong specifically to the extent that it can acknowledge responsibility for being all of itself. Most sensible is the person who can honor *all* of his (her) past living as being ideal self-helpfulness in its time. Whoever can freely declare the most of one's life-experience to be exclusively one's own enjoys the strongest mentality.

Most difficult of all self-meaning to appreciate as entirely my own is whatever I can mean by divinity. This necessity is explicable on the basis that I must conduct my life in accordance with my choice concept of my self-identity, and most difficult of all ways of life is the totally fit divine way that subsumes all of the rest.

It is pure mental hygiene for me to keep uppermost in my mind *as long as I live* the indication to realize that my living is a synonym for growing myself, so that my only matter-of-fact meaningfulness must consist wholly of my own individual creative nature. My consciousness is also a budding mental process revealing my personal individuality. To illustrate, what I name heredity, environment, superhuman, subhuman, society or whatever, must be expressing enlargement of some of my very own self-meaningfulness only. However, only to the extent that I have labored to love all of my mentality as my mentality can I "unlock the door" admitting me into theretofore unacknowledged regions of my psychicality.

I like to exercise the insight I have already mentioned: nothing can just happen "out of the blue." Every occurrence is a necessity. I can never do anything until I have mobilized "all that it takes" to do it, but then I must do it. My necessitating my becoming an insightful, instead of insightless, psychologist depends entirely upon how willing I am to work hard at living self-consciously, that is, at fully understanding my responsibility for being solely and wholly the personal individual that I am. This prerequisite is at once my hardest and easiest way of life. "Hardest" because it demands painstaking heed for my augmenting self-consciousness. "Easiest" because every other conduct of my life entails helpful but distressing symptom formation warning me of my self-nescience.

Each form of philosophy, psychology, religion, or education of any kind reflects the extent to which I have schooled my mind with self-consciousness. Thus any preferred form marks the precise developmental stage of my mentality when I became a drop-out from that schooling. To elaborate by review, at birth I was an individual incapable of any understanding of what it meant to be an individual. However, my welfare during the rest of my life must depend specifically upon my teaching myself what it does mean to be an individual. In other words I cannot drift or idle into mental health, but must work for it in a uniquely special way.

In the course of my development, whatever I have become is my present being. For example, my present mentality must subsume all of the mentality that preceded it, the former being continuous with the latter. *Just how my present living honors its identity in its previous growth is a momentous health issue.* Most desirable for its lifesaving value is the whole truth of presence of mind as standing for the presence of the whole mind. The truth observes: what's past is present.

In the interest of momentary creature comfort I may repress my so-called past living as gone, thereby excluding it from having any conscious meaning for my present good. In that action I succeed in seeming to disconnect myself from myself. This method of living my past is fraught with trouble,

being responsible for my creating distressing mental symptoms warning me of my self-disregard.

In the interest of my continuing welfare I may treat my
so-called past living as not gone but as not sufficiently propitious to be consciously involved for the time being. Thus I
willingly renounce it with the understanding that it is good in
itself and therefore potentially a helpful function. Here by
"renounce" I mean: remaining willing to withhold my resistance from freely examining any consideration, while presently not attending to it. Here by "repress" I mean: remaining unwilling to withhold my resistance from freely examining
any consideration, while presently refusing to attend to it.[2]

I may proceed now to account for certain "schools" of meta-
psychology as being more popular than others, and for the
doctrine of solipsism as being least popular of any. I may
advance many *reasons* explaining why I espouse one school of
thought or another, or why my character is the kind that it is,
but sufficient justification for any conduct of my life can be
found only in the way my personal experience has shaped my
mind. I can account for each of my orthodox and unorthodox
systems of edification with the following understanding of
psychogenesis.

Basically all of my becoming must be the outgrowth of all of
my having been. Being a conscious individualist is a development rooted in my being an unconscious individualist. Only by
being a conscious idealist can I attribute conscious individuality to my fellowman, or whole individuality to any existent in
my so-called external world. Consciously subjective idealism
(solipsism) is the life orientation that requires the greatest
faith in the existence of myself (including my fellow-creature
and my world). It is justly feared to the extent that I have little
faith in my wonderful ability to postulate existence other than
my own. It is intolerable for the unimaginative, matter-of-fact,
objective scientist I am.

[2]See Glossary.

For becoming an objective scientist (behaviorist) devoted to the study of the materiality of the external world, I must first repress or renounce the reality of my own being, namely, that of subjective ideality. My notion of objectivity derives from the negation of my subjectivity. My notion of subjectivity derives from the affirmation that all of my mentality, including my seeming objectivity, is really subjectivity.

For becoming a subjective materialist I must renounce or repress my objective materialism.

For becoming a subjective idealist I must renounce or repress my subjective materialism.

For becoming a conscious solipsist I must difficultly renounce the unconscious solipsism in my subjective idealism. It is noteworthy that only my solipsism can enable me to substitute renunciation for repression.

My *being* is all that can *be* for me. My generating my experience, my producing any activity of my being, can only amount to some modification of my being. I live my every meaning only as an integral growing of my mind. I can "acquire" no addition to my being. Rather I must become, namely grow, it. My teaching myself that all of my education must be my generating my self-knowledge (conscious or unconscious), is the *how* of learning from which appreciation for my self-continent organic wholeness derives itself.

A justifiably vexed student voices his feeling, "You call yourself an idiolinguist, a solipsist, or by some other name meaning untouchable, inaccessible, unapproachable, or inviolable. How peculiar can you be! Would you do away with all common sense, all education as I have always considered it to be? How do you propose to have the civilized world make itself over to fit your notion that all sensation is nothing but impalpable self-growth merely increasing self; that all touch is merely self feeling self? Must all of your literature be rewritten in the first person? How can I dispose of the countless ways in which I now unwittingly live myself, without making a federal case out of it or writing a book about it? I find it hard enough to live myself kindly just the way I am without turning away from that nearly overwhelming life course to try an entirely new way. In fact it is obviously foolish to ask myself to turn on myself unkindly, even in the name of education. Rejection of common sense principles of learning that have evolved gradually in the progress of civilization seems neither wise nor prudent."

It is ever my aim to say and feel *yes* before applying myself further to any of my student's valid objection, for it must be always valid, desirable, and helpful living of his. This particular concern, about the extent of trouble involved in creating a new self-image, is most significant because it is potentially usable as strongest resistance against trying to *extend* lifesaving self-love further. I observe most carefully that my ongoing life means merely extending my lifesaving self-love further. Love of life is the natural, biologically adequate, feeling of being alive.

Of all sources of minor and major mental trouble I know of none more grievous than this one of looking down upon any of my so-called past living as being in any sense unworthy. All that I can mean by so-called past living must be really constituted of my *present* living. I proceed:

"Yes, my raising such sensible objection to honoring full-measured individuality of any individual is often necessary. Also, if putting on the new man would necessitate discarding or belittling the former one there could be only mixed advantage in any kind of so-called growing up. True enough, commonsense self-understanding that I have made my own is magnificent in providing singular provision for my wants, and I can scarcely imagine how long that common sense has been in the making before I grew it as my own. I cannot imagine what it would be like to be without it. Certainly, each degree of my spurning any commonsense claim would estrange my acknowledgeable self from all of my living of my fellowman. As long as I live I continue to need *all* that I ever have lived. I need to discipline my mind to live with love *now* whatever former experience has been mine, regardless of whether or not I judged it was worth living at all originally. Without my so-called mistakes my so-called successes could have no meaning. Without my ignoring myself, my heeding myself must be meaningless. I owe my capacity for full self-trust to my loving understanding of my capacity for self-deception. And so on."

Although it may not seem that way at first, my science of conscious living only of myself does not involve any getting rid of already existing educational methods. In fact I need all of my educational understanding that already exists as the only possible root for my new educational understanding to grow forth from. It is my knowledge of my ever extant capacity for undisciplined and irresponsible living that helps to make the fact of my present wholeness significant to me. I see nothing but (that much of) my own identity in any of my child's seeming recklessness or abandonment. This life-giving self-insight gradually relieves my sense of enormity of any so-called evil, deformity or ugliness in the revealing light of whole-self appreciation.

I define education as my own systematic conscious mental development. However, my established educational practice favors the illusion of learning as being an acquisition of not-self knowledge.[3] Thus Shakespeare could say, "Use almost can change the stamp of nature" *(Hamlet,* III, iv). Learning by rote is a study method that extends to every concept of learning except that of learning by conscious mental growth. The inviolable unity of each unique student can find expression in the concept of wholeness reflected in the word "university" itself.

My university is a wholeness of meaning in my whole-full mind uniquely representing devotion to mentality, dedication to the meaning of *acknowledgeable* individual life and to the life of responsible individual meaning. My university is a unity of purposes with which I help myself to recognize the genius in the commonplace, the imagination in the real, the spiritual in the material, the societal in the solitary, the sanity in the irresponsible, the health in sickness, the depth in the utilitarian,

[3]See Introduction.

the tender in the tough, the concentration in the distracted, the freedom in restraint, the conscious in the unconscious, the strength in weakness, the sameness in difference, the science in disorder, the law in confusion, the continent in the overwhelming, the sacred in the profane, the new in the old, the intuitive in the learned, the underlying growth nature of all behavior, the ever-moral truth of my life in all that I live.

Becoming the naturalist of my own being is the whole advantage that my study of science has presented to me. This truth makes safely valuable all of the concinnate truths it discloses. I seem grateful to myself most of all for my discovery of the virtue of present conscious self-devotion for my understanding my all that belongs to me.

My worthy colleague questions, "What do you really think about Wayne State University?" When I ask myself that question, I realize that all of *my* Wayne State University must amount exactly to what I am able to make it mean in terms of my very own creating of (my) its meaning. My sense of my identity in *all* of my Wayne living is my justifiable claim to being any special kind of educator I may be. One of the "Seven Wise Men," Bias of Priene (c. 550 B.C.), was asked the good of education for a student. He pointed to the marble seats of the amphitheater, and replied, "When he goes there, that he might not be a stone sitting upon a stone."

My long experience as a public school teacher has taught me to revere as supreme: I experience my schooling consciously as moral education precisely to the extent that my teacher fully recognizes that all of his (her) own learning consists of his (her) responsibly growing knowledge in the form of his (her) own self-knowledge, exactly as my developing athletic prowess consists of my responsibly growing body competence in the form of my own physique. My true moral learning has been the consequence of my consciously discovering new self-knowledge enabling me to deal understandingly with my nature (including the nature of my world).

Am I habitually allowing my vocabulary to represent me

without even realizing such a possibility? Am I seeming to be a man of words, rather than the man of my word? How can my speaking or writing be misleading or even make me become self-disrespecting, for example? One way can be by my consistently referring to my reader only as masculine: *he, him, his,* etc.

In order to appreciate my living it is necessary to learn, gradually and reluctantly, to renounce every word of mine implying habitual suffering, so that it can no longer prevent my learning how to enjoy my life. Whatever I do or omit doing is at the time my best method of helping myself, and that includes crying, screaming, "going to pieces," wanting to die or kill, or whatever. A person's chief objection to pain or sorrow can be his assumption that it is not helping him, that it is not constructive, whereas living difficultly is always a strengthening experience. By giving myself up to my own uninformed conception of self-discontent, by resigning myself to the seeming necessity of not valiantly helping myself by whatever difficult experience I endure, I appear to conceptualize myself as helpless, unresourceful, self-sacrificing, biologically inadequate. Indeed, if I consult my everyday dictionary I find it consisting greatly of such life-derogatory terms contributing to my cultivating a habit of self-disesteem.

The biologically adequate way for me to mind *whatever* distressful experience is to *understand* its goodness, to realize that it is my divine truth manifesting itself as necessary, to acknowledge that my arduously living it is really triumphal, rather than lamentable, identification of my personal will with my universal will. I find all source of human woe traceable to *faultfinding* of one kind or another, best concealed in melioration (progress, improvement, betterment, etc.) The lawyer calls it crime, the clergyman calls it wrongdoing, the physician calls it disease, the teacher calls it failure, the parent calls it disobedience, the mathematician calls it error, and so on.

There is no power of helpfulness more deserving of lovable appreciation, more unkindly treated, than pain, including unhappiness of any sort. Thus rejected by me, my pain is not subject to my volitional regulation. Indeed it sets up as if it could be opposed to my joy of living, of which biologically it is but an integral element.

Following is an apt example of how I can seem to feel subjugated to a word rather than be certain that such a word owes all of its existence to my being. The label "solipsism," which means literally *one's self alone,* is a most meaningful case in point. First of all, this term accurately signifies inviolable individuality, integrity of the soul, intact organic wholeness of the self. Whatever is consists only of whatever it is. The individual variant, the basis of medical theory and practice, honors this necessity. Every statement acknowledgeably standing for the complete truthfulness of truth is a solipsistic statement. Nevertheless, temptation may be overpowering to hedge on the fact that solipsistic mentality is the whole truth and nothing but the truth about all of the meaning of my life.

Relying merely upon my reasoning, I can never attain appreciation for the naturalness of my being all one, a thoroughly self-continent person, an absolute individual self capable of living the meaning only of my own growing of my self. Indeed it is my reasoning that enables me to invent innumerable ways of appearing to myself to be able to circumvent the reality that my life is a solitary, non-communicative, independent, non-relatable, inviolably whole here-and-now one. Such reasoning that I am not all and only my own living derives from my capacity to imagine so-called otherness, elseness, alienness.

What then can help me to sanity by realizing my self-identity in my variegated life experience? My education in self-consciousness derives from my capacity to *observe* the meaningfulness in any of my living. It is specifically my devotion to practicing my self-consciousness that confronts me with the evident necessity for solipsistically growing my soul as my own and my all as my soul.

As a rule my good academic colleague, however profound in his knowledge of his subject, dismisses understanding-responsibility-for-solipsistic-necessity with just as much levity as the corresponding degree of gravity it adequately deserves. I tried the experiment once of consenting to lend a professorial colleague my film, *Illusion and Reality*,[4] depicting the necessity for psychic reality, since he wished to decide its fitness for student presentation. I found his acceptance considerably short of kind rejection, without his offering any explanation for his excited resistance. Gratefully I realized then, as now, that rejection is the beginning of acceptance. The key to my education for sanity is the conscious capacity for renunciation of any and all of my knowledge, for only therewith can educational rigidity be spared. Freedom of mind is the only possible freedom.

Like every other dichotomy, that of ends and means attempts to divide unity into duality and is consequently fraught with no end of compensatory demands. As a professional educator I can be victim of a technical notion of gravest consequence for my (including my pupil's) welfare. It consists in my habitually viewing myself as if I am not the end *unto myself* that, as a whole individual, I must be. Thus, I may delude myself into believing that I can somehow be a means unto my fellowman and yet remain an end unto myself. Then I cherish as prized ideal my ability to be of service as a useful means to my pupil, thus living out the illusional role of being a dexterous instrument, a helpful educational tool. Every tool itself is nothing but the reifying of abstraction. But I may not sense only my own continuity in the sequences of events with which I seemingly surround myself.

My habitual life-discounting fallacy (of imputing access and utility to external learning processes) is prevalent throughout my formal educational experience. Even the attempt has been made to justify its practicality on the basis of necessity to make a living, a livelihood unrecognizable as being entirely my own innateness. Thus education as an end has been termed liberal; education as so-called means has been termed vocational (the bread-and-butter studies).

[4]Created and produced by King Vidor in sound film, 1967.

Seeing my learning as being my growing is not achieved by some kind of turning of either my perception or my attention from without in, but rather results from my gradually realizing that all that I have been judging to be "without" or "looking outward" *is* really and only *in* or *inward*. I do not and cannot make an unintegrated self into an integrated self somehow. Rather, all I can do in order to appreciate my integration is to teach myself gradually that I am already integrated, and always have been.

All of my feeling of lack of integration is traceable to my habitual lack of awareness for my ever existing integration. My integration, itself, is always present. It is only my recognition, acknowledgment, or whatever responsible sensing and feeling my self-identity, that may or may not be awakened. My conscious self-education arouses this affirmation that I am whatever I learn, that I become self-knowledgeable through my study, that my innovating life justly involves my owning up to its ever burgeoning meaningfulness in order that I may be able to feel equal to myself. I define my living as becoming more and more of myself.

My integration, as my individuality, is actually mine from the beginning of my existence. My realization of its nature, however, must be constantly learned by me, as such, if I would cultivate a biologically adequate appreciation for being alive. My living is my learning of me, consciously or unconsciously.

Widespread illusion that knowledge is acquired, rather than grown, favors the creation of a dichotomy of intellectual cultivation implying that knowledge and self-knowledge need not be identical, that learning and mental development do not equally consist only of my self-growth, that my education and mental development may exist in no necessary proportion to each other, that the existence of learned truth in my mind does not suppose a corresponding developmental strength of mind deriving from my exertion of growing it, that my knowledgeable understanding of any of my experience can be achieved without even my modifying my mind for the possession of it. The reality is that all of my conduct of my life is integrally organized in terms of the wholeness of my nature. The same architect wrought my hand that worms this writing.

In short, the fictional dichotomy of ends and means allows for all of the appearance of insightless so-called acquisition of knowledge without requiring the learner's responsibly accounting to himself that he is growing his identity in all of his learning. Meaning of my sense or of my consciousness is really *of* either one only, and cannot be "of" aught else. Such as I grow myself, so is my wordage, so is my self-understanding. All of my seeming observation or understanding of "another," must be at the expense of acknowledgeable self-observation and self-understanding.

None too noticeably, my understanding of my own wholeness is my only possible source for my experiencing my fellow-man's wholeness with any understanding. Since all of my learning is my creation achieved solely by my own living, my sole hope for growing to appreciate my growth as referring to my wholeness-development springs from my duly *revering* that my living *is* the only possible source of my learning, study, reflection, or whatever mental experience. Why lose my conscious mind in studying so-called mechanical or chemical explanation of my life by denying I must live what I mean by mechanical or chemical?

For many years now I have considered my *consciously* self-grown self-understanding to be my only basis for realizing my wholeness, my discovery of my wholeness being my liberation of myself from my habitual ("unconscious") ignoring my mind's capacity for mental dissociation. Hence I have assumed, as a major responsibility of my wholeness, my trying to train my nature to mind my own business, education, health, or whatever interest, as being exactly and only my own. *Only* my alert practice of this method of conscious self-education can require my student to grow the kind of educator he experiences in his Dorsey.

The point of view from which any exposition is conducted

must be (consciously or unconsciously) purely psychical. Difficulties in understanding any exposition as a rule arise from not considering it as purely psychical. Thus, my mind cannot mirror my body or building in some other way. Rather all that I can mean by my body or building *is* minded mentality. As might be expected, the question about mind, as about body, has led to an unsatisfying answer because the question has been incorrectly stated. Specifically, the pure subjectivity of the questioner, his question and his answer, is regularly ignored. For example, by calling attention to the purely psychical nature of aphasia, Hughlings-Jackson (1835–1911) clarified the whole meaning of it.

Indication of the theoretical and practical usefulness of the conception of wholeness-entity is discoverable throughout the published works of Sigmund Freud, revealing how either the conscious presence or absence of the whole truth about any subject respectively accounts for its asymptomatic or symptomatic functioning. My self-analysis is accurately describable as my devotion to methodical discovery of my wholeness-nature.

My only life experience that I can observe consists of my mental activity. All of my mental experience is reducible to meaning. My developing a selective vocabulary signifying any particular area of my mind constitutes the naming of a singular set of meanings psychicalizing (unconsciously, as a rule) that specific area of my mind as being *exclusively distinct from any other*. Thus I have already written and published my *Psychology of Language, Psychology of Emotion, Psychology of Political Science, Psychology of Ethics, Psychic Nature of Physiology,* and so on.

The point I wish repeatably to make clear (to and for myself) is that each and all of this so-called studious effort of mine is strictly and inclusively psychical; it is purely the product of my mind, as subject, working upon its own nature only. Whether my scientific interest is directed towards naming all that I can mean by astronomy or anatomy, physics or metaphysics, machinery or metabolism, geology or physiology, the one basic truth about any or all of it is that it must consist only of my life interest as expressed in my mind only.

Furthermore, unless I systematically honor this reality, that all of my living is naturally reducible to me only, I must suffer the helpful consequence of both conscious and unconscious suffering warning me that I can neglect my life only by unconsciously creating symptoms heralding that neglect, instead of consciously creating my enjoyment of my life's augmenting wholeness.

Therefore, whether or not I orderly heed my physiology as applied psychicality is not only of academic but also of hygienic concern— "orderly" implying regularly and steadily, since my responsibility for consistently maintaining my self-consciousness cannot prudently be taken for granted (unheeded).

A consciously solipsistic version of learning is indispensable for a biologically adequate understanding of mind, as well as for the justification of the conscious self-educator's goal. I see no choice other than to affirm that I am all one-of-my-self or to deny so being. And my denial can only unconsciously affirm what I deny. Without the presence of whatever is denied, there can be no denial.

For my formally educated fellowman the word "solipsism," instead of designating truth of individuality as its structure implies (all one self), may conjure up some kind of "abnormality" of self identity, a "megalomania of hypertrophied self-interest," perhaps. The conscious solipsist knows that all that he can mean by society or "externality" of any kind must exist in him. The unconscious solipsist imagines that his own center of gravity can and must be displaced in his rejected selfness which he names society or externality. The conscious solipsist continuously enjoys the "gentle radiance of spiritual illumination."[5] I cannot but believe, with my Emerson, that the true meaning of spiritual is real. How accurately he di-

[5]See John Franklin Genung, *The Life Indeed* (Boston: Marshall Jones Co., 1921), p. 39.

vined atomic energy. Of deity he recorded, "I find the omnipresence and the almightiness in the reaction of every atom in Nature.[6]

Steadily struggling with my contumacy towards the only authority possible in me, namely, my own, I gradually grew to realize more and more of the extent to which I would not claim my life as being wholly my own. I needed my overwhelming guilt helpfully warning me of my self-rejection to continue, in order to spare my having to shoulder my overwhelming responsibility for being all of myself. Guilt is unconscious responsibility.

All of my struggling against my own authority derives from my dissociating the whole of my life's meaning into 1) a region in which I sense, feel, and consider the presence of my self-identity and 2) a region in which I deny the placement of my self-identity. My illusioned duality may be helpfully felt (as conflict), but possibly I have not taught myself to interpret my pain or unhappiness of any kind as being the lifesaving self-helpfulness that it is. Hence I can go on struggling, arguing, fighting, warring —always unwittingly against myself. Mental dissociation necessitating symptom formation is my only alternative to being sincere with myself (including my fellowman). My every word is merely a name for some of my own living. Each of my sciences, or morals, becomes an *as if* postulation by seeming to be able to be an impersonal construction.

When I began to grow glimmerings that I must be *my* own only friend or whatever, I began to sense some of the extent to which I habitually use my language to magnify the region of my mind I cannot claim as mine at the direct cost of belittling the region of my mind which I can and do claim as mine.[7]

Thus I began to understand the vast extent to which I am

[6]"Worship," *The Conduct of Life.*
[7]See Francis Ellingwood Abbot, *The Syllogistic Philosophy* (Boston: Little, Brown & Co., 1906), II, 304–5, 58–91.

inured to using my formal and informal schooling to grow unacknowledgeable self-truth. As my choice self-insight developed I lost none of my ability to use my mind insightlessly however, —a biological necessity of indispensable helpfulness for my retaining my ability to see congenially nothing but myself in *my* insightless fellowman.

My discovering the illusion of "communication" in formal education led to my studying just what does actually happen in my learning process, namely, perception of my intellectual growth. This idea led me to the irrefutable realization that all I can ever do is grow. Surely all that I can grow is my own being. All of my seeing, hearing, or my any other sensing, or perceiving, feeling, and thinking (including free associating) is entirely my growing of each such region of my wholeness.

Before this self-enlightenment, for example, all I was capable of imagining was that I could speak to another who could hear me speak, or that I could hear another speak to me. Of course this illusion prevented my discovering (and arduously heeding) that I never did learn to speak, for the complete act of my speaking includes my listening to what I am saying. No one else can do my listening for me any more than he can do my speaking for me.

What actually happens when I seemingly listen to a speaker? I merely grow *my own* sensation and perception comprehended in a unity in my mind that I denote as speaker. I grow his speaking to himself and listening to what he says as being the only possible way he can ever speak or listen to a sensible man. I renounce my illusion that he can speak to me or that I can hear or see other than my own growing sensation of hearing or seeing. If I wish to approximate speaking or hearing anything (my) he says, my only possible way is to say-and-listen-to-myself whatever I have imagined his saying-and-listening-to-his-self. That means also my respecting the sincerity with which he grows his talk.

Whatever is, wholly is. Whatever is, is real. Reality, itself, must be wholly real. My own individuality is a synonym for my own wholeness. My nature is my whole nature. All of the apparent regionalism of my anatomy or physiology is really constituted of nothing but my indivisible wholeness. All of *my* so-called environment or heredity, or *whatever* mine, can be nothing but my very own holistic living of it. I cannot be "in" any place or "surrounded" by anything since all of my so-called outside meaning is my own inside creation. It is my wholeness alone that is alive and can keep me alive, or make me want to live. Only conscious wholeness enables symptom-free joy of life.

Review

It is my wholeness alone that is responsible for whatever I am, for whatever I do or omit doing. It is the exact source responsible for any or all of my behavior. If I would understand whatever seems to happen to me (including my examination of my fellowman), it is my wholeness that I must keep in the foreground of my speculation. It is my wholeness that controls my health, education, philosophy, psychology, religion, or whatever discipline of my nature. In my wholeness I recognize the spirit of my being. Only my wholeness works, or can work. Assuming responsibility for being my wholeness is the fair price I willingly pay for advancing my understanding of my marvelous existence.

The kind of education I need, health education, is by definition: education to appreciate my wholeness. Naturally I try to verbalize myself so that my fellowman can live his Dorsey as enthusiastically thanking himself for growing this enlivening way of life that is consciously relevant to life. All life is wholly individual life. Therefore the *case method* I use is always that of myself as originating the case. The good in earning esteem for my life-worth out of living, as all else, must be experienced to be understood. The balance of my experience, with consciousness for that experience as being my self-growth, is my definition of my wisdom.

My writing style is consciously individualistic. My use of quotation is also characteristically my own. It is *my* Emerson or *my* Goethe or *my* Shakespeare I quote. My only possible obligation is to myself.

On the other hand, it is my inhibited appreciation for my wholeness that helpfully signalizes itself in innumerable symptoms of unpleasure called pain, discord, conflict, anger, grief, trouble, sickness, dispute, ignorance, distrust, superstition, war. There can be no part, division, or separation, subsidiary or subordinate, in wholeness,—*identity* only.

Continuing existence, implicit in the wish to live, is the vital meaning of any so-called progress. Every other kind of ambition may compel the interest of the whole existent only to *itself* so that one may seem to be under the control of his own striving, obsession-like, rather than the converse, which is the product of one's revered wholeness.

When I call myself one I intend to mean wholly one which I really am, but not consciously am, due to my having repressed so very much of my living by associating it with dislike. Fortunate is one who can teach himself that "No" (negation) is *always* helpful repression. If I do not consciously follow my own living I must feel lost.

I ask myself, "How does my solipsism reconcile itself with the law of nature? How about legality, the rule of law, the law of order?" My next association, or reply, to this inquiry is that, for me, there can be no meaning in such a concept as the law of nature except the meaning I create for it out of my own nature. I can understand such a conception only to the extent that my history as an individual has prepared me to do so. All of my insight supports the declaration that my only possible law of nature must correspond with my understanding of my solipsistic self. In other words, "natural law" that I can defend scientifically states: whatever is, is all and only about itself.

Everything, as everyone, is its own everything or everybody. Whatever is, is distinguished by its own unique wholeness. Self-possession is the true polity. Justice is the recognition of this law. I hold that this concept of law of nature is the one most consistent with the meaning of scientific growth of the scientist, legalistic growth of the lawyer, or theological growth of the theologian.

The first necessity of the insightful (hence self-honoring) educator is to understand the necessity that the pupil is an inviolable individual whose schooling *must* consist entirely of his own mind's educational development, that is, of his own mental *growth* in terms of his willing devotion to cultivating his own conscious self-knowledge. It is expectable that the needs of the insightless must dominate the teacher's practice of education until sufficient awareness for the history of the grievous health problem involved becomes inescapable public information of the responsible health officials.

Scientific study of any concern must begin with the history of the development of that concern. Devotion to human dignity itself is the outcome of personal history of self-appreciation creating and sustaining it. The truth of truth about myself is to be found only in the self of my self. My natural law justifies itself with this declaration of *self* sufficiency. I know of no other life orientation divinely capable of necessitating the allegiance of everyone everywhere, either with or without acknowledgeable willingness.

4

My Psychology: The Study of My Psychicality

A right thinking mind never becomes hateful to itself.
Lucius Annaeus Seneca (4 B.C.–A.D. 65)

I define my psychology as nothing but my own systematic psychic growth, the masterful study *of my* mind *by my* mind. My experience has taught me the necessity to observe the force of habit operating in my mind if I would undertake the study of the spring of my psychicality revealing exciting life value. Each form of my philosophy, psychology, religion, or education of any kind reflects the extent to which I have schooled my mind with self-consciousness.

My Albert Einstein (1879–1952) heeded, "The world of experience as I live it must be my creation," observing that every so-called natural scientist builds his psycholinguistic structures within his own subjectivity. My Ralph Waldo Emerson described the real feat of the imagination to be its showing that everything is convertible into everything else. Such considerations feature the psychical nature of fact, reality, truth.

I help myself by consciously psychicalizing every subject of my study. By psychicalize I mean: to painstakingly acknowledge my every word or meaning as being strictly my mental event only. I recognize that I help myself at enormous cost to my health (by way of obscuring my psychic integrity) in indulging the illusions of externalization and personification.

I define my streaming mind as the organismic development providing my life with its self-meaningfulness, both unconscious and conscious.[1] My Ralph Waldo Emerson considered mind as indefinable, perhaps somewhat like electric-
ity, in that it can be known only as one sees and realizes it in
his living. My working definition of it is that it is my life
force that expresses itself imaginably, both unconsciously and
consciously, in my self-contained activities such as degrees of
motion, tension, sensation, perception, consciousness, thinking, feeling, wishing, affirming, negating, so-called bodily
uses, entifying so-called not-self experience (environment,
fellowman, externality) and the like self-functioning, culminating in my appreciation for the intact subjective identity
and wholeness of my individuality.

As in the days of justly renowned William James (1842–
1910), ordinarily my psychological colleague studies mind as
an object in a world of other objects. " 'Mind,' in his mouth, is
only a class name for *minds.*" Such generally is meant by the
natural-science point of view. James goes on, *"Introspective Observation is what we have to rely on first and foremost."* To distinguish mind from all with which it may think and feel James
considers to be *"the most fundamental of all the postulates of psychology."* This life-fathoming insight invites comment about the
apparent subject-object duality. When I proceed from creating
a thought to any further creativity (e.g., consideration)
"about" that thought, e.g., going from hearing to examining
the product of my hearing (the heard), I proceed from being
subject as creator of my thought to being (as if) object in my
created thought.

Biologically adequate appreciation for the mighty necessity
that whatever is human can exist *only* in the form of human
individuality can have its *only* origin and meaning in the mind
of the private person. This most revealing, enlightening truth
for everyone must remain for each one, alone, to grow and

[1]See Glossary.

know. However, understanding of this perfectly natural fact is seldom attained. As a scientist I have learned to respect that necessity.

The phantom problem created by the mind's capacity to dissociate itself into seeming pluralities (e.g., subject-and-object, consciousness-and-unconsciousness, you-and-I, past-and-future, one-and-many, real-and-imaginary, self-and-not-self, internality-and-externality) continues to perplex today's insightless philosopher or educator quite as it has his predecessor through the ages. Personal insight (self-consciousness), the basis of sanity, is feared as insanity. My living, that is, my experience, teaches me the supreme importance of making a sharp distinction in 1) the real nature of any of my behavior and 2) what that behavior looks like to me. Certainly that distinction becomes immeasurably greater as I observe what my fellowman's conduct looks like to me and then try to imagine the real nature of that conduct. Looked at "from the outside" any behavior is inscrutable. But only the person can view his behavior from the inside, and that merely during the actual living of it. Thinking about any act after it is accomplished is by no means the same as observing it *in statu nascendi*. Despite convincing appearance to the contrary, one mind can never be in any respect an exhibit to another. Renowned psychophysiologist William James insightfully named the confusion of the agent and the observer "the psychologist's fallacy."

I work hard to recognize all of my living as meaning "self-discovery," thereby making self-discovery into *conscious* self-discovery. I find that my present conception of my being is the outgrowth of the way in which I have lived my consciousness. Consciousness is the soul of self-enlightenment. Comes to mind a statement of a favorite philosopher of mine, Irwin Edman: "What the flame is to the candle, that the soul is to the body."

I divide my consciousness functioning into three stages. First, a general consciousness for my discovering the existence

and the importance of my sensory and perceptual functioning. I presume this kind of primitive consciousness is found in
the animal mind. An animal can endure experiences which
would be too terrifying or otherwise unpleasing for me, because the animal is hardly "taking personally" any of its living
as I strive to do keenly.

Secondly, there emerges a specificity of consciousness allowing me to distinguish unities or wholenesses obscuring the
overall integration of my life meaning (mind). Around the age
of two I begin to recognize glimmerings of (a) self-consciousness that I can acknowledge and (b) self-consciousness that I
can recognize only as other-than-myself. This stage is characterized both by very gradual and uneven development. At first
it seems to be desirable, but later it results in unpleasing consequence. Thus I may come to consider it to be as far as I can
safely develop my capacity for self-observation. My most loved
hence trusted one may often seem displeased by my conscious
self-assertion. This beginning self-consciousness obviously appears to dissociate my mind so that its whole underlying unity
cannot be observed by me.

The third and final stage of my consciousness, whole-mind
consciousness, may be never or rarely attained by me. However, it is necessary that I attain it in order to understand with
biological adequacy the solipsistic nature of my whole-minded-
ness. The truth that makes me see my wholeness reveals: I *am*
all that I can mean by my "you," in the same sense that I *am* all
that I can mean by my "self." This ultimate growth of my
self-consciousness also enables me to see (1) my identity in the
kind of self-unity I developed in stage one, plus (2) my identity in whatever seemingly self and self-otherness unities I
grew in stage two. It is important to realize that each succes-
sive stage of my growth of self-consciousness exists along with
each preceding stage. My experience that self-consciousness
involves difficult self-responsibility tends to keep me from
practicing it consistently.

My fellow psychologist may comment, "You seem to have a

foolproof technique. Thus you define psychology as using your own mind to study your own mind. But you also assert that you are just as comfortable with any other definitions of mental science, that your using your present definition is not at the cost of any previous view you formerly conceived on the subject. For example, you state that your notional unity (named solipsism) created by your own subjective or spiritual exertions justifies rather than denounces any of your earlier opinions of mentality. What do you think strength of mind consists of anyhow?"

As I make my own each of these objections I reply, "Yes," to each one. My strength of mind consists of how much of it I can live kindly with full acknowledgment that it is all and only my own. The strong act of my mind is its ability to consider soberly its any and every meaning as being entirely its own creation. This mental development is so arduously achieved that it is rarely attained. Calling my soul (mind) my own and my all my soul (mind) involves shouldering the heaviest personal weight, namely, *conscious* responsibility. Hence unconscious responsibility (guilt) may be easily preferred by way of negation, denial, ideas and feelings of alien control, anonymity, etc.

My patient psychologist again: "The books I consult define *solipsism* as involving the individual's denying the existence of anybody or anything but that individual. I understand that you help yourself by avoiding validation based upon (presumed) impersonal reasoning and seeking validation by the most personal self-consciousness. You consider thinking, such as reasoning, to be an unrecognized form of wish fulfillment. You prefer to let the fact speak for itself."

As I live my you speaking and listening to yourself, I honor this questioning as my own. Yes. However in my mind, being a *solipsist* need not mean only that I deny the existence of all else simply because I can affirm merely my own existence. My having first-hand knowledge of my own being *only*, does not imply that I cannot conceive of the existence of any other

Homer D. Strong and Dr. Dorsey enjoy a moment together at a reception, May 28, 1968, honoring the director of alumni relations, Wayne State University, who held that post for twenty-five years before his retirement.

Film director King Vidor visits the Wayne State campus to discuss a forthcoming psychological film with his friend John Dorsey, July 22, 1968. Photographed in informal conversation after a luncheon in Vidor's honor are (left to right): Charles E. Feinberg, longtime friend of Dr. Dorsey and co-editor of the Walt Whitman Review; Dr. Walter H. Seegers, professor and chairman of the Department of Physiology; Dr. Dorsey; King Vidor.

Dr. Dorsey greets Professor Max Beloff, chairman of the Department of Psychiatry at the University of Milan, November 14, 1968, before a lecture sponsored by the University Professor. Also present was Luigi Lazuriola, Italian consul, Detroit.

Dr. Dorsey autographs a copy of his book American Government: Conscious Self-Sovereignty (1969) for trustees of the Center for Health Education, its publishers. Left to right: Dwight C. Ensign, H. Walter Bando, Emilie C. Sargent, Dr. Walter H. Seegers, Gertrude Grawn (Mrs. Carl B.), Robert F. Grindley, Dr. Dorsey.

A national Black History Museums conference was held at McGregor Center September 27, 1969. Examining books illustrated by Afro-American artists are (left to right): Margaret and Charles Burroughs, directors of the Du Sable African American Museum of Art, Chicago; Dr. Charles H. Wright, director of the Afro-American Museum of Detroit; and William Rea Keast, president of Wayne State University.

Detroit's mayor, Roman S. Gribbs, presents Dr. Dorsey with a citation, February 25, 1970, for his many years of work as chairman of the Mayor's Committee for Rehabilitation of Narcotic Addicts. Dr. Herbert A. Raskin, adjunct professor of psychiatry, Wayne State University, and the incoming chairman of the committee, stands at the left.

Poet Louis Ginsberg visited the Wayne State campus on several occasions, under the auspices of the University Professor. Each time he read poetry to groups of freshman medical students. A visit to the electron microscope laboratory inspired him to write a poem, which he entitled "Electron Microscope." Printed and framed, together with his photograph, it was presented to him October 23, 1970, by Dr. Walter H. Seegers, professor and chairman of the Department of Physiology. He was delighted to receive it and left it for placement at the entrance to the laboratory.

Among those present at the ceremonies marking the opening of the Vera Parshall Shiffman Medical Library, July 7, 1970, were (left to right): Dr. Alfred H. Whittaker and Norman O. Stockmeyer, members of the Wayne State University Board of Governors, and Edward L. Cushman, executive vice-president.

being and live that conception as integral to my own self-identity. Quite the contrary. I can posit the wholeness of other existence just to the extent that I can comprehend my own wholeness. This conscious mind-continence is difficult to attain, hence the antagonistic tendency to dispose of its vital truth by describing it as a dilemma, or predicament, necessarily denying the existence of anybody but one's self.

I cannot create, or in any way grow meaning for, any experience except by living it. All of my sensing is nothing but my growing of it, but by assuming that I can touch, taste, smell, etc., something or somebody other than myself, I appear to myself to be able to suspend or abrogate my own absolute self-continence. The analogical consequence of my sensory functioning for all of the rest of my working mind (and the converse) is far-reaching and, as far as I know, hardly appreciated.

I live my psychologist: "That seems a lofty generality making little sense for me. Please try to be specific and less dry about it. Verify it if you will."

Again I see my identity in my you. Yes. I can live no cogent evidence other than self-evidence. My only possible datum of experience is my mental process. I practice the use of my sensation as soon as it appears and, from that uninstructed psychic functioning my growing mind derives forcible meanings, such as space, time, duration, eternity, infinity, motion, force, substance, plurality, part, change, otherness, externality, presence, absence, light, dark, sound, quiet, warm, cold, emotionality, help, etc.

To illustrate, I create my sensory (mental) dimension of space-and-time. Then I proceed to apply its qualities in innumerable forms to my other (also subjective, spirited) mental functioning, thereby modifying the latter's meaning. Thus I may derive such seemingly structural ideas as beginning-and-end, extension-and-limitation, length, weight, measure, body, preexistence, afterlife or any other meaning that can tend to obscure the fact that all of my being is always here-and-now living of my own internality only.

My psychologist: "How did you become a solipsist? I mean a *conscious* solipsist, for I understand you were born an absolutely self-contained individual and there can be no choice about that."

I answer my own question: Purposefully, by laborious and often painfully dry practice of self-awareness, itself, only. Schooling is always self-education, but rarely conscious self-education.

My capacity to function *alone* creates and cultivates my appreciation for my own immediateness in my existence. This truth of acknowledgeable self-continence, in its totality, constitutes the nature of self-consciousness, the subject of my life's interest. Ancient sages score the consequence of one's functioning, and not functioning. Pythagoras (c. 578–510 B.C.) ordered, "Ponder all things, and stablish high thy mind, that best of charioteers." Heraclitus (c. 540–480 B.C.) recorded awareness of the need to study the constant flow of his self-activity. Empedocles (c. 490–435 B.C.), credited with founding the first great medical school, taught the love of freedom of functioning as well as the separation and strife resulting from the activation of hatred. Hippocrates (460–375 B.C.) held, "The patient's nature is the doctor that cures his illness." Epicurus (341–270 B.C.), who practiced the frugal life, recognized that absence of pain is the only true pleasure of vital functioning, of act and avoidance. He founded the oldest sanatorium for the sufferer of mental trouble (310 B.C. in Mytilene). The counsel of Epictetus (c. A.D. 60–110) to those who fear want is: "Exercise yourself. . . . thus only are men made free."

The science of mentality, as every other science, must eventuate in a well-made language. My scientific work is not reducible to any kind of verbalism, however. Rather, my research is the product only of my mind's growing itself. This creativity precedes my finding accurate naming to describe it. All of my growing of myself, constituting the whole of my activity of any kind, is preverbal, even preconscious. Nevertheless, all of my wording of my mental living is of vital consequence for my cultivating my realization that my living is all and only my own. For this purpose my every word must be examined as to its accuracy for naming the *psychical* derivation of every meaning.

To illustrate, I find usage of each term *psychical* and *psychological* often implying sameness and therefore presumed to be interchangeable, but such is not at all factual. Yet I find the consequence of such habitual usage immeasurably meaningful. As an insufficiently informed scientist I can understand my aversion to considering so-called "psychological" research worthy of my scientific study. I can observe that the term "psychical," however, refers specifically to individual mentality itself (rather than to justly or unjustly assumed study-of-mentality) and offers itself readily as a desirable dimension of my constitution.

The term *physiology* refers to the mind's study of the form and functioning of physique. No ambiguity attaches to the fact that the intention of this discipline is to lead to the certainty of individual organic performance. On the other hand *psychology* refers to the individual mind's study of its own nature, my seldom honored idea which, nevertheless, I consider to be of dominant importance. Appreciation for the psychic (not psychological) nature of physiology (as of every other science or art) is my long-sought-for integrative understanding that unites conception of my brain and conception of my mind, conception of my so-called external world and conception of my divinity. I note that in my religious terms such conscious life integration constitutes what I mean by the salvation of my soul. I find that all of my soul's uneasiness is traceable to my overlooking its wholeness and allness. The intelligibility derivable from my appreciation for my intact integrity is my sufficient source of life satisfaction. It is a system of life felicity with the understandable purpose and order of self-authority and self-responsibility. Whatever I live, like Jehovah, is that *that* it is of me. I can be umbilical only to myself. "External" is a name for nowhere. Whatever is, internally is.

My need to build a connection between my physiological

and psychological meanings (as in psychosomatic concepts) is resolved by my awakening to my mind's observation of my body meaning as being the origin of its psychicality. The need for a "connection" yields to the recognition of the organic psychical (not psychological) identity underlying all meaningfulness, e.g., cerebral anatomy, biology, physiology, biochemistry, biophysics, cosmogeny, history, ethics, etc. My insightless need for "alien bodies" of any description is traceable to my need to repress them (to repudiate them as psychic entities). The description and understanding of human want and conflict as being symptomatic of repudiated psychicality in my individual mind is the new sense and new meaning that my own ongoing self analysis, *only,* continues to produce. I now recognize that my tendency to separate any study of mine from its psychicality is to leave that study in the air without any organic basis, —just the opposite of my former hesitation to attribute organicity to psychic activity.

In the interest of my continuing welfare I may treat any of my so-called past living as not gone but as not sufficiently propitious to be consciously involved for the time being. Thus I willingly renounce it with the understanding that it is good in itself and therefore potentially a helpful function. Living is not a finishing experience until it completes itself.

As Aristotle discerned, man *must be* personally concerned with his living of his fellowman. American sculptor Horatio Greenough (1805–1852) explained, "Whenever there is a wrong, the response is pain. The rowdy eyes that glare on you from the mob say plainly that they feel that you are doing them to death. . . . Your six percent is as deadly a weapon as the old knife and tomahawk." Thomas Jefferson found it only natural to be concerned with how his fellowman was growing his life.

Although I understand that the practice of so-called communication is the source of habituation to a potentially dangerous illusion implying that each communicator can impose his will upon the other, I am also aware that usage of this illusion habitually exists in, and is helpfully cherished by, everyone. The growing child's mind needs this illusion as long as he must remain unconsciously dependent upon his parent.

Thus a so-called humanistic psychologist may be concerned with the "common lot" of "members of the human family" and upholds his "communication" as an act capable of uniting one individual with another, hence good for everybody. It is this habit of mind, formed early in life as a stage of understandable mental development, that may also force the taught mind into a groove that prevents its possessor from devoting his life-interest to the truth of his absolutely inviolable individuality. By habitually (insightlessly) indulging my illusion that I can unite myself with another individual I forfeit my understanding that my every word is created organically out of my linguistic living.[2]

Knowing full well that all of my speaking and writing is by, about, for and to myself, I keep disciplining my mind with awareness for its own law by explicitly declaring (to myself) that I am merely wording for myself certain new ways of helping myself. True, only the *ideal* can be the real, but the "material" can be only the unconscious ideal, after all. However, no new way of minding can be advanced at the cost of any former way. I know the new way is the outgrowth of the previous way and therefore cannot exist without it. Thus, I am able to be just as comfortable using my mind self-continently now as in the unconscious way I began using it. I can still live with love all of my thoughts and feelings about "communication," just as I formerly did.[3] But my so-called surrounding is really my forceful living.

Every stage of my mental development owes its being to all of my preceding mental development. The moment any expe-

[2]See my "Idiolect," *Communication of Scientific Information* (Basel: S. Karger, 1975), pp. 12–27.

[3]"We can afford to allow the limitation, if we know it is the meter of the growing man" (Ralph Waldo Emerson).

rience, even the most exciting, apparently usurps the place of my insight that it is mine, at that moment it is traumatic. My experience cannot take the place of my mind except in the one place where my mind lives it. The physician of his mind cannot be a faultfinder, but rather a seer of the necessary lifesaving helpfulness in all of his mentality, a redeemer of his real wholesomeness disguised as apparent partialism, a discoverer of the perfection in all conduct of his life, however imperfect it may seem to be at the moment, a beholder of the lifesaving helpfulness in every kind of pain, sorrow, and indifference. He knows he cannot be dwarfed by any of his own living.

The "quality" educational psychology I crave is that of my learning to know that *all* of me is identically great, rather than that some-of-me is greater than another some-of-me. I must have an eye constant to the basic truth: Whatever is, *perfectly* is. In presenting my ideas about the specific self-belittlement in the insightless and irresponsible usage of so-called communication, I take care to distinguish the fact-finding involved from the charge of so-called faultfinding that might easily be read into it. I live each of my ever-present illusions with love, recognizing each one as being my own helpful experience. I am as proud of my first as of my subsequent development of mind, recognizing the former as being the indispensable root of the latter. Yet, the deeper I go in my study of my language, the more I can understand it as being my own psycholinguistic growing of the orchestration of my wholeness.

The fact that I cannot attribute wholeness to any of my world except to the degree that I recognize my own wholeness is a truth that I could not grow prior to my creating much informed meaning for my own undivided entirety. Only after my conscious self-unification became evident to me could I realize that the significance of each aspect of my being develops its full sense specifically in terms of the overall meaning of the nature of my complete inseparableness. At last I then understood that I am not made up of parts but rather of developmental constituent wholes integral to my uninterrupted totality. My self-conscious perspective reveals all of my illusional gaps in my personal identity as united in my true altogetherness. It is in this light of self-consciousness that living becomes illuminated as continuous self-fulfillment, as original not a copy, as creativity not fuss, as selective not "chance."

I have grown increasing understanding of any so-called common tongue as necessitating a systematic *unconscious* self-belittlement in its linguist, thereby necessitating (in protest) an augmenting, systematic, unconscious symptom formation in its linguist. By habitually overlooking myself in my wording I become increasingly anaesthetic to the sensation of selfness in my language. The future security of my freedom-cherishing way of life rests upon my continuing ability to distinctify and support my concrete truth of my absolute individuality, as contrasted with my seeming to subject myself to my mind's abstract conception of any form of collectivity. Only what *I* do, or do not, can have any significance for *my* world. Doing is unconscious feeling, including thinking. All being is compositional doing of what one is, namely growing (living) selfhood.

This self-understanding created in the depth of my individuality is the product only of my cultivation of my *conscious* self-education. It is not at all traceable to so-called communication, upon which my formal education seems traditionally based. All so-called communication involves verbal magic, which conveniently appears to be able to bypass the reverberation of inviolable individuality.

The Fund For Adult Education member tries valiantly to recognize and cope with the role of language in the development of man's appreciation for his own freedom.[4] Citizen resistance to consciously cultivating his knowledge as being entirely self-knowledge is so very powerful that he finds it preferable to demand opportunity for "quality education" without

[4]*Toward the Liberally Educated Executive* (White Plains, N.Y.: Fund for Adult Education, 1957).

insisting that it must be conscious self-education. Wholeness-consciousness is momentary wisdom. Only conscious self-education can start or sustain the mental process that creates conscious self-wholeness. A so-called well-balanced education is the growth only of a mind disciplined to balance itself, insightfully. *Just when conscious self-education becomes the backbone of my educational system can it be safe for me to tie my love of freedom to the future of my systematic education.*

Hardest of all for my fellow student to highlight is that any innovation upon his self-understanding must be an outgrowth of his existing understanding, and cannot function at all as repudiation of any of his previous self-appreciation. However, once he has mastered the fact that all his mind can ever do is grow its own experience as self-knowledge, he can begin to sense his benefit in his willingness to consider every creation of his innovative mind as his own living of it, hence as already demonstrably lifeworthy. My *every* meaning is the creation of my own living mind; hence it is insightless for me to oppose my meaning for body or matter or death to my meaning for mind.

For me willingly to take responsible command of my power of flashing self-consciousness is the self-reliance that enables my cultivating my appreciation for my wholeness, my freedom of freedom. All men are created equal, each one equal to his (her) own individuality, but no one is born consciously equal to his or her own human nature. Every American is born with the same governmental sanction for growing consciously equal to his (her) own magnificent being. Such conscious psychogenesis is at once the development of responsible American citizenship and the optimal fulfillment of life. Continuing education on this willing responsibility is my lifetime Americanization project. *Freedom to become aware for the enjoyable whole of one's self is the ultimate benefit of conscious self-sovereignty. It is the uniquely American contribution to the divine goal of world citizenship.*

Painfully I gradually grew wise to the necessity that any so-called community language must be a costly illusion specifically responsible for the linguist's losing his conscious mind through making it his unconscious mind, by giving it a name that does not reveal to him his own personal identity, *only,* in it. "Painfully" because this growth of self-understanding had to proceed against my need to continue indulging my very strongly intrenched habit of mind. I refer to my comforting usage of my language to conceal whatever of my living I cannot yet associate with love, from my living I can kindly unite as my acknowledgeable personal identity.

The *why* of my heeding, as wholly as possible, the necessity I name wholeness, may or may not be obvious at first consideration. However, further deliberation fully justifies it. My every ideal originates in it and, in fact, every possible meaning of my mind owes its existence to it. Goodness, itself, is good to the extent that it is universally beneficial. Beauty is beautiful insofar as it fully satisfies. Truth, itself, means the whole truth. The sound of music is the song of individual freedom to enjoy wholeness, wholeness that subsumes "externals" as physiological.

Discipline with self-consciousness is my mind's attainment of salvation. Believe what I will, it is first necessary for me to believe in my own life, the valid and verifiable measure of all of my understanding. I am my life—I am the meaning of the history of my growth. *Whole-life appreciation for one's own fluent living is the moral law governing the just conduct of the flaring immensity, life.* To dare to pioneer my vital meaning consciously to its perfect freedom of functioning constantly tests the growth of my moral heroism. I deem conscious self-insight to be the most fitting apparatus for psychic research, for investigating all that can be real, namely inness. Whatever the direction, whatever the distance, every observation of dimension must be of the observer's internality, the locality of depth, soul, spirit, essence, identity. The surface is entirely modified gradation of innativeness that goes deep down as the force of life. All externality is the illusion created by the negation of internality, quite as materiality is the negation of ideality. Whatever exists, exists in itself only.

I cannot live my concerted innateness in my "environment" because my environment must be lived as my inbeing. From this consistent experience I observe that all of my so-called externality exists inly, in terms of *its* own internality. By appreciating that all of my looking must be at what is inside me, I can attribute this necessity to every existent of my imagined "outside" world. My scientific duty is to see to it that I am honorably realizing that my every meaning, psychic experience, is all and only an individuation of my individuality. I cannot even want to practice this fidelity for my integrity except to the extent that I can fully appreciate the benefit to myself, including my fellowman, derivable only from thus remaining true to my self. Living with the idea of what it means to be able to live is the consequence of hard mental discipline in that manward development.

My alert reader objects, "You might as well contend that ideality results from repressed materiality." True. However, the concept of materiality is congenial to the conscious idealist who includes it in his scientific deliberations, whereas the concept of ideality is not congenial to the conscious materialist who excludes it from his scientific deliberations. In other words, it is not necessary for the idealist to exclude any of his meanings of materialism from his scientific orientation; it is necessary for the materialist to exclude his meanings of idealism from his scientific orientation. Honored wholeness of mind is at stake.

Each of my meanings for my body is nothing but a mental construct, despite my habit of excluding it from my mind as such. Furthermore, my so-called body meanings constitute the nucleus of my mentality. Thus, all physical hygiene is really mental hygiene; athletic practice is mental exercise; every kind of posture, station, gait, gesture, or whatever doing is my growing of my psychical activity. A great benefit derivable from so-called physical games, including walking, swimming, or various forms of play, is the fact, realized or unrealized, that the wholeness of the individual enters into them.

Clear observation that all of my living is here-and-now living has necessitated my adding present insights to seemingly previous ones. For example, so-called memory provides a striking instance of how I can use my mind in a way that seems to deny the truth that all of my living is immediate living only, that all I can ever be aware of is merely whatever I happen to be presently growing of myself. My illusion that I can "recall" any of my past living, as such, is all at the expense of my conscious devotion to my present being. The whole popular meaning of memory can be explained only on the basis of mental dissociation rather than integration. The fact is that I can resort to imagining that my remembering is far removed from my present psychic life whenever I cannot acknowledge the true significance of that memory content for my present existence.

By imagining that whatever I am now experiencing is really far off somewhere in time or space, I can spare myself from acknowledging the limited extent of my present self-tolerance. Thus my memory can be relied upon as a form of living myself unconsciously while appearing to myself to be awake. Whatever is, only is. All that can be alive of my so-called past is my present growing of myself. My reminiscing is wholly my present creating of self-meaning. My forgetting can apply only to my unreadiness to create present living, not past. My present retentivity depends upon my preparedness to live consciously whatever I might prefer to call past recollection. I do not redeem any of my mind from oblivion but rather create newly whatever I choose to consider memorized.

This here-and-now living appreciation of so-called remembrance is deeply significant for my adequately honoring the allness that I actually am. None of me can be bygone. Every scene of my childhood is dear to my heart, but its fond "recollection" depends upon my present readiness to acknowledge it as mine. Any of my mentality that I dissociate as being not present, obviously cannot rid me of it. I go on living it dangerously, as if I am not responsible for its being. As mentioned, this rejected existence of some of myself must impair my voluntary appreciation for my true wholeness, thereby contributing to my symptom-forming depreciation of my wonderful life itself. Mental trouble is aptly described as presently suffering from unrecognizable reminiscences. To the extent that I cannot grow to recognize that I now possess all of my self, I must conduct my life "like one possessed." All "forgetfulness" is unconscious mindfulness.

Probably the first psychologist could not be interested in staying in his right mind, a condition dependent upon the arduous cultivation of conscious self-responsibility. My beginning to assume complete responsibility for self-direction is the beginning of my becoming an adult. My realizing that my living is a continuous release of my creative power helps me to acknowledge my magnificence, including the magnificence of my everyone. My every function, my every word, is an expression of the necessity of my wholeness.

My only alternative as a beginning psychologist is to conduct my mental power of observation as if it could somehow get outside of my mind to report on what I must consider to be external to me. Then, unable to recognize my mind in such latter meanings, I resort to that dichotomy of dichotomies, mental-and-physical. Soon such helpful fictions as theoretical-and-practical, ideal-and-material, sacred-and-secular are created. And thereby, little by little, a vocabulary supporting my individual irresponsibility for my own marvelous being becomes the so-called language "of the people," seemingly not referable to my person alone. My own career is a case history of a research scientist finally discovering his own living only in whatever he lives.

One mind blindness possible as a psychologist can become most overlooked of all others, namely, my unawareness that as a psychologist I have nothing, and can have nothing, but my growing of my own life to go on, in my efforts to explain any and all of that life's experiencing itself. I need a language of biology for describing any of my living, including my every doctrine.

In my educational literature I find increasing mention of
the ideal of freedom of the *whole* man, for example, "What the
industrialist wants is the individual who possesses the imaginative comprehension which comes from understanding the
whole condition of man."

Why does my freedom occur? So that I may liberate myself
from imposing my unconscious will upon my living as if it
could be foreign to my conscious will. I am free, in the sense
of *consciously* enjoying my freedom, only to the extent that I
govern myself willingly in terms of the wholeness of my life
which includes my repressed mentation. My choosing is wholly
just that grows out of my awareness for my organic integrity
—a process of synderesis as distinguished from syneidesis.

My schooling is liberal insofar as it disciplines me in appreciating my wholeness, my allness, by my recognizing that my
education is the growth of my self-knowledge. With regard to
the meaning of my self, my living is my making up of my own
mind. However, my growing reverence for that truth is the
heart and soul of my education to health.[5] William W. Jellema
noted well, "The concept of the wholeness of man, moreover,
implies that what is taught ought to recall his wholeness and
not further fragment him."

It is the diremptive power of the mind that can explain the
seeming divergence of the psychic devotee of the East in his
study of (his) subjectivity from the psychic scientist of the West
in his study of (his) objectivity. Certainly I need to grow understanding of the rich yield of yoga, as of Western psychicality. To illustrate, I taught myself the traditional neurological
language, or perspective, that my vegetative nervous system
can operate only unconsciously, being alienated from my control and therefore named my autonomic nervous system. Or, I
may have taught myself the language indicating that my primary unconscious mind is alienated from my possibility of my

[5]See "Living Education," *Michigan Education Journal,* April and May,
1957.

ever achieving mastery of most meaningful linguistic self-growth essential for my appreciating the wholeness-nature of my being.

However, the wordage used in the study of yoga constitutes a language largely foreign to my accepted psychic vocabulary so that I must learn to translate its terms into my scientific syllables. To be sure, great efforts to attain this conscious unity have already proved successful for the occidental and oriental student exerting them. For example, the advance of self-insight realized by the western bioenergetic scientist is most encouraging biofeedback. Scientific exploration of my visceral internality, formerly considered to be inaccessible for research, is now extending the vistas of introspection in a manner and to a degree most promising for supporting realization of the inviolable wholeness of human individuality. The fact that such investigation of my hidden internality meets with my strong resistance is expectable in view of my same tendency to ignore most valuable self-information, during my self-analysis, of regions of my mind other than those of my body.

Resistance

I have been studying (researching) the development of self-consciousness to find the nature of resistance to that sure source of life appreciation. Whenever I protest against my necessity to live any of my experience, I feel a strong resistance even to considering it kindly. My self-conscious mind, which provides me with my feeling of acknowledged self-wholeness, is unwilling to extend its recognized sameness to whatever I live with dislike. Hence it is I can understand my colleague's need to resist kind consideration for whatever psychicality that has not already integrated itself into conscious self-identity. The significance of resistance for producing repression and its associated symptom formation is rarely recognized. Rather I can practice resistance with little or no appreciation for its necessarily dangerous consequence. It is this mental condition of "taking for granted" that I can resist my own living with impunity that is the hidden source of my health trouble, including "criminality." Therefore I elaborate on the biological role of resistance in my growing of my conscious self-knowledge. It is a sign of my present unreadiness to see my lovable identity in whatever I must live under protest, and therefore an indication that my appreciation for my wholeness is that much obscured.

In his "History of the Psycho-Analytic Movement" (1914), Professor Sigmund Freud describes his original theory of repression as "the foundation stone" on which his psychoanalysis rests. From the start he observed his mind's tendency to seek pleasure and avoid pain. He recognized the ease with which the habit of regarding pleasure as good and pain as bad might be set up to the subsequent disadvantage of overlooking the lifesaving understanding of the helpfulness of each. Specifically, he discovered unenlightened resistance to honoring the existence of any of his psychicality must require some compensatory symptom formation. He noticed that unpleasurable feeling can serve as the initial force accounting for the act of repression, for the process of conscious activity becoming unconscious activity and continuing to operate as such. He also noted that repressed meaning, denied conscious manifestation as willingly lived, reveals its thus alienated energy in a compulsive, obsessional (involitional) form. With keenest scientific acumen he pursued the expression of unpleasurable feeling, detecting its potential and actual significance for favoring unconscious employment by resisting self-conscious behavior. If exercising my psychic power produces pain of any kind, that distress tends to impose restriction upon my freely using my power. In this sense, my associating unpleasure with any of my life's meaning may and does function to limit my conscious freedom and augment my unconscious occupation.

Transference and *resistance* are key words in psychoanalytic work. Each term refers to my difficulty in growing my wholly lovable mind with realization that it is all and only mine. "Transference" is a process which enables me to displace my emotionality *as if* it might apply to someone else, thus: "It is you I love (or hate) not myself," "You make me angry, I certainly do not make myself angry," "I fear you, not me," "I am jealous of you, not of myself," and so on. Transference therefore enables me to bypass my otherwise disabling resistance to acknowledging that my emotionality, as all else that I live, has to do only with my own being.

I begin to develop my transference and resistance patterning early in life, as soon as I achieve meaning for my self-identity enabling me to distinguish it from all of my living for which I cannot yet work up conscious self-responsibility. What I cannot live with as conscious self-responsibility I must live with unconscious self-responsibility, namely, guilt. My original sin of necessarily denying my wholeness can leave me guilt-ridden for life unless I resolve it with my self-insight.

Whether I live my experience with like or dislike can have nothing whatsoever to do with the experience itself, as Professor Freud's mentor, Professor Jean-Martin Charcot, observed. Liking is all and only about liking, itself; disliking is all and only about disliking, itself. This truth about resistance is the only key that can open the door of my conviction that my life is a whole individuality that is all and only about itself. Furthermore, my living any of my experience with any form of unpleasure (disliking such as pain, hatred, regret, indignation, scorn, fear, envy, or whatever) merely indicates my present unreadiness to live that experience with the corresponding form of pleasure (liking such as enjoyment, love, gladness, engagement, praise, courage, pride, or whatever). I begin to become ready to renounce my resistance in favor of acceptance only when I begin to discover that sufficient truth must be on the side of whatever happens in order to make it happen. Every kind of unpleasure is a corresponding form of life-affirming pleasure that I have negated (made unconscious). Every form of unpleasure is already a resistance feeling.[6] It is the feeling of resistance, itself, that motivates me to try to do something to alleviate my unplea-

[6]See my *Psychology of Emotion,* pp. 85–136.

sure and thus restore my free joy of living. In order to control my emotionality I must first of all experience it, quite as if it were controlling me. Then I must gradually teach myself that my every emotion is subject to me, rather than all of me to it. Then I can soon learn to renounce being resistant to my resistances, just as I can learn to renounce being intolerant of other intolerance.

Resistance is my conscious mind's lifesaving defense against overwhelming itself with excitation which it is not yet strong enough to acknowledge as worth living. Resistance resolves itself when it is recognized for being what it is, namely, a helpful illusion that what is myself is not myself.

Being a "sorehead" or having "blind spots" are illustrations of my allowing my feeling of unpleasure (of any kind or degree from severe pain to mild aversion) to decide the extent of my development of my self-consciousness. Professor Freud insightfully regarded dreaming as the "guardian of sleep," sparing my awakening to unpleasing realities of my existence. In quite the same sense, my every resistance may and does guard me from awakening to the truth that I *am* my "dislikes" quite as I *am* my "likes," merely by limiting my realization that the wholeness of my individuality alone prescribes the limits of my solipsistic self-identity.

Ideally, I conceive my mind as existing for the purpose of my appreciating the wonderfulness of my life. Ideally, it provides me with the meaning of my life. Ideally, it behooves me to use my mind to be able to consider whatever experience it presents and, ultimately, to find that experience good. I not only live it, but I live by means of it, whatever it may seem like.

The "cure" of my helpful signs and symptoms consequent upon my desperately dissociating my mind into I and not-I (resisted) compartments lies in my teaching myself to understand how all of my life has been a struggle to maintain whatever degree of conscious self-identity I might achieve with my limited understanding (hence limited control) of the innumerable resistances to calling my soul my own and my all my soul.

Habit

It is not surprising to me if I turn my eyes in one so-called external direction or another as if to look at something outside of me, and then the consequence is that I seem to be able to see what I am trying to look at. Similarly, turning my attention in a direction which I know is within me results in my lighting up conscious self-observation which was before impossible. Such attention led me to examine the role of lightless habit in obscuring my true nature. Habit ("second nature"), in the form of conscious-self nescience, regularly supervenes to eclipse the self-illumination providable only by acknowledge-able self-responsibility.[7]

Unquestionably, habit steadies and lends the seeming of security. However, my ponderous habituation that exists is hardly ever recognized by me. Yet it obviously exists at the cost of cultivation of my conscious will, and it certainly diminishes my appreciation for the truth that my life is always fresh, constantly new. All of my so-called impersonal education that I cannot recognize as habitude must exist as my unconscious mentality; hence the lifesaving importance in my realizing that all of my knowledge is my newly self-grown mind.[8] (My) Pestalozzi anticipated the psychoanalytic finding: "The picture of its mother, which accompanies it everywhere, becomes itself the conscience of the child."

I accustom myself easily to a life of enjoyment rather than unaccustoming myself difficultly to enjoyment of my life. Actually to make myself ignorant by customary conventional

---

[7]"Habit is second nature," the wise saw of Diogenes.

[8]See Paul Radestock, *Habit and Its Importance in Education: An Essay in Pedagogical Psychology*, trans. F. A. Caspari (Boston: D. C. Heath & Co., 1889), pp. 49–62.

education must remain my necessity unless I attain understanding of the loss of liberty I must sustain by progressive
habituation that substitutes obscure mannerism for consciousness honoring my mental development. Little wonder that I
suffer insightlessly from monotony, boredom, ennui, disspir-
ited sensations (my only passion being for some experience
that I can enjoy as new), as long as my habit has obscured the
truth that all of my living is of necessity always newborn. Only
by teaching myself that I am a growing individual identity
completely founded in itself can I discover the soft and soften-
ing illusion in the unsensed contradiction defining habit as
"second nature." Learning is the new unity produced by the
learner's creating his own lesson.

Throughout this volume may be observed considerations of
the powerful force of education as habit (unconscious self-
experience) or as the growth of self-knowledge (conscious self-
development). Most of my so-called conscious living, conducted while I am supposedly awake, is not conscious at all in
the true sense of being systematically acknowledged as entirely
my own living. I can assume that I am fully awake even
though I am not acknowledging that I am awake to myself
only and entirely. My habitual processes are not consciously
performed as a rule. The ability to sense consciousness wholly
as *self*-consciousness serves as the scale of mental strength.

It is important not merely what I do, but also why I do it.
For example, I can appear only to belong to this university
committee or that, to this city board or that, to this civic foundation or that, and so on, furthering this academic interest,
advancing this city development, perpetrating or correcting
this social "error," or whatever—all the while fully realizing
also that *my* university, city, society, or government all belong
to me, exist meaningfully as living interests in my own individual mind, quite as I understand that all of my experiences of
my fellowman exist entirely in his (her) own mind. My writing
chronicles my real *present* living of seeming past experience,
otherwise it would seem to be "a heap of nouns and verbs

enclosing an intuition or two" (Ralph Waldo Emerson). Secret magnanimity!

Review

Freedom, as every other meaning, is psychic and is the product of consciousness for the solipsistic nature of whatever exists. To be free is to be aware that whatever is, is all and only itself. Tolerance for being all of my wholeness is the greatest conceivable strain upon my wholeness. Hence my resistance to consciously psychicalizing my every experience routinely as evident respect for the truth of my necessary self-continence. Hence my unseeing search for my freedom, which I must hunger for as long as I refuse to see how it is employed in being entirely and only itself. Meanwhile, I am free to live *as if* my life experience is not all and only its own. However, by thus appearing to deprive my life of that much *(as if* living) of its true meaning, I forego biologically adequate appreciation for my real wholeness, as my consequent symptom formation confirms. I try to make my brilliant reasoning do, for what only my mere self-observation can do.

The problem of human unity arises from disregard for the only location of meaning of human totality, which can exist only in each human individual. All union, binding, cohesion, or whatever unifying power, in order to be wholesomely meaningful for the individual, must be recognized as existing ideally only in each one. My work as a psychologist properly addresses itself to as great as possible elucidation of this rarely recognized fact.

Such effort requires difficult toleration of extending difficultly lovable self-consciousness. Only conscious self-love can enable biologically adequate appreciation for sufficient self-truth to comprehend self-wholeness. Hoping for such self-development is a necessary form of initially experiencing it. My disciplined honoring of the truth of my innate wholeness is integral to my making myself consciously whole.

Despite all of the religious, educational, and scientific evidence constantly attesting that every individual can and must create his (her) own world within him (her), nevertheless I find self-understanding, derivable only from augmenting appreciation for one's inviolable individuality, is the chief desideratum in self-development accountable for every possible so-called "social" problem including war, poverty, crime, illness, and the like obvious belittlements of human individuality. To feel lost in the perception of a so-called external object and to activate the self-consciousness of sanity at the same time is impossible.

Language can become a habitude that strengthens the illusion of self-alienation, thereby weakening appreciation for the truth of inviolable individuality. The sense of truth of self-wholeness cannot be grown into a habit. Rather the act of self-consciousness always involves conscious will. The fostering of the sensing of self-consciousness engenders aesthetic, moral, and religious appreciation, particularly by honoring the truth of truths, namely, one's ever-innovating life itself. Self-consciousness is self-mastery.

From all of this realization of how habit appears to be able to bypass self-consciousness, and specifically conscious will, it becomes understandable how (my) Jean Jacques Rousseau (1712–1778) could claim, "The only habit which a child should be permitted to acquire is this, that it habituate itself to nothing in particular." Rousseau wanted the child "to be always master of itself and always to follow only its own will as soon as it shall have one." Free and independent self-decision, appreciation for one's own absolute originality and controllable conscious and unconscious mentality to care for, provides motivation of the greatest power for arduous intellectual labor. Only self-consciousness can generate conscientiousness; only self-unconsciousness can engender disregard for consequence.

Taking notice of my own unique nature is the only true foundation supporting due accounting of my growing-of-self-understanding, the basic principle of all of my consciously free psychicality. Necessarily it is never too late, always just the right time, for me to begin health education that can be secured only from disciplined devotion to the truth of my very own authority and responsibility for living my conscious oneness. My United States Government officials are sworn to uphold this ideal of acknowledgeable self-sovereignty! But it must be my private personal will to go to work to honor all that I can be in the individual that I am. My beyond is ever inness of my wholeness.

My beginning consciousness permits no appreciation for the existence of my whole individuality as such. It involves neither my authority nor my responsibility for being my self. Somewhere around the age of two or three years I begin to be fleetingly aware of the personal nature of my united selfhood. Even then I soon find that my considering my nature to be a special one is attended by painful feeling of separation, of aloneness, so that I tend to avoid pursuing further the truth of my self-possession. Yet I must develop my self-consciousness in order to discover the self-continent unity of my life. First, through the persevering exercise of my self-consciousness I must try to find out just what it means to be a whole self, an individual. Then and only then do I become capable of attributing the same kind of unique wonderfulness to my every fellow person. It is my awareness for my intact oneness and allness that enables me to conceive my self as a subjective soul and, as such, an individuation of the soul of my universe.

⇒》《⇐ 5 ⇒》《⇐
My Science

I cannot find language of sufficient energy to convey
my sense of the sacredness of private integrity.
Ralph Waldo Emerson

I find that the direction of all scientific discovery is towards realistic simplification of illusional complexity, observing the unity underlying variety, observing the subjectivity comprising "objectivity." Creative functioning of the ingenious concept "conscious individuality" engenders understanding of the revealing wholeness of psychical living. Full acceptance of my full self consequently functions to advance my seeing my identity in all my so-called external world, just as my firm grip on a whole tool functions for any other work. All of my understanding is the issue of my uniting into a recognizable whole whatever I wish to understand.

Man has been described functionally as a tool maker. In his creation of every word he can observe his image and likeness, the creator. Most unique of all he is a wordsmith who enlarges his wordage without recognizing that all of this increase consists simply of a naming of meaning constituting only his own growing mind. As usual, seer Ralph Waldo Emerson discerned this self-enlightening view: "A man hardly knows how much he is a machine, until he begins to make telegraph, loom, press, and locomotive, *in his own image*" (my italics). Even then he may, and ordinarily does, develop a vocabulary of mechanics, physics, biology, or whatever, by means of which he appears to be able to lose, rather than find, his own mind in each of his own mind's verbal creations. All of my writing has one meaning for me only: my life. My conscious solipsist Søren Kierkegaard recorded, "The critical judgment which excludes a writer from the realm of literature does not limit his sphere of action; but the criticism which assigns him a definite place within, may well be cause for apprehension."

I stop to realize the full extent of the irresponsible verbal life that I let lead me in my earlier existence, the childish helplessness in my plight of limited ability to recognize my mind as a functioning apparatus for creating and appreciating only my own life's meaning. My greatest good is the biologically adequate functioning of my organic meaning, an achievement that depends specifically upon my working up my capacity to discover that I *am* all and only whatever I live. This truth about myself would have overwhelmed me, if I had tried to comprehend it all at once.

My child self must be unskillful in the use of my mind. Then I hardly know that I know my mind exists. For example, if I were to observe myself using any other instrumentality of my world as I did my mind, my natural life awkwardness (limited agility) would be instantly apparent, providing me with the incentive to add to my proficiency.

Naming is an important psychic act of powerful consequence deserving heedful consideration. My every word is a name given by me to some meaning integral to my own mind. In fact my every word is sanely conceivable as a synonym for my name.[1]

To the extent that I do not take my wordage seriously, responsibly, as being a manifestation of my ideality, I thus far ignore the organic truth of my own wholeness. The truth is that every kind of kingdom I can know anything about exists within me, in the form of a systematic vocabulary I attribute to it. The effectiveness of that truth depends upon how much

[1]*Psychology of Language*, pp. xxi–xxxiv.

importance I make of it. My scientific tendency is to overlook it entirely or merely take it for granted.

For example, when Carolus Linnaeus (1707–1778) invented biological nomenclature and divided all of his world of nature into the three kingdoms, minerals, plants, and animals, his verbal equipment undoubtedly included the word *spirit,* as he was the son of a clergyman (Nils Ingemarsson). Furthermore, the connotation of "spirit" corresponds with the subjectivity of psychicality as none of the three named kingdoms can. Yet, as his father Nils, a peasant, became a spiritual guide, he had adopted as his own family name *Linnaeus* from a great linden tree growing near his home.

As an organic chemist I can create for myself a most efficient system of chemical names describing structure and indicating function of chemical properties, so that the temptation to forfeit awareness for its all contributing to the truth of my wholeness can present itself without my realizing it. The consequence can be that of my losing rather than finding my sense of identity in my own production. My field of study can seem to completely isolate itself from its only truth, namely, creativity of my own individuality.

But, how can my *scientific* irresponsibility for being myself go on and on?[2] The fact that no one can know anything about whatever he may be overlooking explains the whole thing. For example, as a mechanic, certainly I can never deal with anything *but* my very own problems and possibilities, but if I lack the insight that I am the creator of all that I can possibly mean by my motorcycle or car, then it must seem obvious to me that all of the "mechanical" living of mine must be alien to me. Or, as a laboratory researcher, certainly I am the creator of my every meaning of my research, but if I lack that self-interpretation, then all of my living of my laboratory work must seem alien (objective, impersonal, dispassionate, bloodless) to me.

---

[2]See my "Scientific Immorality," *Biosciences Communications* (Basel) 3, no. 1 (1977), 52–55.

The fruitful study of the law of individuality, its practicality and unappreciated utility, is positively demonstrable to each one who gives this soul-searching his sustained consideration. There must be a tormenting feeling of self-insufficiency in me until I can realize that my self-possession subsumes my all. I must endure my goading ambition until I can acknowledge ownership of all of my owndom. Only with recognition of my growing my individuality can I attain willful control over it. True science is working the mine of my mind for its own subjective treasures.

Whence come my insistent demands that my mind be what it is not and not be what it is? Why must I expect to be able to get at something or somebody other than myself, and the converse? How can I explain my need to get out of myself, or to claim I am what I am not?

Thus, I may go on using my mind automatically, as it were, without much awakening to the whole-making truth that it *is* all mine. Indeed I may thereby dismiss many a life-activity of mine with the belittling notion, "It is merely verbal." Such attempt at heedless conversion of my life experience into a kind of dead language prevents my duly appreciating my continual life in my living.

Not merely in writing, but as certainly in thinking, my tendency to conform to the grammar of the vernacular may be steadily indulged, mostly without my noticing such unwitting disregard for consequence. Assuming responsible attention for the vast extent to which my mentality is expressed in my use of language is a heavy burden that I put off as often as I can. My need to remind myself of myself, so to speak, is unremitting but my recognition of that need is all too seldom aroused.

John Locke, M.D. (1632–1704), may be referred to as the father of present-day psychology in that he founded his understanding of mind upon its innate sensibility, including emotionality and meaning. My sensibility may be understood as my touching *myself* by living each sensation (including each meaningful emotion). What cannot be reduced to such excitability is not mental. It is the absence of this organic irritability that is called death. Again, nothing can be responsible for any meaning but mind activating itself. Only by feeling my way can I go straight in exacting, or correcting stray, behavior.

Whether I use my mind to arrange its meaningfulness into a certain circumscribed order that I name physiology, spirituality, mineralogy, or extrasensory perception, the only factuality about any of it is that it is a more-or-less orderly series of sensation or feeling truly identifiable only as my mind. By definition there can be no individual experience save that created by the given individual, her/his self. Unless I can view my experience where all of it must occur, namely, in my own living, I shall be in danger of insightlessly expecting my biological resources to become what they are not or to not be what they are.

I define my science as all study of my life at the level of its individuality. Continued consideration of my unexpected discovery that nothing can happen in my life unless and until all of the truth necessary to make it happen is present led me to acknowledge that when all of that truth is present the happening must occur. Growing this mindfulness gradually educated me to regard such recognition and appreciation of the ever reliable and consequential self-sufficiency of truth as my most helpful insight, deserving to be heeded as the basic law of my nature. It completely resolved all of the confusion I created for myself by habitually dividing my knowledge into two categories, sacred and secular.[3] This dissociation had substituted my awareness of my mental integrity with the appearance of mental duplicity.

By recognizing in the scientific law of sufficient verifiability a restatement of the ethical law implicit in the justice of truth, I enjoyed a mighty access of unity that has conferred its economic efficacy ever since. All-of-my-living consists entirely of

[3]See Introduction.

my continuously being made by myself. I am my only possible textbook of my life.[4]

As I grew further self-understanding to reveal my every duality (good-bad, right-wrong, God-devil, just-unjust, etc.) as my convenient device for solving my current inability to observe ever prevailing unity, my realization of the health importance of revering the truth of oneness or the oneness of truth became strong, strong enough to teach me to have devotion to it and to fear neglecting it on any count. Scientific progress that does not augment self-consciousness is advance in finding a new way of feeling lost. Only the science of one's own living can be built on valid and verifiable data. Its method is historical. Its element is each scientist's inwardness. Its unit of measurement is each scientist's self-authenticating observation.

To this acknowledged ideal of fidelity to *conscious* self-learning I have addressed my educational force as University Professor. My method of operation in the conduct of my office has been to practice conscious self-continence to the best of my ability, and to observe and record the immeasurable benefit I, including my fellowman, derive from this purposeful furthering of reverence for my individuality *now*.[5]

I *am* only. I *am* my life. All of my living is now-living. Instead of postulating a past or future as such, I observe there *is* a region of meaning in my mind existing truly in my present being which I can designate *as if* it could consist only of my past or future living. I make much of this all-comprehending fact of life because, in order to be able to appreciate life with biological adequacy, I must be able to revere it *now*.

Nothing can ever happen except *now*. Every depth of my nature is alive and active now. Observation of this silent necessity enables me to understand my growth as the evolution of my subjective ideality, of my continent individuality. Consider-

[4]See my *Living Consciously: The Science of Self*, with Walter H. Seegers (Detroit: Wayne State University Press, 1959).

[5]Cf. Baruch Spinoza, "Ethica," *Opera Posthuma* (1677).

ing as I do that all of my symptom formation is traceable to my trying to substitute the illusion of objective externality for the truth of my subjective internality, my discovery of the nowness of my existence becomes evident as of greatest importance for my health care.

To begin with definition, a human being of any age is a unique whole who already has a consequential history of his (her) existence. The nature of a human being is that of a growing individual whose lifesaving need it is to be able to create opportunity to cultivate his (her) appreciation for what it means to be a growing individual. This appreciation is the product of gradually and wilfully assumed responsibility for his (her) own self-identity. The strong willpower needed to work up further conscious self-responsibility derives from further cultivation of acknowledgeable self-consciousness, an achievement motivated by recognizable self-interest, life benefit.

What is not wholly and only itself (i.e., solipsistic) cannot exist as an entity. Self-activity is the necessary life principle in all viable existence. The source of appreciation for this principle, giving conscious unity to my existence, is conscious self-observation. It is precisely and merely this source of self-understanding that provides the self-responsibility resolving the seeming problematic difference "between" conscientiousness and consciousness.

By trying to consider any subject without realization that it exists all and only as mentality of mine, I am committed to imprecision from the start. To turn my word for everyone and everything into acknowledgeable illustration of my autobiography has been the central purpose of my self-insight-oriented writing. None of my mental activity can hold adventitious interest for me, despite every convincing appearance to the contrary. I must judge my worth and wisdom by the reach of my acknowledgeable self-possession.

I can and do imagine existence other than mine, but I also learn to prize this lifesaving imagining as integral to my whole mind. Stern and relentless discipline has helped me to find satisfaction in the truth that absolutely none of *my* so-called world experience can be sourceless in me. Again, the amazing reality is that I originate all of that so-called worldliness. I, and I alone, create, grow, whatever I live. At first, however, I fearfully found my necessity to reverse completely my habitual allocation of meanings I attributed to so-called real and imaginary worlds.

Gradually I had to accept the scientific evidence of my senses as providing me with self-evidence only, and not with any evidence of my external world. Formerly my mind had habituated itself to defining its own subjectivity as somehow unreal or imaginary, in contrast with the real objectivity it gratuitously attributed to the *as if* objectivity of its so-called external world. With shocking truthfulness I observed that my *only* real scientific evidence must be my self-evidence and that my only real recognition of anyone or anything external to me must be ideally imaginary. World experience of mine must be my native self-identity growing itself consciously and unconsciously. My universe must be contained within the circumference of my living being.

The critical concern at issue here is that, because of my habit of allocating my admitted selfness to my denied selfness (so-called externality), I had to resist as strongly as I could the incalculable benefit in my consciously integrating my mind. Habit had made my consciously self-belittling way of conducting my life so effortless that I had cultivated a preference for it. In other words, I found it easier to go on helping myself by denying my own greatness than to take the trouble to start gathering evidence of, hence responsibility for, my real magnitude.

Of course my argument of loneliness was the strongest resistance to my teaching myself to live with love the incontrovertible truth that only I can live any of my own life, my solipsistic reality. *Argument can never beget anything but argument.* Only my adding to my *self-consciousness* can provide me with the conscious willpower to kindly renounce any and every "argument" seemingly against it. If my self-consciousness seems to extend beyond that of my fellowman's self-consciousness, my effort to get him to accept whatever he must now only reject of his mentality would be a simple case of expecting my blind fellowman to be able to see, in order to reinforce rather than shake my belief in my own vision.

Adding a little self-consciousness only, I must ask of myself three revealing questions. 1) How can I be only lonely for living whatever I am already living, such as my "lost" anyone? 2) Why am I unable to realize that my most recent extension of my self-consciousness is an outgrowth of all of the self-consciousnesses I previously grew, each of which includes the decree that requires my feeling lonely when-separated-from-another and furthermore continues its existence within me? 3) How could I possibly extend the range of my self-consciousness by forfeiting any kind of previous extension of it? It would amount to extreme disability if I would become unable to think and feel as I did in each foregoing stage of my mental development! My ability to run does not rule out my ability to creep or wriggle my toe!

I was in for further shocking proof of my having scientifically disciplined my mind in self-disesteem, on every occasion when I would try to translate my not-I mentality into ideal consciousness (admitted I-mentality). It had never before occurred to me that I might be hating to learn what could become most useful to me if I would but recognize its repudiated presence in myself. Intending to study my world I succeeded in neglecting the truth that I must be the sole creator of *my* world.

It is this specific scientific neglect that helpfully troubles my mind by creating signs of self-neglect I cannot understand, such as anxiety, irritability, jealousy, etc., and the corresponding unhappiness expressed in my mind's body region (so-called physical signs or symptoms).

My formal educational experience, specified as teacher or student, clearly demonstrates the singular rarity with which I, including my fellowman, appreciate the fact that I, alone, am and must ever be responsible for the substance, shaping, and directing of my mind. With powerful obstinacy and marked complaisance I may resist the truth that I am and must ever be solely in charge of just how I grow and cultivate the incalculably great mental power that is mine alone. It is tempting folly for me to assume that I can "drift" into sufficient self-understanding to enable me to steer my life course wisely or sanely. *Only by painstakingly studying in the interest of the wholeness of my nature can I discover how best to regulate my full self-consequence.*

For growing able to obey the law of my wholeness-nature my most fruitful scientific learning is that about power of mine I call emotionality. When I have given free rein to my *feeling* on any subject of my constitution I can have nothing more to interest me in it. I must leave to my further living of affective experience the awakening and directing of my further concentration. From examining each emotional nuance thoroughly I can learn from each unhappiness how understandably I might resort to the most hazardous and frequent symptom formation of all, namely, faultfinding.

The singular service of any kind or degree of so-called faultfinding is to attract my attention to the fact that I am ignoring truth sufficient to attest the faultlessness of that about which I seem to be able to find fault.

The all-abiding and all-pervading truth is that only perfection can exist. Unless *all* that constitutes any existent is present in it, it cannot exist. A consciously whole individual can imagine the helpful delusion implied by such a word or meaning as "fault," or "lie," or "sin" without feeling dominated by it. To illustrate, the plural term "opposites" may imply the illusion of more-than-one. However I can be most conciliating in honoring the necessity for the appearance of duality in any so-called opposites. Each opposite serves to support the underlying unity in each polar term of the pluralistic conception *opposites*. The stronger my cowardice, the greater my bravery in renouncing it; the stronger my vice, the greater my virtue in renouncing it, and so on.

Whenever I find myself, in any degree of enormity, helping myself by resisting sober consideration of the goodness of any possibility whatsoever, right then and there I always find myself unimpeachably justified in assuming the corresponding degree of helpfulness for my welfare in 1) my being able to repudiate any of my mental activity whenever and where I must resist acknowledging it as mine, and 2) my gradually becoming willing to realize, however, that I *cannot* experience any kind of mental activity other than my own, including whatever possibility I am presently unwilling to consider. Accompanying each increment of self-consciousness are the increments of conscious self-love and conscious willpower, enabling me to honor the right to exist of some of my meaningfulness. Even the meaning of my life-denying power is also life-fulfilling.

What I am not ready to live consciously as my self-identity I can live unconsciously as not-I. *I actually owe my being alive to my just being able to live through whatever I do experience.* Later, gradually, I can grow the conscious self-interest to live it with grateful appreciation. It is my lifesaving discovery that my free mental health depends solidly upon my ability to reduce to the real being of my conspicuous self-consciousness all of my mental activity that passes for science, logic, religion, philosophy, sensation, perception, observation, emotion, or whatever other mental "seeming."

Anew, I am *all* of my own living. All that I can know of my so-called external world constitutes the lifesaving realm of my creative imagination. This biological necessity of mine entails my being either responsible or irresponsible for the whole of my allness.

It is undeniably up to me, being born a whole individual, to find out from my own experience precisely how to teach myself to take biologically adequate care of my whole individuality. *Biological adequacy means due concern for the wholeness of my organismic constitution.* Unquestionably my conscious life fulfillment must depend specifically upon just how I can educate myself to honor the truth of the absolute wholeness of my creaturehood.

As a scientist I may not recognize that I cannot understand any element of a subject except in terms of the wholeness of that subject. A whole is not an assemblage or collection of interacting forms deriving its unity from attached independents. Unity, itself, is the innate withinness of the characteristic individualism constituting wholeness. Union is not an intervening force existing between bodies to hold them together. As all else possible, union exists only within itself, in the form of whatever is united, whole or individual. As a scientist I may disregard that necessity if I have not mastered the truth that a whole must consist only and entirely of wholeness. My human being is a whole organism of which my evolving personality is its most vitally protective form exerting my life energy consciously and unconsciously (that is, responsibly and irresponsibly).

For my wholeness to function with full competence, my awareness for the truth of its functioning is indispensable. Otherwise I tend to regard myself as a person or organism of parts, a notion most unfavorable to my revering either the power or glory of the free world of my own creating. *Of course my denying the truth of any of my living is proof positive of its existence,* but my mind may be too distracted by its so-called otherness to be able to make that unitive observation.[6]

Since there is always most of my functioning life which I do not appreciate as being my own self's identity, in order to accord with the organic wholeness of my mind I invent a reconciling device which can seem to separate it into two parts: one, that which I can "like" and claim as my own present identity, and two, that which I can "dislike" and claim is not-I, or foreign to my own present identity. My mind's capacity for self-denial or self-negation ably serves this function.[7]

Originating as (consciously) unwilling experience of hurt,

[6]Sigmund Freud, "Negation," *The Standard Edition of the Complete Psychological Works of Sigmund Freud,* trans. James Strachey and Anna Freud (London: Hogarth Press and Institute of Psychoanalysis, 1953–), XIX, 235–39.

[7]Anna Freud, "The Ego and the Mechanisms of Defense," *The Writings of Anna Freud* (New York: International Universities Press, 1946), II, chapters 6 and 7.

negation allows for the intact organic wholeness of my life's meaning by readily seeming to provide quick conscious riddance of mental activity I cannot live with the pleasure of my self-identity. However, this defense of my acknowledgeable mentality is at the (helpfully) grievous cost of immediately creating emphasis of unacknowledgeable mental activity in self-repudiated symptom formation characterized by obsessive or compulsive force.

My concerned reader observes, "I have helped myself by noticing what I thought was the fitness of man with his surroundings, his relation to his fellowman, indeed his dependence upon his external world. According to you he must be absolutely unrelated, absolutely self-dependent, absolutely unfit for anyone or anything but his own existence. Do you not go too far in your meaning of oneness? According to you it is the necessary form of whatever meaning that can be."

Yes. I help myself also with each solitary feeling or view I live my reader owning up to. In fact my extension of my meaning for individuality grows out of just such preceding meaning for it. My Emerson declared in his London lecture "Politics and Socialism" (1848), it is individualism men need, rather than having all things in common. I help myself also by daring to assert that all of my fitness is in and of me only; all of *my* relatedness is uniquely mine; all of *my* dependence must be dependence that I alone develop, and so on. My continuous self-growth rules out the possibility of my experiencing any fortuitous occurrence, such as a so-called accident. All apparent chance is really the only possible momentary choice.

My reader again: "Not only common sense but *every* appearance is against such a notion of disunited human being! The very idea is untenable that only by being your own best friend can you succeed in being your neighbor's best friend."

Yes. Certainly I may seem rarely fit for willingly assuming responsibility for all of my meaning for my world. The very term "common sense" implies more-than-one person. The very word "appearance" involves not only whatever appears but also who is creating the appearance. In fact, my every language I know strengthens my concept of plurality at the enormous cost of weakening my concept of individuality. The word "unity" can apply only to oneness as constituting the unique integrity of oneness. I cannot become united or dis-united with *my* fellowman for (my) he consists entirely of what-ever I live as *my* fellowman. Hardest of all is it for me also to succeed in living or loving my every fellowman as really being my own living, my own lovable being.

My reader supposes, "What if you cannot like your fellow-man but must hate, scorn, resent or otherwise only suffer him?"

Yes. Often my first, or even long-lasting emotional re-sponse to some of my living is to associate it with dislike of one sort or another. Then I tend to avoid being aware of even living that hurt love as long as I can. I cannot let myself think about it, and even avoid occasions where it might come up. The trouble with that ostrich-like psychology is that it permits all of that hurt living of mine to continue enforcing its significance without my ever trying to become able to see, or feel, that it is my own living, so that I can learn how to take care of its consequence.

My reader may observe, "But how can I ever learn to con-trol my hurt feeling when I cannot even learn to respect my pain as lifeworthy?"

An excellent question. Hardest of all of my lessons of grow-ing up is that of my learning gradually to honor the lifesaving helpfulness of pain or unhappiness of any kind. I wrote a whole book on this subject pointing out how my unpleasure protects my present indispensable self-image by banishing hurt care from it until I can work up the understanding 1) that I save my life *only* by whatever I am able to live and 2) that I can prosper to justify and learn to love *whatever* I live, once I know sufficient fact about it to explain its goodness.

Whatever I experience is always in perfect proportion to what I need to experience in order to stay alive, but that understanding is indeed hard to come by. I grow my most valuable life lesson by studying the biologically functioning goodness in all of my emotionality, pleasurable and unpleasurable alike. "Pain" is the term I use for unhappiness in the body meaning of my mind. My daring to call my life my own, and my "all" my living of it, can only *seem* foolhardy, for it comprises the epitome of gentle wisdom. I can bring myself to rely only upon my own reckoning of wisdom. I find all conscious wisdom characterized specifically by its mansuetude.

I have finally grown the clear realization that nearly all of the wordage of my world is mostly the issue of each linguist's limited ability to imagine that 1) *his* world is all his own creation, 2) his study of *all* the truth of his world must reveal its *perfect* design and 3) his full understanding of all of his pain or unhappiness would reveal it as pleasure or happiness inhibited by lack of realization that the sufficient truth must always be on the side of whatever happens before it can happen.[8]

My reader speaks up, "Do you never close your mind to distress, not shut your eyes to trouble? For example, do you live an unrivalled existence, or think you do? I see you would define man as being essentially an imaginative creature."

Yes. I can help myself by so-called retreat whenever I choose to do so. My night sleeping is a necessary method for restoring my vigor, and degrees of sleep ("absentmindedness") are natural restoratives throughout my so-called waking day as well. However, it is one issue to be able to invest my interest in a certain way, and quite another issue to feel impersonally compelled to do so. As to rivalled living, my rival can be none other than the creature of my own creating, whether I momentarily choose to honor that fact or not. For example, my living of my rival as if he is not-I can excite similar meanings of my childhood which I enjoy for their nostalgic value, as in a story or play.

[8]See my *Psychology of Ethics*.

About imagination, its providence is illimitable. It is the mentalizer of life, ultimately capable of idealizing the individuality of self-identity as the soul of divinity. What cannot be imagined! Of all power acknowledgeable freedom of imagination is most deserving of lifelong protection and cultivation. Whatever is, imaginatively is. The meaning of meaning itself is imaginative. I am whatever I can imagine I am, for example, my moveable observatory of my own universe, my world of my own divine being, my psychicality of my own physiology, my theopathy of my own theology, my design of my own perfection or my perfection of my own design.

In other words, it is my duty to myself to obey the law of my whole nature as best I can. Hence it behooves me heedfully to cultivate by extension, in every direction possible, my *acknowledgeable* self-identity so that it comprehends as completely as it can the true extent of my nature's inclusiveness. Thus my Aristotle noted it: Man is by nature a political animal.

I must function *only* as an organic whole, whether I acknowledge that necessity or not, and thereby hangs the true story of my life. I have resisted the full meaning of this all-important appreciation for the inviolable wholeness of my organic constitution, only on account of the forceful fact that I have had to grow my mind initially as if it were not entirely and inclusively my own. Early in my life I began forfeiting my enjoyment of the feeling of precious innocence (holiness) associated with the free wholeness inherent in my uninhibited self-recognition, unknowingly making my necessarily true wholeness into a seeming mass of being designatable as self and not-self.

As my conscious process of seeming self-belittlement continued, my unconscious process of my otherness-aggrandizement grew apace. Had I not awakened myself to the self-blind way I was conducting the wholeness of my life, I would certainly have ended it with a feeling that I did not, and could not, amount to much; whereas "the world" or "God" or something else of my own repudiated "otherness" must be correspondingly as great as I was small. Beyond all else in consequence, to the extent that I must deny that I am my own otherness, must I deny that I am all divine. I am my own divinity. My consciously self-devoted Jan Christian Smuts expressed his profound appreciation for the wholeness-nature of human individuality in his excellent book, *Holism and Evolution* (1926).[9]

My research on how my mind works its excitements goes on against powerful resistance. Forceful resistances to living consciously are: 1) habit and 2) the extent to which I became a "dropout" in growing understanding of the use of my mentality. For example, I did not learn fully how to use my eyes to see until I grew the ability to acknowledge that I am all that I am seeing. The same requirement of force applies to the functioning of all of my sensibility. Conscious and unconscious sensation and emotion energize my organismic constitution. I must see the meaning of all of my sensitivity first as all about itself only, and second as associated only with my own functioning. Thus, hate is all about hate. It is really love that is inhibited in direct expression and therefore forced to show its oppositeness as its only form of expression. It always associates itself with my own behavior that was formerly lived only with undisguised love.[10]

The use of force is necessary for disciplining my mind with self-consciousness. Nothing can happen except motivated by force. However, when all of the force is factually present to make it happen, then it must occur. My conscious willpower is the force with which I apply myself to acknowledging that I am my "dislikes" just as I am my likes. My unconscious willpower is the force with which I resist such conscious self-observation.

Whence my conscious willpower for making myself aware that my repudiated meaningfulness is truly deserving of being

[9](New York: Viking Press, 1961).
[10]*Psychology of Emotion,* pp. 125, 138.

lived with love? Here the force of my wishing for this achievement must be present. I must first, so to speak, "hunger and thirst" for this attainment of self-insight. Then I must allow my mind freedom to function as freely as I can, without allowing my judgment to prevail by maintaining rejection of meaningfulness I formerly disowned. Thus I can observe elements of my mind that need to be lived with loving understanding. With each such increment of self-awareness are associated increments of conscious love and of conscious willpower. I succeed in securing greater conscious willpower at the expense of diminishing my unconscious willpower.

It is the truth of my conscious sensibility combined with my power to discover my conscious touchability that I resist recognizing for its scientific importance. Albert Einstein unified the assertion: "Science without religion is lame, and religion without science is blind." I am touchable through each of my senses and each of my emotions. My responsible awareness that all of my touch is self-created and self-felt is necessary for my development of conscious self-continence.

Review

All of my scientific investigation is based on my conscious self-observation; all of my self-observation is based upon the necessity that my living of all of my being, including my observing, consists of my *growing* it. Bias or dogmatism in my scientific technique must be the product of my willingly practiced insightless empiricism. My experience systematically corroborates my hypothesis that my strength of mind, including my development as a scientist, increases in direct proportion to the extent that I can live all of my mentality consciously, that is, as being entirely and only my own.[11] For achieving such self-insight I must teach myself to understand the origi-

[11]See Stephen C. Pepper, *The Basis of Criticism in the Arts* (Cambridge, Mass.: Harvard University Press, 1945), pp. 17, 38, 40.

nal helpfulness of my first resistance to seeing only my own identity in my personal experiences associated with dislike. It is such "disliked" living, unattended by insight, that favors my dying.

As I allow my previously repudiated idea to appear consciously (as in my free association), I also sense the unpleasant feeling I associated with it in rejecting it in the first place. My motivation to undertake this (helpfully) disagreeable task is my wish to free myself from the symptomatic mentality (occasioned by the initial repudiation) which necessarily impaired my recognition of my wholeness and allness. As I proceed to endure consciously living my dislike, I not only strengthen my endurance but also attain volitional control of my dislike. Thus I become able to learn that "disliking" is the disguised form liking must take when I do not have sufficient knowledge to appreciate the lifesaving helpfulness of whatever idea I must otherwise associate with dislike.

Any idea whatsoever that I live is necessarily of lifesaving value by virtue of the fact that I am living it. Therefore it is imperative, in the interest of my life itself, that I gradually strengthen my conscious tolerance to become willingly responsible for all of the whole of my mentation. But that is not as difficult as it may seem.

To illustrate, I need not ask myself to believe or favor or in some way prefer any given conception in order to revere my integrity. Not at all. All I need achieve is the ability to consider that conception soberly, acknowledge its right to exist, recognize its meaning for what it is worth to itself, and thus live it as integral instead of alien to the wholeness and allness of my mind. It is this just appreciation for the truth of *whatever is* that empowers my mind with the all-embracing peace it has never known without it.

The extent of my sanity depends directly upon my mind's disciplined capacity to consider kindly any meaning (thought, feeling, perception, or whatever mentation) as having its perfect right to exist, as being integral to the wholeness of my psychicality. The extent of this requirement of sanity is essential for my attaining and maintaining my mental balance, demonstrating that my psychic experience has become really subject to *my* wholeness of mind rather than seeming to be able to usurp the mastery of that wholeness of which it can be only an individuation.

6
My Religion

The shudder of awe is humanity's highest faculty,
Even though this world is forever altering its values.
Goethe, Faust, *Part 2*

It is biologically adequate that my proper mental posture be one of awe at the immeasurable magnitude of my own marvelous nature. Growing my understanding of religious belief and scientific fact reveals discoverable (divine) truth everywhere. I can say as did Emerson when asked as to his religious opinions, "My views are to be found in what I have written." The moral law of truth is the pith and marrow of all observation possible to me, namely, conscious self-observation. What I call good comes of conscious (free, willful, responsible) obedience to the law of my unconscious growth, to the joy of living my immeasurable, incommunicable, indescribable being. "Such as men themselves are, such will God appear to them to be," observed John Smith, seventeenth-century Cambridge Platonist.

Here I define my religion: appreciation for my own divinity as integral to my belief in the divinity of my universe. All of my life's conceivable meaning is based solely upon my ever experiencing anew my individual nature. During my University Professorship years I grew my heedful consciousness for my very own growth with ever deepening meaning for its being all and only my constantly creating my wholeness afresh. With increasing insight I recognized the accuracy of my designating *my* Wayne or my Detroit or my Michigan as my mind's organically growing of its true unaccustomedness. Certainly that growth-of-new-meaning orientation describes precisely the nature of *my* campus, my city or my state, namely, my developing all of it as integral to my creating or growing all of my own meaningful wholeness. My fellowman's referring to his growing his factory development as his "plant" sprouted rich consequence. To grow strong in realization of the momentary nature of living, I grew further understanding of the specific helpfulness in growing self-consciousness temporarily, as it were. Now is eternally now; here is infinitely here.

*My constant hunger for order arises from the necessity that the truth of my wholeness-order be constantly expressing itself in the form of integrity (oneness, wholeness). My acknowledgeable divinity-meaning cannot safely be "taken for granted" any more than can any other power of mine. Rather it must function, it must work itself. Every so-called organ of my being must work itself in order to maintain itself. Budding and blooming consciousness for this truth, *divinity is scientifically observable,* reveals enhancing joy of, hence appreciation for, being ever a new person, unused, novel.

I am stressfully aware of the boldness of my endeavor to record my strictly solipsistic orientation, particularly about my investigation of the nature of theodicy in the light of examination of the development of my own religious living. For me religion and ethics are one.[1]

Perhaps it is already evident that a person's poor self-opinion, as his being imperfect, necessitates his taking care of himself as if he does not amount to much. It may not be quite as evident that a person's proud self-estimate as divine necessitates his cherishing his life as most worthy of his utmost care. Every appreciation of a man for his being may be weighed as his own divine aid to help him do his duty, to work up his moral ability. His "whole scientific enterprise" may be weighed as a man's seeking the understanding of sufficient facts of his

---

[1]See my *Psychology of Ethics.*

life to be able to obey his divine will. His sublime self-confidence, based upon his understanding of the absolute reliability of factual being, may be weighed as his faith in God. His vital, wonderful mental power, his conscious imagination, may be weighed as his indispensable function for factually divining himself as deriving his being and sustenance from a divine providence integral to him and he to it. His spontaneity may be weighed as the source of creativity in his life force. His telescope and microscope may be weighed as self-extensions of his self-knowledge, not as sources of self-abasement, for finding new evidence of his greatness and glory rather than for losing himself between the infinitely small and the infinitely great; his "control over nature" may be weighed as control over his own human nature; his ideas of progress may be weighed as his continuing pleasure in his ongoing perfection!

The question is often posed, Why does one always speak of "a universe" rather than of a "multiverse"? Or why does one always have in mind *"one* world" when he refers to all of his cosmos? The reply is that each human individual cannot be more or less than one, although he may conceive of his oneness as subsuming either innumerable individuations in itself or as not being whole itself. However, more-than-one or less-than-one is always an illusion created by crediting either single view with more than its accurate, complete singleness. Every allusion to more (or less) than one (for example, every collective noun or fraction) is itself a single allusion connoting the impossible "plural" (or "part"). In all of man's history no one has ever been able to demonstrate two anythings or less than one anything (such as two anyones, or any fraction which is not *its* whole self). If I conceive my oneness as constituted either of manyness or of less-than-oneness I can do so only by disregarding the fact that the conception itself is a single individuation of my wholeness.

Plato described the helpfulness in the power of knowing-by-wholes (totalities). Mind's self-activity is the source of the whole of its mentations. The mind's power to imagine an "impersonal" world-view is what is responsible for the doctrine of pantheism, a philosophy which must be considered insufficient by me if I am aware that my sense of value itself is constituted of its personal meaning for me. Contrary to philosophic reasoning, my universe is not "at once" both one and manifold, any more or less than I am. *Unity* is all there is to my every meaning.

It is impossible to attend to the feeling of full self-appreciation (or even to Emerson's "lords of life" such as the self-helpfulness in perseverance and contrivance) while engaged in "unwilling" activity. In willing work, quite as in play, immediate conscious inclination decides self-activity, and the will to work is manifestly the person's own impelling force. His own evident being furnishes him with life-giving enjoyment. He can grow to see the whole of his working condition and "circumstance" as his greater self. The costly process of depersonalization underlies all my living from which I must withhold my feeling of personal identity. Only the recognition of the self as creator of new selfness in all experience enables self-consciousness, the immediate recognition of my own wholeness. All meaning must be an expression of personal experience, a truth unconsciously affirmed by every negation of it.

My resort to my divinity as my only source of helpfulness may be rarely realized by me if I have helped myself mostly by dissociating my concept of my self from my concept of my godliness. I may readily delude myself with the conviction that my God is too far away to help. Yet the enduring value of the conception of the divinity of life, of the divinity of all existence, lies in the fact that it, only, is always and everywhere repeatably observable, demonstrable, and experimentally validatable. It involves no other-worldliness, is not merely the ideal of exceptional spirits, cannot be fully understandable just as a means or instrumentality, and requires no leap of the imagination or rare attainment of reasoning. Rather it is the fundamental meaning of reality, the only reality of meaning itself. Even this truth of divinity finds necessary expression in the divinity of truth. The allness, wholeness, perfection, oneness, omnipresence, almightiness, inclusiveness, omnipotence, and all such infinite and eternal attributes of God baffle every effort to describe the meaning of one's divinity. For sure, however, discouragement from striving to acknowledge and appreciate the divinity of all of my world exists in protean forms. If I yield to it I create my most dangerous inhibition, namely, that of the functioning of my wish to live my realization of my consciously divine wholeness.

My reader objects, "If divinity is the only true reality, how can you explain all of the war, crime, accident, murder, suicide occurring every day?"

When I ask myself that question, I reply that all such manmade life difficulty is the *desirable* outcome of the force of truth. No human event can occur until sufficient force of fact is present to make it occur, when it must occur. My study of the history of any development always sufficiently accounts for it. If I do not want it to occur, then I must teach myself how to do all possible to bring to bear sufficient force of fact to prevent its occurrence, in favor of the development I prefer. By dint of scientific discipline I can observe that reality, based upon the force of truth sufficiently justifying it, is all that can ever be present. And that applies to my geologic, atmospheric, or whatever cosmic happening as well as to my other human behavior.

"Do you mean that God evolves quite as all else does, that he undergoes development, too?"

Certainly I can grow such an idea. However, my experience (further growing) teaches me to renounce this tempting view as being a comforting illusion, although helpful, also responsible for disastrous conditions signalizing its inadequacy. Rather than being the result of gradations leading up to its final perfection, divinity is perfection to start with, just as it is all else from the beginning.

I can easily mislead myself in my search for God-meaning (as if all meaning is not divine), particularly by mistaking "ne-

gation" for reality. Especially the negation called unconscious-
ness habitually spares me acknowledgeable responsibility for
being my whole self. The negation "imperfection" similarly
spares me acknowledging that I do not know sufficient truth
to thoroughly justify whatever I find fault about.

Consciousness for the life-giving, lifesaving, and life-taking
truth that divinity is all that exists or can exist is entirely
another consideration indeed. Divinity is never absent, but
consciousness for the presence of divinity is a rare event in the
life of all but the person who has discovered it in and of his
own being. Therefore, for the good of one's world it is most
consequential to clearly distinctify 1) *divinity* and 2) *conscious
divinity*.

It is the lack of this distinctification that enables or requires
the fabrication of such illusional dualities as God-devil, good-
evil, heaven-hell, right-wrong, just-unjust, condemnation-
redemption, sacred-profane, better-worse, spirit-flesh, and
innumerable other affirmation-denial combinations. The consequence is that there is no theme less unfashionable or particularly uncongenial than that dealing with a pure culture of
ideality such as soul or spirit or even imagination itself.
Seemingly my Walter Lippman's observation, "Whirl is king,"
helps to make understandable my distraction from the abiding truth of my own divinity, as it readily occurs. It is easy
for me to feel that my will and my desire can be in unending
conflict as long as I persist habitually in overlooking the truth
that my desire is my unconscious will.

The Scholastic called totality "a perfect being." Responsible
self-activity is conscious freedom. My American self-educator
William T. Harris clearly stated his linguistic insight: "Univer-
sals are only *flatus vocis*—mere names or mouthfuls of spoken
wind: only individuals exist." His use of the plural term "individuals" was no doubt recognizable by him as *one* word the
literal meaning of which ("more than one") cancels itself.[2] This

[2]Quoted in Leidecker, *Yankee Teacher*, pp. 533–75.

comprehension of unity is accessible to every devoted practitioner of appreciation for the full-measured meaning of individuality. Particularly since Hippocrates, every physician's medical ideal is: full respect for the absolute individuality of the individual.

Whatever is, justifiably is, or it could not exist. Whatever is, is therefore moral. However, to be consciously moral my being must be conscious being. In this circumscribed autobiography I am consciously wishing to elevate my living with the force of moral insight provided by my discovering the real identity in seemingly disunitable interests such as past and present, society and individual, religion and science. My scientific study therefore does not lose (in classification, statistical treatment, or whatever temporary concentration of attention) biological reverence for the ground truth of my individuality. Similarly, all that I can learn from study of my history is that I *am* all that I "have been" and am "becoming."

To be able to approximate this reverence for wholeness I am following my inclination but also consulting my competence, a design that must add disciplined vigilance to my natural exertion. Whatever I am, including becoming, is the issue of my natural history. I keep minutes of my sensing new self-understanding, for my further guidance in growing new self-confirmation, since I value my sense of my self-identity as my most comprehensive sense. It serves to open my every other sense so that I can find rather than lose my self-appreciation in my own self-activity.

All of my recognition of truth, goodness, or beauty is the product of my own growing of it. It is precisely my creating my life experience that secures whatever end I would possess. All that can make my living important is *that living* itself —a seldom heeded but most consequential fact. My vision is not merely fitted to what I can see; it *is* whatever I can see. The tremendous power and influence over my behavior, attributed to *my* so-called circumstance or surrounding, becomes agreeably understandable only when I realize that all of it consists only of my living of it as my very own power. I am all of my own "circumstance."

My University work has been largely devoted to attesting that my, including my fellowman's, absolutely necessary self-continence is most deserving of thorough notice. Otherwise it must remain strange to me why wisdom decrees that I must learn to love my enemy (or whatever I live with dislike) quite as I must learn readily to love whatever I live easily. I *am* identically whatever I live, easily or difficultly.

Of necessity all influence is self-influence; all meaning is self-meaning. Valid purpose of my science is to discover and master the evident truth that makes acknowledgment of this necessity valuable to me. My finding that all of my "relations to external nature" are really prodigal physiological processes in my mind becomes most exciting and intelligible by my purposefully making it applicable to my welfare.

Marvelous advance in self-appreciation can result by my growing from "What is there in it for me?" to "What is there of me in it?" Biologically adequate self-care is the direct consequence of biologically adequate self-appreciation. Only I can be observable to myself—a biological necessity so inconspicuous that it is rarely heeded.

Only acknowledgeable self-observation is ideally serviceable to health. Once fully realized, this repeatably demonstrable scientific fact of life is sufficient inducement to make me admit that my self-interest is integral to my every educational occupation. Each occurrence of purposive self-consciousness invigorates. As Antaeus wrestling with Hercules renewed his vigor by touching his mother earth, I discover that I (including my self-unconscious fellowman) can restore my strength by my every resort to my lifesaving, biologically true, acknowledgeable self-interest.

The hygienic corollary to the easily attested fact that active self-appreciation promotes free health is the easily attested fact that active self-depreciation promotes inhibited health. In other words, any of my scientific work in which I seem to

On April 15, 1971, Dr. Dorsey was honored by university and civic officials at a retirement party, and presented with resolutions of appreciation from the Wayne State University Board of Governors and the Detroit Common Council. Left to right: Dr. John M. Dorsey, Jr., President William Rea Keast of Wayne State University, Mary Louise Carson Dorsey, Dr. Dorsey, Dr. Edwin Carson Dorsey.

April 15, 1971. Mel Ravitz, president of the Detroit Common Council, presents the resolution of appreciation to Dr. Dorsey.

April 15, 1971. Ruth Hilberry (Mrs. Clarence B.) congratulates the University Professor.

April 15, 1971. President Keast congratulates Dr. Dorsey, as Michael R. Sibille of University Information Services looks on. Mrs. Dorsey and Mary Keast (Mrs. W. R.) are glimpsed in the background.

April 15, 1971. Wayne State University friends with Dr. Dorsey are (left to right): Richard R. Kinney, Jr., art director and production manager, Wayne State University Press; Julia V. Boone, secretary, office of the vice-president; Thomas C. Rumble, dean of the office for graduate studies; Edward L. Cushman, executive vice-president.

Dr. Dorsey is pictured with Dr. Winfred A. Harbison at a reception, May 24, 1972, honoring the former vice-president for academic administration on his retirement from Wayne State University.

Colleen Moore Hargrave, Hollywood star, and King Vidor visit informally with the Dorseys at their Highland Park home, September 14, 1972. Photo by John Collier, Detroit Free Press.

A group photograph of the Wayne County Medical Society Library Committee was taken at the dedication of the William John Stapleton Reading Room, Shiffman Medical Library, September 24, 1970. Left to right (seated): Drs. Alfred H. Whittaker, John M. Dorsey, Don W. McLean, Rose E. Herrold, Edward D. Maire; (standing) James J. Aiuto, C. Jackson France, Donald R. Brock, Ralph R. Cooper, Robert H. Berman.

forget myself certainly does not rid me of myself. It does rid me of that much voluntary appreciation for, and control of, myself. And self-possession is my only real, or attestable, possession.

Horace Mann wrote (December 9, 1836), "Emerson showed me what I have long thought of so much,—how much more can be accomplished by taking a true view than by great intellectual energy." As I review the life endangering extent to which I have seemed to be habitually in the service of my language, instead of the converse, I am amazed at how powerfully my pejorative words have contributed to that verbal enslavement. Meliorative terms conceal pejoration but function in the same self-belittling way. Whether I judge one condition worse than another or better than another, each judgment contains the presence of faultfinding concerning one of the terms. Whatever is, perfectly is. I would not trade the reality of *perfection* for the illusion of "progress."

My amazement at this discovery that my language not only conceals me from myself but also hypostatizes faultfinding is quickly followed by dismay over the extent and consequence of my self-deception. This painful astonishment is helpful for my understanding why my recognizing my submissively subjecting myself to my language, instead of merely the converse, did not occur to me before. Simply by associating liking or disliking with any experience, I can evaluate the former as desirable and name it "good," or the latter as undesirable and name it "bad" (so-called value judgment), whereas each is perfect and necessary functioning of my own ideal being.

Compiling the facts of my divinity at will constitutes collating them. I find that I can omit no fact whatsoever from my divine category and conclude that it is impossible for any act of mine to be other than as providentially helpful as possible whenever or however it occurs. Any and all of my behavior is nothing but the momentary manifestation of that much of my growing of myself and, as such, is as provident as it is possible for it to be.

In ancient biblical times the thoughtful sage recognized that steadily exercising his will to practice goodness, justice, or understanding must result in his growing his life's meaning in this worthy direction. He found that the consistent way in which he used his mind invariably developed his cultivating his concept of his self-identity according to the trend of his devotion.

Isaiah conceived this truth, one grows as he plants, "Look unto me and be ye saved." Ezekiel alluded to it, "Turn away your faces from all your abominations." Plato heeded this necessity in self-creating self, "Lift the eye of the soul above its slough and set it toward its summit." Mark's Jesus named it the Watch, "What I say unto you, I say unto all, Watch." My Sigmund Freud devised his method enabling one's watching and seeking for his greatest good, that is, the good of his wholeness or allness. Professor Freud taught himself life-consciousness by constantly disciplining his mind with the practice of acknowledgeable self-observation. He set the working of his mind toward its revering all meaning as consisting of its own vital production. He kindly renounced negation, recognizing in it merely an unconscious effort to annihilate some of his own mentality not sufficiently understood for its helpfulness.

All education is self-activity. *Consciously* self-taught is the specific way for being *consciously* God-taught, or consciously divinely guided. *Heeding* that I am growing *all* of my knowledge as my self-knowledge is divine insight based upon the principle of beholding deeds *in order,* life's first law. When first I grew this solipsistic conception I felt its magnitude as a strangeness, even hostility, in contrast with my then habitual sense of continuously "repeatable" self-identity. My further experience taught me that all of my meaningfulness had to be all of my own conceiving and that, therefore, out of sheer self-interest I must gradually make the best of it, that is, make myself appreciate it as my own helpful being. Thus I allow functioning of my own nature to light up in my mind meaning before which I have formerly quailed, so that I can gradually learn to love and labor such conscious-self knowledge as my ever helpful self. Here "I" represents my present conscious and unconscious self-identity.

By *conscious* self-knowledge I mean specifically: full awareness for the truth that any or all of it (my knowledge) must be created by my own mind out of its own mentality. My *conscious* self-knowledge bears the stamp of its psychical origin in my clearly understanding it to be entirely and only the product of my own subjectivity. I trust its meaning as being constituted of functioning of my own self-activity.

Only my individuality-revealing consciousness can contribute to my self-wholeness edification, thus honoring my organic integrity with biological adequacy. It is from my gradually growing appreciation for the magnitude of my own unity that my gradual development of my theologizing wholeness-consciousness is taken.

I have made my own, by *creatively* reading (responsibly authoring) it, the determinative concept of divine understanding produced by long, scholarly and consciously subjective (spiritual) labor of many a religion-oriented theologian. This divinity emerges as all and only one, completely self-sufficient, autonomous, free, whole, responsible, real, identical, omnipresent, omniscient, omnipotent, unchangeable, unconditioned, subjective, absolute, perfect, just, and self-adoring creator of its providence. All that can be meant by preservation appears to be new creation.

Only to the extent that I cultivate self-consciousness as self-revelation can I redeem appreciation for *my* own wonderfulness, and through that process become able to succeed in attributing to my divinity all that belongs to it. As I record these words I am heedfully aware of the self-reference in each term.

How can I trace every divine power to my own living? Merely by allowing my imagination free rein for the purpose, I can discover miraculous power of my mind to attain every kind of achievement of power and wisdom in the spirit of truth. Indeed I must draw upon my very own imaginative power to be able to endow my world-divinity, to which I imagine my self-divinity integral, with each spiritual attribute I have created as my own mental production. I conceive my religious experience as uniting me into my personal world, quite as I imagine my universe to be constituted of its divine unity. I am always the founder of whatever meaning my mind can create.

By becoming self-conscious enough to create my so-called external world in the image and likeness of my own arduously worked up wholeness-identity, I can postulate my imagined world-order as being integral to its God presiding over it. My true religion cannot be localized, except in me, on account of my boundless allness-nature, my religious element.

A negative feeling ("attitude") can be *nothing but* an inhibited positive one. My ultimate understanding of this necessity brought me profound peace, security, and conscious self-help-fulness, opening up for my investment with conscious self-identity vast regions of my being essential for my appreciating fully the truth of my wholeness.[3]

I instinctively avoid pain and seek pleasure, and therefore unless I teach myself how to conduct this instinct of mine as subject to me, instead of the converse, I shall be unable to discover the lifesaving and life-giving function of my pain (including any unhappiness). Immeasurable extent of my living experience must be painful. All of my growing up contains painful elements. Whatever I live must be gradually endured as being my own living, if I would grow consciously whole. Furthermore it is my biological providence to be able to try to honor whatever I live, for that "whatever" is indispensably integral to my living as long as I live it.

Endurance, hardihood, perseverence, understanding—such life-rewarding virtue is the product only of suffering discomfort for all of the comfort that it is worth. All of my pain,

[3]See my *Psychology of Language* (Detroit: Center for Health Education, 1971), pp. 27, 120.

including unhappiness of any kind, is really inhibited pleasure associated with inhibited function. I need to start understanding this physiological truth that all present suffering is helpfully prevented functioning of my previously created pleasing behavior.

My joy of living consists of the pleasure inherent in the activation of my being ("functional triumph"), in my freely using myself as I please. However, interference with my exercising myself freely is associated with unpleasure. Thus, the same motion of my hand associated with joy in using it easily, becomes associated with pain in using it difficultly (when it is injured). Or, the agreement associated in perceiving or thinking of my once kind friend becomes disagreement when I perceive or think of this kind friend who has since seemed unkind. And so on.

From studying realization of the uncontrolled functioning of painful experience (even though I judge it as undesirable), the enormous benefit to be derived from my understanding my pain's lifesaving goodness may become evident. It is my profound insight that my every emotion, whether freely felt as pleasure or unfreely felt as unpleasure, is entirely about itself only. It cannot signify anyone or anything except itself, signalling whether or not certain of my being is free or unfree in its functioning. It is specifically this self-understanding that has revealed to me the disconcerting extent to which I have led myself to name whatever pleases me presently as good (hence desirable), and whatever displeases me presently as bad (hence undesirable) living of mine.

Certainly tremendous relief was not long in following my dismay, namely, immediate feeling of comfort at having solved the problem of evil, sin, or whatever "seeming" imperfection. All imperfection really amounts merely to perfection consciously negated in the interest of the necessity to secure sufficient truth to reveal the underlying perfection fully accounting for all possible so-called imperfection.

My present inability to live any of my existence positively

(since I cannot feel all of the truth in it) is signalized by my symptomatically living that much of my existence negatively. This conscious-self defense named *negation* is, as every other resort to self-repudiation (repression), of lifesaving helpfulness also. It serves specifically to preserve my ability to sense and honor my particular amount of already recognizable self-identity, of already achieved appreciation for my personal responsibility for keeping alive, that I can presently acknowledge as being mine.

Following my relief upon freeing myself from habitual subjugation to my helpful feelings of evil and sin, I experienced another wonderful self-understanding. My immediately felt wish was to extend my newfoundland of conscious self-possession to my fellowman somehow. Then my enlightenment came that this wish could also be a cover-up of my own need to grow this same kind of insight throughout my mental extent, a process technically termed "working through."

Each of these growths of *conscious* self-functioning is helpfully united with my growing appreciation for my need to work through my whole vocabulary in its every linguistic usage, to be able to renounce my (unconscious) habit of using my wordage for the purpose of *not* calling my soul my all.

My meaning for the word "renounce" of course is not at all that of faultfinding rejection inherent in negation—quite the contrary. By my term "renounce" I mean merely: *make free to become integral to my volitional control.* For me, renunciation is the act of redeeming sacred selfness. By renouncing any meaning of evil or sin I recognize and honor its helpfulness not only in my former living of it but also in my continuing ability to live that meaning *whenever I will to do so.* I keep myself busy in renouncing lifelong practices of experiencing 1) my own fellowman-meaning as if it is not I, and 2) my fellowman's own self-meaning as if it is not (my) he.

When I repress any of my life's meaning, its vitality may seem to me to be ended. However, the fact is that repressed meaning can manifest its true importance under repression (by entering into symptom formation) that it could not manifest as conscious mentation, namely, its perfect right to be. When I repress (make unconscious) any of my life's functioning, its precious vitality continues to be actively discharging its force, unconsciously of course. It is only ultimate expansion of conscious self-esteem that clearly establishes the insightful fact of the one and only value, namely, *perfection,* of every fact of life.

My recent living or growing of me is characterized by what counts most in my momentary existence, namely, appreciation for my life itself. It has been a forced awareness to the extent that nothing can happen unless the force necessary to make it happen is present. In this sense, for my life consciousness to be unforced must mean that it cannot exist. Also, it is not difficult for me to observe precisely the kind of activation it is that operates for the production and strengthening of that basic love of life itself that I name conscious self-realization. It is and cannot be other than my creating and sustaining my conscious self-observation as such, my disciplining my meaningful capacity in regular exercise of noticing (studying) its power of mindfulness. Self-authentication is the only possible form of any so-called proof.

By voluntarily exerting myself to exercise my life appreciation, and only by this purposeful directing of my will, I can attain biologically adequate emphasis of my life power that comes of careful and caring life cultivation. I see this seemingly belated willful growing of my life appreciation as my volitionally evolving the necessary organ requiring my honoring a lifesaving truth that has always existed in me, namely, life worth itself. Whatever I am forced by my power of truth to invest with self-love begins to live freely.

From the beginning of my being I am an individual in sole charge of my wholly subjective (soulful) nature. I may, or may never, gradually take cognizance of this conspicuous necessity. But whether I ever teach myself to do so or not is ever the most important decision I can call upon myself to make. Ab-

sence of self-conscious mind can become insensibility amount-
ing to my greatest improvidence. My every thought, word,
and deed, as all of my possible passion, is nothing but a kind
of discharge of my native essence.

Conscious self-continence is the law underlying *the law of
sanity*. Only the degree of my devotion to myself specifically as
the possessor of my life enables me to observe the validity and
verifiability of my preferred definition of sanity. Insanity can
be only negated (denied, inhibited) sanity revealing my withholding "the divine look" from living of my very own that I
cannot yet appreciate as such. The ultimate and immediate
source of whatever I can mean can be found nowhere but in
my living it. I may call that mental condition psychism if I
wish, but "psychism" is only a name I give to label an idea I
create.

There can be no so-called necessity except that natural and
completely desirable necessity imposed by the omnipotence of
truth. Here ascends the design of designs, the inescapable
evidence of universal plan:

*The demonstrable, repeatable, and incontrovertible finding is that
only the presence of sufficient fact (power of truth) to fully account for
any happening can ever, and must always, wholly produce that event.*

To understand this declaration of fact is to experience what
God's forgiveness means, to understand how the scarlet of sin
can become the white of innocence. Such is the unshakeable
foundation of undeniable reality, the realization of self-consciousness as the light of life, the attestative basis of sanity. It is
too true not to be good. Truth cannot be found except in its
own activation, as St. Paul thought, "For what man knoweth
the things of a man, save the spirit of man which is in him."

It is of the grace of my religion to maintain the truth of the
dynamic, subjective or spiritual, force of life *and* the illusion of
the mechanic, objective or material; to advance the claims of
growth and identity to *be* the power of cause and opposition; to
understand every personal experience as *the Coming of the Lord;*
to appreciate all well-doing as well-being only; to recognize the

healing element of wholeness in whatever sin or wretchedness; to see every book as the book of life of its author; to discern only the present in history and prophecy; to know the seamless unity underlying polar opposites; to equate spirit of being and freedom of function; to achieve reconcilement of mutually exclusive views to inclusive wholeness; to let reverence for my life be my sufficiently trusted guide; to interpret *all* of my life as myself being newly made whole here and now; to envision self-consciousness (insight) as my willingly responsible alternative to guilt-ridden servitude.

A difference of opinion distinguishing the historic scientist and theologian, that is, whether man is the product of evolution or of special creation, resolves itself in the realization that each individual creates her (his) own self. Whatever exists, is all and only its own being. Beginning with conception every individual lives all of her (his) own growth. Such autogenesis is integral to the self-creativity implicit in the name "Creator." All being is entirely within *its* own existence, mutation or no. My growing the dimension of self-consciousness in my individuality forces such changeable self-consequence as to merit the name of mutation. The largeness of the order or law of my self-insight reveals my boundless subjectivity, frees my imagination, empowers my will, inspirits the reality of my functioning innerness and naturalizes my love of the wholeness, allness, and absolute freedom of my perfect life.

Revealing reflection upon the necessity that nothing can be or happen unless all of the truth essential for making it be or happen is present (when it then must happen), clearly demonstrates the ethical character of all of nature. Whatever is, perfectly is. Whatever is, should be, ought to be; whatever is not, should not be, ought not to be. In other words, nothing can be except what absolutely perfectly can be.

Possibly the most meaningful description of divinity itself is expressed in the term *perfection*. "God's will be done" is the religious statement of the scientist's discovery that whatever happens, necessarily happens, on account of the presence of relevant factors sufficient to require its happening. To understand this providential way of God fully justifies the divine nature of whatever occurs to seeming disadvantage—poverty, health trouble, catastrophe, or whatever.

Whatever I experience deserves glorification, but only my knowledge of the sufficient force of truth prevailing to make it happen can enable me to appreciate its divine justice. It is this purest of wisdom inherent in every unique existent that surpasses every other kind of sovereign power, that creates the best of all possible worlds. Protected by this dominating self-insight (divining the design of Providence), it is lifesaving to strive to be able to wish for whatever my divinity wills, to recognize my God's will as my will, to appreciate my awareness for my own unity in comprehensible godhood.

I imagine that it is the degree of my appreciation for the life of my perfect Self that determines the degree of my appreciation for the reality of the perfect Soul of the Universe of Which I imagine my Self to be an integral Element. The ground of all of my truth is my belief that I can and must be entirely and only my perfect self, consciously or unconsciously. To live my experience truly means to acknowledge it within the development of my original self-existence which itself is divine. Love of all of my Self must be an individuation of my love of God. My Emerson recorded this moral conviction in his own words of piety: "Self-existence is the attribute of the Supreme Cause."

I advance this self-understanding deliberately, for I find it to be the sole method by which I can hope either to establish ethics upon solid scientific ground or to establish science upon solid ethical ground. So far, the only eminent way to either whole religious or whole scientific life orientation, I believe to be through conscious self-observation. It is the unique privilege of the *conscious* solipsist to consider the history of either scientific or religious study from the acknowledgeably psychical viewpoint. The seen can be found in, derived from, only the unseen.

Review

For me to be in my self-conscious frame of mind means I am minutely alert to my responsibility for being all and only my momentary self. The longer I live I wittingly direct the course of my behavior along my historical path. Only thus can I escape spending my life as if an hysterical demonstration. I find pursuance of this developmental way of life to be the one most consistent with my understanding my living as nothing but my growing of my innate possibilities.

I live for myself only, recognizing that any other effort must be not only supererogatory but also heedless of the necessity imposed by the fact of my individuality. Somewhat as Novalis recorded, my thinking is meaningful movement of my being, including my muscles. Of course I entertain today, as easily as in my childhood, every wishful claim to live more and less than my own life. Like water my self-estimate can rise or fall as high or low as activated sources of my own power and capacity.

What has given man pause, the pause that precedes conscious life appreciation, is the belief that a power greater than himself exists in the world, the Creator of the All. It is this clue to the meaning of divinity in his own life that can become understandable to him as inspired revelation of his own godliness necessarily integral to that universal deity of his faith. Rare of every generation is the individual sufficiently self-possessed *consciously* to be able to consider fairly his own divinity meaning as being entirely of his own creation. That I justly make my God in my own image, whether affirmed or denied by me, is a necessity of my humanity.

The original discoveries to which I have led myself by my (conscious) self-analytic exploration, by systematically applying my Sigmund Freud's method of free association, cannot be at the expense of any other ethical system or religious belief I formerly cultivated, but rather are necessary outgrowths of the same. My approach rules out any worthy intention of writing a complete history of either my religion or science. It *is* my intention to keep only my present self-consciousness in the foreground of my account.

Although the helpful conception of *development,* perhaps earliest comprehensively applied in Friedrich Schelling's nature-philosophy (1799), is now largely taken for granted by my biological scientist as a theory which he cannot well do without, it is seldom strictly appreciated in the only form in which it can really exist, namely, *self-development.* Only the truth of *self-development* can derive its meaning from the source of personal experience. All I can ever do is grow, and all I can *ever* live is a growth of my individual self. Emerson put it briefly, "Every form is a history of the thing." Sobering realization!

His cultivating his wholeness identity delivers the scientist from his time-honored dependence upon dividing his investigation into the two perspectives: the *normative* that evaluates fact according to the law of how it agrees or disagrees with a given norm; and the *explicative* that upholds identical value for any and every fact.

By revering my every fact for what it is, *and therefore ought to be,* I can renounce my dependence upon my symptom-forming duality: "seeming" and *being.* Somewhat as my Goethe I can aspire: to "seem" nothing, but to *be* my everything. It is comforting to know this security: I must be what I ought to be, I should be as I am (including my any wish to add to, or subtract from, my being). It is only my *same* living of it that can confer its sameness value upon any fact of mine.

My freedom of will consists in my choosing to live my being, including my freedom to end it. No one else can choose any of my living, including dying, for me, despite many an appearance to the contrary.

I write in the first person and present tense as consistently as I can, indulging my wishful opinion that what I try to do herein may in some distant here-and-now be required of each author aspiring to compose scientific or religious literature.

So-called religious thought and feeling appear to constitute primary sources whence blessed sanity is derived. Man's growth of morals from his supernatural, then his social, and on to his acknowledgeable self-meaning, parallels the growth of his devotion from impersonal and personal godliness to his ultimate discovery that all of *his* divinity must be, necessarily, his own divinity. This last speculative enlargement enables him to grow the whole understanding not only that he is all of his own divinity but also that he is all divine.

It requires my discovery that all of *my* reality must be my psychic reality, to empower me with willingness to make room for my "resisted" living in my conscious mind as integral to my conscious self-identity.[4] The pain of realizing my own conscious mind's sturdy resistance to welcoming the incursion of its further life-consciousness is assuaged somewhat by my further realization that my conscious mind will similarly defend that additional self-identity once it can recognize it as such.

In brief, I find that the practice of self-consciousness is the most exacting way of life and also the precise conduct of life that necessitates its practitioner's acknowledging his (her) divine nature. All of my existence is *here* and *now* living. Eternity consists of nowness; infinity consists of hereness. Such understanding of the necessary *presence* of my mental activity discloses the necessarily illusional nature of memory, including forgetting. It can also rescue me from my addiction to my deadening illusion of being a "mortal" one conducting merely a "mortal" existence.

[4]My so-called "external" reality must be a convincing product of my faith in its existence.

7

My Health

Health is no more than learning.
Thomas Jefferson

My true-to-life enthusiasm, inhibited by fear of daring to revere my wonderworking nature that I have been subjecting to
the threat of nuclear warfare, began to enliven itself again to
biological adequacy following persevering discipline with my
consistent discovery that I, always including my every fellowman, can have no vocation or any functioning other than that
of growing my astonishing self, with or without consciously
observing that provident necessity. Thenceforth I wished to
recognize as my sane education, formal or informal, only my
acknowledgeable self-development in my living mind. Under
this *conscious* management of my living my character began to
change considerably, becoming less neglectful and more wary
for steering my sole welfare including the welfare of my
world. Such has been the education of my acknowledged will.
All lucid consideration of health involves the life significance
of wholeness, inviolable self-oneness.

As University Professor I find vocational satisfaction daily in
regarding every indication of so-called health trouble as being
indispensable meaning for my mending, and thus saving, my
life. My liberty to see nothing but my own identity in every
aspect of my self-produced campus happening enables me to
explain lustily, not listlessly, each person or occurrence to my
self as being a manifestation of meaning in myself.

171

Conducting my mind as if it consists of separate meanings obstructs my observing that my understanding any one region of my mind is the key to my understanding my essence in all of my wholeness. To reinforce, my sensing the importance of one of my life concerns may seem to prevent my acknowledging that *all* of my minding is important. I may seem to myself to consist of innumerable interests conflicting with one another rather than of harmonious wholeness, particularly if I have educated myself to notice only differences and resemblance, but not my wholeness identity underlying each.[1]

I am sure that my self-wholeness can be realized in my present conditions merely by localizing each one where it is all occurring, namely in my living it as my mental condition. Thus, I teach myself all that there can be to teach, namely, the evolving power of my individuality. Individuality is all: Whatever is, individually is. Responsible holiness equals conscious wholeness.

My self-identity cannot be discriminated away into otherness of one kind and another, but it can *seem* to me as if this self-dissolution is the perfectly natural good of becoming educated. However, the true scholar is the true master of conscious self-wholeness.

It is the ubiquitous principle of self-help that enables me to renounce my illusions of "external" laws and jaws. Only by crediting my mind for what it can be and do, can I gradually come to appreciate the wonderfulness of my life itself. Conversely, by withholding the magnificence of my mind from my self-understanding I can gradually come to value my life itself as hardly worthwhile. I behave according to my opinion of my life's worth.

Self-understanding, as all of my mentality, is intuitive, and not to be acquired somehow at secondhand. All of my mental trouble, every symptom, is always the helpful sign of withheld

[1]See my *Psychic Nature of Physiology* (Detroit: Center for Health Education, 1977), pp. 73–84.

self-esteem. It calls for no remedy other than its being recognized for what it is, namely the indication of my life depreciation as discoverable in my lack of devotion to the truth of my organic wholeness. The greatest change of my University Professorship office being to study all of my eventful life as becoming understandable only in terms of its history (its roots), I naturally apply this same principle of truth for my understandingly appreciating my fellowman's developmental way of immediately helping his (her) self.

That scientific literature is true to life which records not only ideas but also includes the marvel whence they come, the subjective life of the scientist. Enduring throughout my whole existence, I consider my most difficult hygiene to be that of adequately appreciating my amazing life, as such. I find that my every self-dissatisfaction is traceable ultimately to this specific source: biologically inadequate life *appreciation*. All that I have ever read or written is most meaningful as constituting the health doctrine of appreciation for my life. Recognizing this necessity makes contentment, ignoring it creates instructive discontent ("health trouble").

The strongest distinction of which I have a notion is I-and-not-I, a distinction without any difference at all except that traceable to my developmental need as an infant and child to live very much of my self without realizing that I *am* living it. Unique power of mind is its potential ability to assume responsibility for being itself only. Throughout my writing I discipline my mind by exercising health principles that need exercising. It is the force of my weak mindedness that objects to such exercise, calling it useless repetition, monotonous routine, etc. Invariably I find that my annoyance with "repetition" or "monotony" is a displacement from matter (content) to manner (style). To illustrate, I would prefer not to keep reminding myself of my habituation to overlooking telltale roots of my surface mentality. Again, growing up, my mind is not strong enough to endure much of my living as being entirely all that it can be, namely, my own creating of my own life's meaning.

The trouble arising from my unrelieved necessity to maintain fixative unawareness for my I-and-not-I mental dissociation is that I must go on feeling that all of my not-I living is involuntary, beyond my responsibility, entirely foreign to my nature. Most distressing consequence of this apparent splitting of my mind is my dangerously impaired realization of the intact wholeness of my individuality, enforcing hazardous limitation of my sense of unified self-identity. For every meaningful pursuit it is merely my mind I need to be able to use, and my *accredited* presence of mind is always most salutary. All of my love of nature can be only my love of my very own nature. All of my exercise of my senses creates self-meaning only.

My ideal University Professorship functioning bases itself firmly on consciousness for one actively functioning responsibility: My personal opinion is all about itself and can never have the meaning of rejection of established opinion. I reject no so-called established opinion whatsoever but, rather, recognize *its* indispensable helpfulness also. Each mind must devote itself to what appears of value in its own experience. My *every* man is a true godful man. There can be no mind but one individual's mind. My materialism *is* unconscious idealism.

Individuality is all that can be the real source of mankind, and, therefore all that can be needed—not more than one, as in the abstraction "the people." Emerson divined, there can be no union whatsoever except that existing within (not "between") each individual. My insightless insistence upon being able to be more or less than one is not only providently symptom-forming but also my only source of symptom formation ("mental trouble"). William James, M.D., in 1907 wrote to Carl Stumpf (1848–1936), German psychologist, that each one of us does "lead a life of non-communication."

My fellow scientist may valiantly endeavor to settle the whole truth of his inviolable individuality by yielding to his illusion that his mind is an image of the so-called external world that he somehow actually experiences. Even my cherished term "datum," literally meaning *gift,* is itself a helpful illusion except insofar as I intend it to mean my giving my own created discovery to myself. Surely whatever I live I give to myself; and the donation can be explicable only in terms of my creating (my) *it.*

Despite all appearance to the contrary, there can be no demonstrable correspondence whatsoever of any kind or degree *between* me and anything external to me. In my mind cannot be found any link uniting my nature and any so-called other nature. It is to the health benefit of everyone that each one's absolutely whole individuality be, and be recognized as, all and only its completely identical self. Effort is well spent that is devoted to the thorough elucidation of the full meaning of oneness. My English language, mother tongue, Esperanto or medical vocabulary cannot adequately word this unrelative self-enlightenment. Of necessity only acknowledgeable idiolect can record it.[2]

Again, to become willingly conscious that I am all of my own living I must develop the corresponding heedfulness of mind that enables me to live such weighty responsibility with love. It is my appreciable love of my living that furthers my affirming it is mine; it is my unappreciable love of my living that furthers my denying it is mine. My "appreciable love" is felt as pleasing (safe freedom) by me; my "unappreciable love" is felt as unpleasing (dangerous hindrance) by me. During my early psychogenesis it is very easy for me to find only my self-identity in the way I please myself; but it is correspondingly difficult for me to find only my self-identity in the way I displease myself.

Hence it is I may grow my mind without realizing that it is *wholly,* all, mine. Unless I learn how to teach myself the basic identity of my pleasure and pain (as of all so-called opposites), I have no course other than to affirm my growing self-identity in all of my own experience I associate with pleasure, and to

[2]Ibid, pp. 13–19.

use my mind's own power of negation for denying my growing self-identity in all of my own experience I associate with unpleasure.

Thus becomes evident the lifesaving benefit to me in laboriously working up thorough understanding of the obscure but true sameness underlying the conspicuous but illusional difference of what I name pleasure and pain. But how can I ever teach myself to honor the selfsame goodness in my pleasure and pain alike? How can I ever grow the mental strength to observe sincerely: I need to be able to *feel* that infuriating myself is as lovable as enjoying myself?

How can I see love-making in my hate-making or the converse for that matter? Can my crossed (inhibited) love turn itself into rampant hate? Can my rejected adoration take the form of unleashed loathing? Is it possible that every rejected meaning of my mind, or every individuation of my individuality, can struggle to preserve its freedom to function in such a violent way? How can my denial of the right-to-be of any meaning of my mind enable that meaning to flaunt its unfreedom by exposing its most painful nature, namely, the meaning of its oppositeness?

Is it even possible that my learning the indispensable helpfulness of pain or any other unhappiness is my only possible way for me to attain a biologically adequate appreciation for my wholeness? If all of me is wholeness, is my every life distinction indicating not-I an illusional localization? If I am all one whole, and wholeness is the only true identity of any of my being, must I teach myself to live with love whatever I am already accustomed to classify as no good? In order to honor the wholeness of my true nature must I teach myself gradually to restore with awareness the identity of all that I have categorized as divine and evil? Must I gradually acknowledge that any and all of my perfect faultfinding is perfectly traceable to my perfectly insufficient fact-finding? Can my true "triumph over pain" really be my triumph over my ignorance of any of my suffering as being absolutely indispensable for my teaching myself biologically adequate appreciation for the glory and power of being a whole-souled self?

My reply to each of my questions is, "Yes, certainly yes." A well-made question indicates my mind's inability to live with love the whole meaning which that question posits. I find that my mind is all-inclusive, that my ability to affirm any meaning does not rule out my ability to negate that same meaning. Opposites, *as well as all differences,* rule each other in, not out. My power of negation is mental only, and it can refer only to my effort to dispose or reject my own mental content only. Once this necessity is fully appreciated I can save myself no end of falsely believing in the ostrich-like psychology that my shutting out my power of observation is the ideal way for me to escape troubling my mind over any pain (unpleasure, unhappiness).

However my denying, or saying "No" to any possible consideration does seem to have the magic power to rid me of it temporarily, or apparently render it inconsequential, or at least make it less potent than would my saying "Yes" to that consideration. However, the biological function of negation is to serve as the unrecognized and unwilling beginning of acceptance of present and necessary living of my wholeness. This insight is the creation of conscious self-analysis (integration) only. Conscious wholeness cannot be imparted.

It is my biological destiny to be born with no consciousness for my self-contained nature, but to be compelled in the interest of my welfare to teach myself that my intact unity is all that I am. My first sensing of my personal identity is the very beginning of my teaching myself of my natural integrity. From then on my furthering of my manward appreciation for my wholeness depends entirely upon my ability to extend my sense of my personal identity to include *all* of my life experience. This lifesaving course of conscious-self accountability is beset by any and all of the pain (unhappiness) I difficultly teach myself to understand as perfectly desirable good. Self-observant William T. Harris oracled, "Wisdom is the insight into the ideal of man, the totality of his potential nature and the ideal laws which govern its nature."[3]

Whenever my physician brother defines health in terms other than those strictly applicable to an individual's teaching himself (herself) enjoyment of the full use of his unique creaturehood, I nevertheless respect his aiding himself habitually by whatever theory of health his ever helpful imagination finds practical. Indeed it is enlightening to study how he works his mind to come forth with his views upon this concept which is central for all medical effort. As a rule, he tends to consider a specific condition of health to be: freedom from debilitation, dysfunction, disease, and distress. Insightfully he may continue to specify that one cannot enjoy freedom from any condition which appears to subordinate him to itself, which appears to subject him as a willing individual to its alien control, which seems to violate the integrity of his conscious individuality in some way or other.

To illustrate, I enjoy healthy regard for my fellow physician who renounces his traditional dichotomy of health and sickness, discovers that each sign or symptom is entirely a wholesome constitutional mobilization of vital energy, and recognizes that every so-called "pathological" development is really nothing but the cultivation of his patient's heroic physiological efforts to preserve his organicity. I approve when he consistently subordinates his painful feelings to an understanding of health based upon searching for, and use of, *the facts* perfectly explaining and explicating each patient complaint, thus obviating necessity for any possible kind of faultfinding in any of his medical profession.

It is equally satisfying when I see my young student medic learning to renounce (rather than repress) the traditional dichotomy of mind and body, to observe that each of these terms is but a word naming manifestations of the same one human life, to recognize that the fact of the integration of the

[3]Leidecker, *Yankee Teacher*, p. 585.

individual necessitates an accurate naming of each of the
forces of life which does no violence to the truth of the
oneness of that life, to forego indulgence of his deeply in-
grained habits of attributing to his science merely the orientation of the medical philosophy of materialism of the nineteenth century, to cultivate and discipline his imagination as
being the most practical resource of his human nature, and
to prize above all achievements his ongoing recognition that
his all-creating life is completely and sufficingly his own.
Knowledge of such enlightened conduct of life is welcome
heal to the frequently sore heart and head of the lifelong
medical self-educator. Trust in fact-finding, as proving ever
confirmed trust in a dependable providence, reveals the comforting abiding truth of the inherent goodness ever-present
in due appreciation for that never-failing force of being
called *fact*.

A fact of fancy is as real as any other. Every fact has the
quality or character of being *lived* entirely by and in the mind
of the individual actuating it. The universal validity of fact is
intrinsic to its real substance: being actual and actual being. Its
presence or its absence is tantamount to present living or absent living, for each fact is an activity of a given life. It is
customary to imagine a realm of "fact" which is "objective" as
distinguishable from a realm of "value" which is "subjective."
This soft doubleness is at the bottom of any and all of my
irreverence for whatever existent I find myself unready to
identify as *my* being (as only and entirely of my own making):
it is at the bottom supporting my contradictory attitudes towards my life: but it is also at the bottom supporting the
growth of the kind of self-image which is compatible with my
current idea of a consciously integrated life which is fully worth
living.

Despite every demonstrable evidence of the absolute perfection of my universe, nevertheless in pure self-defense it is
necessary for me to live on screening my very same perfect *self*
experiences into those which I recognize and value as personal

and those which I do not recognize and value as personal (quite as during my infancy and childhood I identified with what experience felt "good" in me and withheld my sense of personal identity from whatever did not feel "good" in me). Whenever I can extend my capacity to live with love whatever I could formerly live only with dislike, I attain a clearer recognition of, and hold on, my life.

The solution of this problem created by extensive self-disrespect (in the form of disrespect for "unpleasant impersonal facts") is an obvious but extremely difficult one. It consists in sufficiently studying each such unwelcome fact enough to be able to cherish the certainty that its existence completely justifies itself. Careful study of any fact of mine reveals that its existence is 1) absolutely necessary, 2) most lovable (livable) in origin, 3) most propitious in occurrence, 4) most desirable in meaningfulness, 5) most essential for furthering helpfulness, 6) perfectly right in every respect, 7) indispensable life intuition for my present living.

"Fault" is the helpful symptom which is ever ready to substitute for recognition of the factual evidence of the basic helpfulness in *any* seemingly undesirable human experience. "Fault" is a useful condition of mind helpfully calling my attention to a gap in my full appreciation for my uninterrupted oneness. Only my further making of observation (fact-finding) can fill in that gap of self-disregard and thus not only relieve me of the feeling of guilt excited in faultfinding but also release me to my strengthening and healing power of life appreciation. That pursuit of pleasure is most rewarding, in terms of health, which leads me to search for the facts of the overall fact of my life. My faith in God rests and ranges in this life orientation. What I cannot find fault with I must see as good, as perfect, as deserving of every traditional feeling ascribable to divinity. I have observed that the expression "simply a human idea" rules in (and not out) "simply a divine idea." Similarly I have observed that negation of perfection in any and every place implicitly asserts the omnipresence of perfection.

Review

That view of man that he actively creates his own "environment" and therefore cannot be the "butt of circumstance," that his mind is always active and never passive in the creation of his every cognition (including sensation and perception), that his whole universe is nothing but the ontogenetic creation of his own understanding, that his idealistic world is his divine creation, that he is his own immanent divinity, that his imagination (his use of his mind) not only enables him to create his divinity in innumerable ways but specifically empowers him with the ability to conceive God as subsuming each man's own personal self—that healthy regard for individual man's immeasurably immense self-identity respects the wholeness of his being.

If so-called "external environment" (other than merely my imagining my own "externality") is a factor in my development, then my individuality must be a joint product and therefore my claim for appreciation of wholeness of my being is not fully warranted. Internal human experience is all that can be. "Externality" cannot apply to it.

Since due realization of wholeness of my being is considered to be the essence of the meaning of health, and since full devotion to such realization can deliver me from any of the negations of any restricting humanistic position, it must contribute to my well-being to dilate upon the hygienic benefit desirable from self-discipline to full measured self-esteem.

The question at issue is whether the whole truth, hence healthful evaluation, measures a man as a "worm of the dust" and his world as "a vale of tears," or whether sufficient facts support the view that a man is inherently perfect, creating his perfect world according to perfect specifications and needing only freedom, self-enlightenment, and the full use of his imagination in order to attain the ideal health status and true blessedness of thoroughly appreciating his perfection. How this questioning is settled can solve many a problem vexing a physician as well as increasing his vulnerability towards his actual dangers and life-taking risks.

The term "psychotherapy" may carry some pejorative connotation of the nature of faultfinding. Beginning with the sane view that all is always exactly as it should be, on account of the force of truth (fact, datum) present to make it exactly the way it is, I find that I must revise my time-honored conception of diagnosis and treatment. Accustomed to consider illness as something "wrong" with health and therapy as a riddance of that wrong, I can consistently overlook necessary historical facts fully explicating and thoroughly justifying every kind of health trouble or whatever else may seem to me to be undesirable at the time.

Every so-called illness thus may be readily misunderstood by the mind of limited experience as implying a "bad" condition or at least as a kind of living that ought not be at all. Indeed, unstudied feeling implying rejection, the wish for riddance, escape, and the like, is biologically adequate for immediate instinctive avoidance of life-threatening unpleasure and seeking lifesaving pleasure.

Sufficient fact-finding convinces me that whatever happens or can happen is for the best. For example, what appears to be destructive turns out to be constructive; whatever appears to be loss turns out to be gain; whatever seems to be an accident reveals itself as a necessity; whatever looks to be pathological proves to be helpful; whatever I call bad is justified as unrecognized good; whatever "displeases" me becomes understandable as wholly pleasing; and so on.

My reducing all of my possible activity, including its every meaning, to the one truth of my continuously growing myself discloses my successful resistance to acknowledging any of my experience as an enlargement of my self-identity (repression), as being my effort to inhibit my self-growth. The strong act of the well-developed mind is its ability to consider soberly, kindly, whatever it experiences as being lifeworthy. Generous, good-natured life appreciation is the product only of discipline in the practice of self-consciousness.

Being a physician I am most experienced in my doctor-patient duality, a beneficial illusion depending entirely upon my helpful delusion of displacement of self-meaning upon my patient and that patient's similar delusion of displacement of self-meaning upon her/his doctor. I may or may not take the trouble to be aware that my strength of mind depends upon my difficultly developed conscious responsibility for being *all* that I live, including my every meaning that I may associate with my patient. Yet my mental health (conscious mental integrity) is the consequence of this specific strength of mind.

To illustrate, my mental functioning involves me constantly in enlarging the content of my mind. Much of my experience is lived by me at first without my assuming responsibility for *being* it. My conscious wholeness of mind (mental health) is the outcome of my arduously working up my appreciation for my experience as being my own and as being totally desirable (in that I can continue to live only by being able to live whatever I must live). It is my difficultly attained acknowledgment, *the truth must be on the side of whatever happens,* that sustains me in this strenuous effort.

My resistance to realizing that *all* of my living necessarily *must* be good for me derives from trying to avoid overwhelming my mind with conscious self responsibility, the only possible source of growing up insightfully but also the only possible source of caring conscientiously for my self-world. The greater my resistance to difficultly loving my necessarily enlarging self-identity, the more I tend to grow my unconscious forcefulness at the expense of my conscious interest in, and devotion to, the welfare of my true wholeness. There can be nothing for me to resist but self-consciousness. The peace of conscious self-wholeness is possible through augmenting conscious self-identity. My referring my feeling of unpleasantness to anything or anyone but itself only, is the necessary origin of my consciously disowned mental content, the motivation of repression, the origin of the "problem of evil."

Self-insight (self-consciousness) is the unit of mental health. So-called recovery from any complaint (sign, symptom, syndrome) or any source of unpleasure is not riddance of it, but rather is the sedulously cultivated appreciation of its right to be, its constructive helpfulness, its desirable presence essential for my continuous fulfilling of my existence. So-called psychotherapy resolves itself into my gradually acknowledging that any and all of my behavior is momentarily my greatest possible therapeutic effort.

It can seem right to indulge the *habit* of regarding pain (unhappiness of any kind) as unworthy living and only pleasure as life-worthy. Pain points up self-consciousness. Habit bypasses self-consciousness and on that account may be construed as a valuable economy. However, on that very account it deserves special study, which discloses its limitation. Any behavior that obscures self-consciousness may detract from the furtherance of life appreciation itself. Living is necessarily growing. Dependence upon habit easily becomes associated with fear of growth. Renunciation of habit is always attended by fear of loss of the wish to live. *The fear of growing up may soon supplant the wish to grow up, once the latter reveals itself as involving increasing conscious responsibility for being one's self.*

My fear associated with developing my powerful being expresses itself in my restricting my use of my imagination. Thus I refuse to allow free functioning of my mind. For example, doing, as a rule, is unconscious minding. Whatever I am able to think over, I can have some choice about doing. Otherwise I may find myself doing what I would not even allow myself to think about.

My medical treatment, every kind of so-called therapy, can be a dangerously misleading concept precisely to the extent that it may imply that I can safely relieve myself of any responsibility for my health. My every sign or symptom is the helpful indication *to me* of the biologically inadequate way I am conducting my life. My every remedial measure (medicinal, technological, or whatever) is my self-helpfulness. *All* of its meaning is just as psychic as is every other meaning that I live. Yet I may be seldom mind-conscious enough even to consider the dominance of my mental power in *all* of my behavior.

As doctor or patient I am the only possible one who can and must take charge (either consciously or unconsciously) of any and every aspect of my health regimen. My inability to be keenly aware for this necessity (as in coma or in habitually feeling irresponsible for my health condition) is a most distressing desideratum in that it inhibits mobilization of natural efficacy, the invigorating consequence of my freely acknowledged self-wholeness.

The sooner I can consciously shoulder my health responsibility, the quicker I can feel motivation to find out just how to alter my way of life to make it fit the real nature and needs of my whole constitution. The marvelous resilience of my well-being enables me most of the time to restore my wholesome health balance, despite my frantic efforts to relegate my recuperative power to any kind of source that I cannot recognize as being entirely within me.

My search for an accurate perspective for my health education leads me to testify (to myself) that my personal insight is my most valuable possession, next to my life itself. The condition of my health is defined by how I have disciplined my self-consciousness to function. My (unconscious) unwillingness to apply myself diligently to this most rewarding practive accounts for my dispirited attitude when necessarily confronted by the innumerable distresses of my life that I disguise as of "the outside world." My conscious devotion to practicing conscious self-realization renounces the illusion of externality and accounts for my ability to evaluate whatever health hardship I may (necessarily) create as a valuable learning experience which may reveal to me how to preserve the *internality* that is all of my life.

Thus the condition of my health may reveal itself by the way in which I experience a blow from a bludgeon or a bacterium. I may be able to make the best of it and thereby continue to practice whole-self consciousness favoring my healing; or I may be able to feel wholly subjected to it and thereby continue to practice mostly "accident" or "sick" mindedness adding limited self-consciousness to my woe.

Only as I keep adding an increment to my stock of self-consciousness can I ever enlarge my understanding of the wisdom of my body sufficiently to discover that I am the only one who can be responsible for making myself well or unwell.

My studied process of "transmuting life into truth" (Emerson) has clarified the extent to which I tend to dream my life away, not only while obviously asleep or in so-called daydreaming, but also during any of my behavior that does not feature self-consciousness as such.[4] Thus I recognize my extended self-unconsciousness in all of my ordinary living of communication or any social behavior that is unrelieved by my insight that it is all necessarily occurring within me.

It is to the disciplined freedom of my imagination that I owe constantly replenishing appreciation for my life itself. I imagine my mastery of my wholeness to issue from mastery of my imagination. Thus, certainly it is possible for me to engage myself *insightfully* in conversation, dialogue, or whatever appearance of living more or less than myself alone. But such conscious solipsism is unwonted mental activity, resisted by me as unwanted, unbearable responsibility for being all of my own living.

---

[4]Sigmund Freud, "Formulations on the Two Principles of Mental Functioning (1911)," *Standard Edition*, XII, 218–26.

Summary

The most distressing thing about Western medical
science is the outcome that excess concern with
pathologically altered parts of the body has
for the individual patient.
Daisaku Ikeda, Choose Life

I often describe myself as being a one-idea man, meaning that
my every other idea must be an individuation of my conception of myself as a completely continent individual. It is this
self-view that I brought to my University Professorship and
consistently cultivated.

My resurrection of all that I can mean by my body to full
consciousness for its true significance as consisting all and only
of mentality has, of course, proved to be of enormous importance to me as a layman and as a physician. Fortunately for *my*
living my colleague peacefully, this insightful development
cannot occur at the cost of my repudiating either my earlier
sharp dichotomy of my body and mind (then conveniently
denying the existence of one or the other), or my later so-
called psychosomatic or psychophysical compromise, or my
still more recent effort to resolve the issue by making both
body and mind meanings subject of the same organic level
(psychicality). What I have ever found to be helpful (namely,
lived by me) I continue to be able to cherish as helpful. This
insight has been indispensable for my unifying myself as University Professor. My power of reasoning with myself focuses
my attention upon reasoning, itself, which regularly obscures
the abiding truth of my self-wholeness that is ever, but only,
accessible to my responsible self-consciousness.

I can still teach myself common sense based upon the use of my senses. Emerson noticed, "The perception of matter is made the common sense, and for cause. This was the cradle, this the go-cart, of the human child." My early conscious mind, growing forth from my unconscious mind, was not then luminous enough to acknowledge itself as being the creator of the whole of my sensory living. Only by brightening my conscious mind specifically for that vivid purpose can I arduously achieve recognition of the exclusively psychic nature of all of my so-called "perception of matter." Until I attain that strength of luminosity I must live myself *as if* subject to "material objectivity," never discerning that this latter designated "not-I" experience of mine is really only some of my own disowned mentality.

Steadily accumulating evidence of my most exact scientist attests that the seeming solidity of matter reduces ultimately to elements of force. However, such recently lived truth cannot suffice to allow me to renounce my habitual concept of illusional substance. Nevertheless, my own disciplining of my mind with enlightening consciousness can gradually result in sufficient growth of self-insight to necessitate my acknowledging that I, and only I, am the sole creator of all of my meaning named matter or spirit, or whatever. However, this cultivation of my mental clarity does not, and cannot, rid me of my prior illusion of being able to use my senses to explore external reality, to be impersonal and objective, to find meaning beyond my subjectivity, and so on. Again I exercise the self-sight: growth is ever an extension from, hence totally dependent upon, previous growth.

It is now a great source of pleasure for me to have written down the marvelous lifesaving benefit that can come to me only from my succeeding in acknowledging that all of my living of my so-called *environment* consists entirely and only of my very own flesh-and-blood existence. Whatever I am accustomed to view as my surroundings is really meaning of mine that is integral to my organic functioning quite as is any other physiological activity such as my metabolism.

It is my forceful habit of mind to imagine my body as if it could be outside of my mind also, thus encouraging my attributing so-called objectivity or impersonality to it, as to the rest of my strictly (personally) imagined external world. Therefore it is well to note that my psychical physiology includes not only all of my living of experience that I imagine occurs beyond the confines of my body, but also all of my living of experience that I imagine occurs within the confines of my body, e.g., my "environmental" experience as well as my ordinarily conceived physiology, biochemistry, or biophysics. Only meaning presumes a mind; only meaninglessness presumes no mind.

Thus self-understanding, which identifies all of my so-called external world experience as really being my own self-experience, is a supremely helpful achievement of my own making. I can neither bring to mind any other burst of my comprehension like it, nor do I even expect to look upon its like again. Although from my reading I know that similar self consciousness has been cultivated by my other earnest students of their own minds before me, this whole-self consciousness developed in me with all of the apodictic force of original discovery. In growing from strength to strength my mind steadily prepared me for appreciating further greatness in my human living and, ultimately, this superaddition of conscious self realization prepared me for appreciating all of me in my divine being.

When I momentarily or lastingly see the sights, hear the sounds, smell and taste the fruits, or feel the touch of the innumerable forces seeming to be "around" me, all of that seems a far remove from the activities I can sense as going on within me in some already acknowledged organic order of mine. However, as I accumulated evidence to convince myself that there can be no "distance receptor," that projection of spatial sensation is pure illusional displacement, that all existence is within *itself,* that "out" or "outside" must be no-where—then I gradually began to see the possibility of main-taining my illusions as acknowledgeable illusions providing the roots for my growing my real, but erstwhile incredible, consci-ous mental power enabling my willingly creating my own world in my own image. I can understand how my Isaac New-ton could speak of space as the sensorium of God (*Optics*).

Before this wholeness-enlightening growth of my self-consciousness occurred I had to force myself to conceive that I could live the appearance, at least, of externality, because I could not credit myself with creating all of the magnitude of that indefinable expanse as mere but mighty meaning of my own mind. Furthermore, the force of habit of all of my previ-ous illusional living of my designated not-I mentality compelled me to continue, as of yore, yielding to the comfort of its custom, thus preventing the discomfort of conscious innovation.

Specifically by learning how to love myself difficultly, that is, by making myself understand my dislikes as temporary conscious-self defenses, I could cultivate the mental strength necessary for assuming responsibility about being my whole self. Most difficult of all of this growing of conscious self-knowledge concerned my envisaging my sensory and percep-tual living as *innate* forms of my mentation. This advance in appreciating my wholeness was greatly aided by my realizing that I (self-deceivingly) attributed meaning to my so-called ex-ternal experience and, therefore, *that* meaning had to be oc-curring in my own mind. Similarly, I attributed emotionality to my so-called external events and, therefore, *that* emotional-ity had to be occurring in my own mind.

As my conscious self-continence aggrandized I reaped the conscious benefit derivable only from biologically adequate conduct of my life. For example, my knowing just where to look for any and all of my trouble, namely, in myself, is most economical saving of my precious energy. My realization that all of my so-called relationship is nothing but my own organic identity not only makes conscious all of my unconscious illusions of alien control but also allows me to credit myself with meaning essential for my cultivating my appreciation for my continent wholeness and inness.

When that consciously great physician William Osler was asked by his residents where they might learn about the nature of the human mind, he replied, "Read Emerson." From his early life my Ralph Waldo Emerson was strongly attracted to the development of the study of his mind, as such. He offered courses on "Natural History of Intellect," "The Natural Method of Mental Philosophy," and "Philosophy for the People." In his notebook he wrote, "The First Philosophy, by which is meant the original laws of the mind." Sometimes he would name this subject "The Natural History of Spirit." In 1848 he wrote his wife from England in praise of Richard Owen: "His lecture gratified me the more, or entirely, I may say, because, like Agassiz, he is an idealist in physiology."

Whatever I read or write is *my* living itself, not a discontinuity of my life. Observing my mind as a continuum of my mental being honors the truth of my organic integrity, heeds "the requisite wholeness of good tissue" (Matthew Arnold). Only the functioning of my self-consciousness can put me in my place. My every negation creates the illusion of absent presence. My self-awareness *only* enables an ever-needed revival of my mind, the origin of all of my life's meaning.

When I am not mind conscious, the necessary condition of all of my life appreciation, I am mind unconscious, the necessary condition of all of my mental trouble. My Emerson affirmed, "Omit all negative propositions; it will save ninety-nine one hundredths of your labor and increase the value of your work in the same measure," and, "The law of music is law of anatomy, of algebra and astronomy, of human life and social order. . . . It is certain that the laws are all versions of each other." Every observation I make, regardless of whether I call it external, physical, material, or whatever, can contribute to my understanding of my whole mind because it, itself, is being lived by me as integral to my whole mind. And I know

Wilbur J. Cohen, dean of the School of Education and professor of education at the University of Michigan, delivered the Whitney M. Young, Jr., Memorial lecture March 8, 1973. The semi-annual lecture series honoring the memory of the civil rights leader was established at Wayne State University in 1972. Left to right: Cornelius L. Golightly, associate dean; Kurt R. Keydel, member of the Board of Governors; Professor Cohen; Dr. Dorsey.

Dr. Francis A. Kornegay, executive director, Detroit Urban League, and Norman O. Stockmeyer, member of the Wayne State University Board of Governors, greet Professor John Hope Franklin, Department of History, University of Chicago, on the occasion of his Whitney M. Young, Jr., Memorial lecture, November 1, 1973.

Dr. Dorsey presents the Certificate of Appreciation to Dr. Karl A. Menninger, Menninger Clinic, on the occasion of his Whitney M. Young, Jr., Memorial lecture, March 13, 1974. Seated at the table with Dr. Menninger are George E. Gullen, Jr., president of Wayne State University, and Dr. Francis A. Kornegay, executive director, Detroit Urban League.

Julie Harris, celebrity of stage and screen, is the guest of honor at a luncheon sponsored by the University Professor. Ms. Harris, who received the Outer Circle Critics Award for her acting in The Last of Mrs. Lincoln, 1973, was the recipient of an honorary degree at Wayne State University commencement, June 25, 1974. Left to right: President George E. Gullen, Jr.; Leonard Leone, director of University Theatres; Julie Harris; Ruth Gullen (Mrs. George E.); Dr. Dorsey.

U.S. Circuit Court Judge George Edwards, longtime friend of Dr. Dorsey, autographs a copy of his book Pioneer-at-Law *(1974) for President George E. Gullen, Jr., and Mrs. Gullen at a reception, October 30, 1974, sponsored by officials of the state of Michigan, Detroit, and Wayne State University.*

With Dr. Dorsey is Leonard Woodcock, president of the International Union, UAW, who delivered the Whitney M. Young, Jr., Memorial lecture, November 5, 1975. Woodcock's association with Wayne State University dates from his undergraduate days at the old City College of Detroit. He also served two terms on the Board of Governors.

Dr. Dorsey presents the Whitney M. Young, Jr., Memorial Lecture Commendation to Vernon E. Jordan, Jr., executive director of the National Urban League, March 18, 1976. With them are President George E. Gullen, Jr., and Dr. Francis A. Kornegay, executive director, Detroit Urban League.

Dr. Dorsey, editor of The Jefferson-Dunglison Letters (1960), delivered the address at the Bicentennial Convocation, Thomas Jefferson University, April 14, 1976, in celebration of Thomas Jefferson's birthday. Left to right: The Right Reverend Robert L. De Witt, Episcopal bishop of Pennsylvania and longtime friend of Dr. Dorsey; Dr. Dorsey; Dr. Lauren H. Smith, University of Iowa classmate of Dr. Dorsey; Dr. Samuel X. Radbill, biographer of Thomas Jefferson and Robley Dunglison; George M. Norwood, Jr., interim president of Thomas Jefferson University. Photo courtesy of Thomas Jefferson University.

Former governor of Michigan George W. Romney delivered the Whitney M. Young, Jr., Memorial lecture November 3, 1976, on the topic "Race Relations and the Urban Problem." Left to right: Arthur L. Johnson, vice-president of Wayne State University; Governor Romney; Dr. Dorsey; Lenore Romney (Mrs. George W.); Douglas Dow, McGregor Fund trustee and longtime friend of Dr. Dorsey.

Clifton R. Wharton, Jr., president of Michigan State University, is greeted by Dr. Dorsey on the occasion of Dr. Wharton's Whitney M. Young, Jr., Memorial lecture, "Human Rights and Human Capital," November 28, 1977.

Margo Franklin Fleischaker (Mrs. Stanley) greets Dr. Dorsey at the reception, January 10, 1978, honoring Dr. Max Kapustin, recipient of the Leo M. Franklin Memorial Award in Human Relations for 1978. Mrs. Fleischaker is the daughter of Dr. Franklin, in whose memory the award was established.

no finer academic base than that selected for his University of Virginia by Thomas Jefferson: "the illimitable freedom of the human mind to explore and to expose every subject susceptible of its contemplation."

Emerson wanted to construct a language of mind with "the exhaustive accuracy of distribution" with which other students endow their sciences. In all sciences he would have the student discover that he is always working in wholes, and in every detail, after the laws of the human mind. Every so-called worldly or materialistic word of my vocabulary signifies a real fact in my mind indispensably enabling me to imagine that I can help myself with existence other than my own. I have the strongest belief in the use of a course of acknowledgeable self-study called "The Psychicality of Being and Seeming," with which each student can teach himself or herself to appreciate functioning life, in the only way possible, by appreciating the immeasurable power and glory of his (her) own subjective mind.[1] My habituation creates the illusion that my living need not involve the stress of change, whereas growing myself necessitates the changing natural to development. It takes great courage and self-understanding to stay young, in the sense of welcoming inevitable change of growth.

Devotion to self-consciousness is achievable through effort only. That means that permanence of the idea of immeasurable greatness of life, itself, is a meaningful attainment demanding sustained exertion. It is a struggle to live, but to live consciously adds to that trial in proportion to the fullness of my functioning. Why live then? Especially, why live consciously? Each is a question that answers itself with awareness that self-love is the essence of life, that triumph of functioning is life satisfaction itself. The comfort of habit may be regularly preferred to the labor of love. It can seem harder to live self-observation than to practice observation that does not fea-

---

[1]*The Psychic Nature of Physiology* attempts this goal.

ture its selfness. *Dislike is readily associated with difficult living and regularly even identified with it.*

It is my lifesaving advantage to research my biological need to conduct my mind difficultly in just proportion to its magnificent wonderfulness. Only thus can I preserve my absorbing interest in my wholly marvelous life. Nothing can be more important for me than that I discover and ever bear in mind the truth that I am all and only the spirited subjectivity, growth, creativity, perfection, source, meaning, will, interest, being, wholeness, power, freedom, initiative, song, continuity, and love of life.

Habit feeds one of the persistent hungers of human nature, sleep. Every form of self-unconsciousness is a degree of sleep, all the way from momentary self-distraction through day and night dreaming to deep sleep. Habitude can become a kind of ossification that substitutes itself for the rigors of self-consciousness which alone can produce one's life assurance called "presence of mind" or poise. It is my self struggling that I can ably sense as such that brings poise, not pose.

The poise of a consciously whole person is based on feeling the creative stir, the refreshing love, of being wholly (truly) alive, all dear *life* no near life. The right idea of being an individual always reveals selfness, the saving sense of growing (originating) one's owndom from moment to moment. Again, the practice of habit cannot apply to living self-consciously because the latter must be a flaming product of *conscious* will. Habit demonstrates the decisive pulsating power of unconscious will.

The willing exertion to practice self-consciousness is my one and only way to discipline my mind with outcropping of love for living difficultly. The true magnificence of human being, pioneering orderly personal development, really cannot be conducted effortlessly. Every new mental development must appear difficult to bear until it is lived with biologically adequate appreciation for its lifesaving worth. I may ask myself as I would of one of my machines, "Am I *working* well?" For example, in my seeing, hearing, or any of my functioning, am I able to recognize myself fully and only in whatever I am sensing? Am I working up sufficient stamina, conscious determination, to claim being the creator of what I am becoming? Whatever experience I am living with pain or sorrow or sheer delight is necessary for the attainment of my most precious living called interest in conscious self-wholeness.

Thus, working my mind to the limit of its present endurance is my only reliable method for preserving and extending that endurance. Conscious self-wholeness is conscious self-endurance. I possess this idea, and by "I," I refer specifically to the unity of my life that I name my wholeness. It functions most inconspicuously, I do not even think of it often, but without it I know that my life must be "at sixes and sevens" with itself. I cannot appreciate (master) any of my experience except to the extent that I study it willingly as being my own wonderful living of my development. All of my becoming is a true manifestation of my growing nature, either consciously or unconsciously. The bountiful understanding provided by conscious self-continence discovers all giving to be receiving, hence the biological urge to manifest my solipsistic creativity. My every function, including all meaning, is tributary to my wholeness.

My study of my own mind as being all that there can be for *me* to study began with my work with my most highly esteemed Sigmund Freud and has proceeded along the lines of my continuing self-analysis. I cannot express adequately enough my heartfelt appreciation for the unique insightfulness of my Professor Freud's work. I find it manifest throughout what mind understanding I have grown for myself.

I am only and nothing but uniquely individualistic. That is the most and the least that I can assert of my fellowman also. I cannot be overlooked or appealed to as an authority, except as my only possible authority to myself. I may seem to be discovering new unities but my mind, itself, consists of nothing but unity. My only possible form of government must be self-government, either acknowledged or unacknowledged.[2] My educational career is specifically devoted to observing and recording the tremendous health consequence of my self-insightful way of life, not only for prolonging but also appreciating my continuous growth of self-helpfulness.

The necessity that nothing can exist except in and of itself is the absolute first and unconditioned elemental principle underlying all of my mentality. To assert, *I am,* may imply that I am I, but in the interest of conscious self-continence, I cannot declare too often: *I am all and only that I am.* This intrinsic necessity not only pervades but also constitutes my world, as self-creativity, tantamount to the divinity of all meaning. As the *sine qua non* of freedom it reveals the unity of necessity and freedom. I can be neither sure nor unsure of anything but my life, the one truth my consciousness may habitually slight. My study of the nature of my functioning is advanced by my realizing that my performance seems to precede my knowing its meaningful justification. Søren Kierkegaard stated it: One lives forward, but understands backward. However, by allowing my mind to function freely without any restraint I can retrieve the flow of mental content anterior to any presenting mentation.

As my reader, I may feel weary of considering the ideal of attaining full consciousness for my capacities, of fulfillment of my appreciation for my intact wholeness and allness, but I must acknowledge that I know of no exertion more honorable, practical, or hygienic. Literally, sacrifice means to make holy, and such sacrification is surely laudable. My every move is for its own sake only, as all of my activity is for my own sake only.

By nature I want my fellowman to achieve conscious self-helpfulness, for example, by observing the self-benefit he can grow, quite as he sees his Dorsey growing it. It has become obvious to me that I, including every one of my world, must be

---

[2]See my *American Government: Conscious Self Sovereignty.*

a mystic as far as every other individual is concerned. My only choice is whether I shall be a conscious or an unconscious mystic. Thus I enjoy the consummate comprehension of my Eduard von Hartmann (1842–1906): "I should like to call every original philosopher a mystic, so far as he is truly original."

My necessity to live my fellow existent as my own existence is the natural basis for my developing my political organization and every other societal device. Furthermore, my necessity to imagine clearly that my every existent is just as much an inviolable individual entity as my self, increases my conscious responsibility for cultivating my self-understanding. Such is the conscious unity I aim to preserve in my living generally and in this writing specifically.

Perhaps in briefest terms, I have conceived the office of my University Professorship to be that of standing for the helpfulness of the way in which I learned to use my mind. It may not have occurred to me even as a serious student that it might be necessary for me to learn how to think efficiently, how to use my mind in a way corresponding to its specific nature and needs. If such a notion did ever become conscious, I may have dismissed it as I did many another fleeting insight of biological adequacy with such resistance as, "That's too far fetched," "That cannot apply to me," "I already know just how to think," "Thinking is instinctive and does not have to be learned," "Such self-consciousness is objectionable," "Self-consciousness should only mean the embarrassment of thinking of myself as being the object of my fellowman," and so on.

What, whence, and why is my "resistance" to gladly observing as my very own a clear recognition of the primary significance of self-awareness for providing my wholesome mental development? Resistance, itself, however, is my defense against disturbing in any way what self-awareness itself I have already been able to cultivate and practice. I identify my idea of my whole life with my present amount of self-recognition and the fear of giving up the one seems tantamount to giving up the other. Hence it is that my resistance against developing further self-consciousness is for the purpose of preserving the only self-consciousness I have already grown and *practiced.*

Force of habit yields only gradually to further evidence of self-benefit. A habit of living in any way can seem identical with the wish to live, itself, so that opposition to it is associated with distressing tension such as fear and pain. The joy of living derivable only from conscious self-determination, consequent upon the hard work of learning how to use consciously my illimitable power, is hardly imaginable by me to the extent that I have cultivated the habit of believing that adequate joy of living can be accessible through overlooking my real subjectivity in my triumphant scientific inventions.

Conscious self-determination must wait upon conscious self-development which always augments and never diminishes conscious self-identity, thus furthering the correspondence of my self-awareness with my self-wholeness. It is this degree of acknowledged self-creativity that ultimately honors healthy character training, by observing that one's biological nature subsumes one's sociological, as every other, development. It is wise to consider the *good* enabled by conscious self-responsibility only.

Responsible thinking, that is, self-conscious mental functioning, is my only source of 1) recognizing that my life is entirely my own, hence all that can be important to me, 2) understanding my uniquely wonderful individuality as such, 3) strengthening my conscious will, 4) cultivating my self-control, 5) directing insightfully my own growing personality, including determining its character, 6) observing in myself the truth of my own wholeness or natural integrity, by esteeming *all* of my previous experience as I do my present life meaning, 7) heeding the subjective, idealistic, spirited composition of my each and every meaning, 8) realizing that my meaning for my so-called external world must be based upon unfaltering faith in its existence and in my being integral to it, 9) attributing worth of free inviolable wholeness to whatever I live in the name of my fellow creature, including my world, 10) deciding the thrilling necessity that nothing can happen or not happen unless sufficient truth is present on the side of making it happen or not happen, 11) identifying my divinity with my truth, justice, spirit, earnest exertion (work), self-continence, love of life-affirmation, 12) freeing myself from the helpful but distressing signs symptomatic of my efforts to depersonalize and externalize elements of my own difficultly conceivable integration.

Glossary

Following is a list of my present definitions for key words of this writing:

Absolute	completely free; whatever is, absolutely is.
Abstraction	*seeming* objectification of real subjectivity.
Alone	all one; solipsistic necessity.
Altruism	grown-up egoism.
Balance of wealth	every poor man lives all of his own rich man; every rich man lives all of his own poor man; the health of each depends upon this insight.
Becoming	nascent being.
Being	fruition of becoming.
Biological adequacy	serving all interest of self-wholeness.
Body	nucleus of mind.
Communication	delusion of social intercourse compensating for repudiated intact integrity of the individual; illusion based on disregard for language as being each linguist's idiolect only.
Conflict	symptom of negated psychic unity.
Consciousness	personal meaningfulness; subjective ideality; immaterial or spiritual reality; insight; awareness; mind illumination or speculation; exploratory function of mind. *See also* Self-consciousness.
Control	exertion of self-power with conscious self-possession.
Courage	fortitude; perseverance of conscious self-love that is the only possible source for conscious love of life.

Deify	to recognize already existing divinity.
Depersonalization	withholding sense of self-identity from any experience.
Discipline	consciously exercising my mind in a trying direction of my choosing.
Divinity	select term for ordinarily repressed ideal way of living; perfection regularly repressed as too good to be true; enthusiastic, spirited, self-sufficient self-sentience; it is divine to be human and human to overlook it.
Duration	quantitative measure based on illusion of time.
Emotion	organized pattern of self-feeling, providing a sensorium for the mind beyond its body sensation.
Environment	my creation of my vitality I call my surroundings.
Existent	whatever is, divinely is.
Experience	whatever I live.
Faith	conscious and unconscious self-trust.
Familiarity	illusional: disregard for novelty or necessary strangeness of all living.
Faultfinding	inhibited truth finding concealed regularly in pejorative or meliorative term.
Fear	inhibited wish.
Free association	willing wording of uninhibited stream of consciousness.
Glory	exalted distinction of worth unavoidably created by gradual discovery of the extent of one's immeasurable wholeness.
Good	living is all good; conscious living is conscious good.
Grace	art of living conferred by my *conscious* wholeness.
Growth	movement of continuous life development; the basis on which I can render any act intelligible, any cause explicable.

Help	all that is humanly possible. All of living is always divinely helpful, consciously or unconsciously.
Hesitation	unique form of mental activity signifying consciously controlled readiness to function or not to function.
Idiolect	everyone's only language; my language for naming my own living *only*.
Imagination	all mental activity.
Individuality	whatever is, individually is; whole, all one; indivisible; (solipsistic) being.
Inhibition	opposite of facilitation of free functioning; withholding.
Insight	understanding all observation as being *self*-observation.
Knowing	self-generating extension of self-identity in the form of meaning.
Language	everyone's (solipsistic) idiolect only.
Life	absence of death; self-generating, lovable, self-affirmation.
Mankind	I attribute to my every fellowman the same divine human nature that is mine.
Maturity	Whatever is, maturely is. An infant is a mature baby. An embryo is a mature embryo.
Meaning	organization of sensibility or emotionality constituting the mental unit; functioning mentality; unit of mind; self-contained power of functioning inherent in existence of mind.
Means	inhibited end.
Memory	unrecognized *present* being only; illusion of "past" experience.
Mental health	appreciating life worth by affirming all of my experience as my pacific own.
Mental trauma	overwhelming excitation obscuring sense of self-identity.
Mind	my power to feel the way I live my self. Organization of my vital energy that is activated when

	I develop sensibility or feeling, including meaning for my conscious and unconscious being. My life-meaning only.
Morality	need for return of repressed innocence when self-wholeness is overlooked.
Mystic	internal nature of all being; intrinsic quality of truth; entifying solipsistic unity of any and all reality; realized allness of self.
Nature	I am by nature whatever I can be. I grow my all; I *acquire* nothing.
Negation	affirmation of oppositeness; return of repressed meaning (*see also* repression).
Objectivity	unconscious subjectivity.
Pain	inhibited functioning; repressed joy of living.
Peace	conscious self-consciousness for my wholeness.
Perfection	whatever is, perfectly is, wholly is. *See also* Divinity.
Personification	attributing self-power as if it is not all my own.
Possession	all of my possession is my self-possession.
Present	my life's only moment of existence.
Progress	meliorative term compensating for disregarded omnipresent perfection.
Psychology	when conscious, is mind studying mind; when unconscious, is mind studying unrecognized mind.
Reality	whatever *is*; perfection; conscious-self orientation; my acknowledgeable living of my self-meaning; universal solipsistic I-am-that-I-am.
Relationship	illusion compensating for some disowned selfness.
Religion	conscious or/and unconscious sensing of one's own divinity.
Renunciation	insightful withholding from consciousness of any meaning, recognizing its right to be; opposite of repression; ability to direct attention (interest) freely; to be able to take or leave any experience freely.

Repression insightless association of any feeling of unpleasantness with anything except unpleasantness itself; rejection, as undesirable, of living of any of my mental content; necessary withholding of sense of self-identity from any meaning.

Right the demand for conscious integration in behalf of self-wholeness.

Science organized system of self-knowledge regularly overlooked in the illusion of objectivity; a specially made language.

Self my whole organic being; a name for the all of me.

Self-consciousness acknowledged consciousness as entirely self-observation or self-report; personal experience, life-mindfulness; mind reality; *being* rather than "seeming"; attention to self-interest; recognized personal point of view; appreciation for individuality; honoring necessity that all existence is *within* itself; my only possible consciousness.

Self-identity feeling of personal existence. All self-development is automorphic (my Herbert Spencer's word).

Sensibility any self-sentience beginning with sensation, including emotion, and culminating in divine self-consciousness.

Sex genetic element of living; male lives all of his own femaleness; female lives all of her own maleness.

Sickness health struggling to restore its vitality to free functioning.

Society my imagining of a plurality (of "individualities"); extension of self-meaning.

Solipsism term used literally to mean self alone (all one); name for the inviolably intact wholeness, allness, of divine human individuality. My everyone *necessarily* is either a conscious or unconscious solipsist; key term for reaching conscious reality; whatever is, is all and only itself; wholeness.

Soul	the essence of self; whatever is, is all soul; subjective wholeness.
Spirit	life consciousness; wholeness feeling; will; reality sense; cosmic emotion; freedom of independence; identity possession; extensive consciousness for existence; the imponderable nature of subjectivity.
Subjectivity	mind's only reality; living truth.
Thinking	meditation; verbalized and non-verbalized emotion and sensation.
Unconsciousness	the opposite of consciousness; varying degrees of denial of consciousness, from every kind of negation to deep, even if not dreamless, sleep or coma; pre-conscious life meaning.
Universal	essence of individuality.
Vocabulary	all of my terminology of, and for, meaning of my own living only.
Wish	will, motivation; function seeking.
Word	original poetry.
Work	my wish to live derives from pleasure in my functioning as fully as possible—hence the life risk in so-called retirement.
Wrong	unrecognizable right; faultfinding.

Appendix

Teaching, Training, and Research, 1938–1961

In 1938 my fondly esteemed psychoanalytic colleague Norman Tufford visited me in Ann Arbor, where I was Associate Professor of Psychiatry at the University of Michigan. He outlined certain professional opportunities in Detroit. Senator James Couzens had created the Children's Fund of Michigan in 1929. Hugo A. Freund, M.D., the Senator's personal physician, was named president and William J. Norton, executive vice-president of the fund. The Child Guidance Division of the Children's Fund was under the direction of Dr. Maud E. Watson. At the instigation of Dr. Tufford, working with Dr. Freund and Mr. Norton, Dr. Watson arranged a part-time position for me as training psychiatrist of the Children's Center of Detroit. With this arrangement I began my practice of psychoanalysis, continuing lecturing in postgraduate medicine for the University of Michigan. My very good friend, Dr. Leo H. Bartemeier, already had an established psychoanalytic practice in Detroit. He, Dr. Tufford, and I met regularly to further our psychoanalytic experiences and ultimately to become charter members of the Detroit Psychoanalytic Society.

My work with the Children's Fund of Michigan provided the beginning of a fine collaboration with Mr. Norton. He was a member and later president of McGregor Fund. During my early years at the Children's Center, Dean Edgar H. Norris of the Wayne School of Medicine approached me on several occasions to become professor and chairman of the Department of Psychiatry at Wayne. However, I was not ready for the step at the time. In 1946, I was asked to help secure a professor of psychiatry for Wayne. The next development was my being offered the position, this time by Dean Hardy A. Kemp. My salary and the beginnings of my department were to be subsidized by the McGregor Fund. This opportunity was discussed on various occasions with Mr. Norton, whose position about it remained most helpfully neutral. In all of my work with this scholarly gentleman, I found him similarly wise. When I accepted the post of University Professor in 1961, and throughout all of my University Professorship years, he was careful to leave all of my decisions up to me, letting nothing but the facts speak for themselves.

Early as professor of psychiatry, McGregor Fund trustees offered me the use of McGregor Center of the McGregor Health Foundation for my teaching program. I did find new and great clinical teaching, training, and research privileges thus made available to me. The names of the first McGregor Health Foundation Board of Trustees were as follows: Warren B. Cooksey, M.D., Elva M. Forncrook, R.N., Emilie G. Sargent, R.N., Louis A. Schwartz, M.D., Frank J. Sladen, M.D., Alice H. Walker, R.N.

At McGregor Center I benefited greatly from the able collaboration of Suzanne Copland (later Mrs. William D. Crim), executive director, Thomas A. Petty, M.D., medical director, and H. Harrison Sadler, M.D.

Names of later McGregor Health Foundation trustees are: Rev. Malcolm Ballinger, Mr. H. Walter Bando, Dr. Leo H. Bartemeier, Mrs. Jackson Bingham, Mrs. Martin L. Butzel, Mrs. William Robert Bryant, Mrs. William D. Crim, Mrs. Eleanor Cranefield, Rt. Rev. Robert L. DeWitt, Mrs. George Edwards, Dr. Dwight C. Ensign, Mrs. Carl B. Grawn, Mr. George E. Gullen, Jr., Rev. Sheldon Harbach, Mrs. Earl I. Heenan, Dr. Charles G. Jennings, Mrs. T. Hollister Mabley, Mrs. William E. Matthews, Mr. Neil C. McMath, Mr. William L. Newnan, Mr. Frank D. Nicol, Dr. Mario A. Petrini, Dr. Paul T. Salchow, Miss Emilie G. Sargent, Dr. Louis A. Schwartz, Dr. Walter H. Seegers, Dr. Editha Sterba, Judge James H. Sexton, Mr. George C. Tilley, Mr. Thomas C. Tilley, Mrs. Charles C. Zabriskie.

Dr. Warren B. Cooksey recommended that every Wayne medical student have a period of externship at the center, and this plan was immediately put into execution.

The center could not continue without substantial annual McGregor Fund grants. In July, 1967, arrangements were made to discontinue this hospital for health, education, and rehabilitation, six years after I accepted my University Professorship. The property was sold and the monies therefrom made up the fund of the Center for Health Education, the McGregor Center trustees becoming the

Center for Health Education trustees. The purpose of the Center for Health Education was to continue the support of the health education orientation I carried on at McGregor Center for the development of medical students, this time to apply to my university-wide health education activities.

During my tenure as professor and chairman of the Department of Psychiatry and as University Professor I continued to receive financial help from McGregor Fund, and later from the Center for Health Education. I always enjoyed special autonomy for all of the activities of my office.

Trustees of the McGregor Fund

My McGregor Center Medical Perspective

In 1961, upon completing my McGregor Center hospital duties as chief-of-staff, I briefly outlined its meaning for me as follows:

At McGregor Center I organize my medical research, education, and treatment to conform to my difficultly gained personal professional understanding. Conducting a human life safely and sanely (that is, with cheerful appreciation for its constant wonderfulness) is hard work all the way and I must take the trouble to learn how to conduct my life consistently in a most specific manner if I will avoid or resolve health complaints of every description. And what is this one and only self-training? It is necessary for me to learn how to live the awesome truth that *my* world is all my own and thus grow my wholesome appreciation for my life, or I must create signs and symptoms (felt as unhappiness and pain) that I am not learning this vital life-lesson. *I must continually discipline myself to recognize and make full use of my one basic medicinal and spiritual truth: the sacred integrity of my inviolable individuality.* Full self-consequence, full self-esteem, are the most needed and most efficacious developments of the medical world. Whenever my individuality is unheeded or taken for granted or otherwise overlooked, my scientific work-up seems spiritless. Fully conscious spiritual self-discipline, rather than fully unconscious objective self-discipline, is my personal, including professional, ideal.

Although *everything* a man wittingly does is motivated always by his current idea of helping himself, and although there can be no kind of help but self-help, nevertheless one must learn the lessons of greatest self-helpfulness or submit to the limited efficacy of unstudied self-care. The healing power of recognized independence and self-reliance is always amazing.

If I do not study and practice how to live myself healthfully, I shall have the benefit of feelings of distress about my unwise living. Although it seems easy to see the benefit in my feeling pain when I am injuring the surface of my body, it does not always seem easy to

223

see the benefit in my feeling unhappiness (fear, hate, despair, and similar mental pains) when I am injuring myself by any of my other shortsighted personal attitudes and practices. Only conscious self-possession can enable conscious self-responsibility. I claim no "objectivity" for my individuality except in its true meaning of unconscious *subjectivity*.

Every sign and symptom of health trouble describes 1) the nature of the disturbance, and 2) the nature of the cure. Therefore, painful as it may be, it is the course of wisdom to regard every indication of my health ordeal as being positively healthful, in view of its profound and indispensable meaning for my learning how to mend and thus preserve my life. My only possible quorum or forum is the one I create within my native being.

Encouraging features of my McGregor Center cure-all (strengthen-and-heal-my-self-with-insight) are: 1) it demonstrates itself to the eye of the scientific investigator, 2) it really always works wonders, 3) it is never too late for it to start working, 4) it acts as a preventative, besides as a cure, of the self-obscurement underlying my unseeing complaints of so-called "attack of illness." The individual-self factor is the whole matter of *all* of my experience. My every study can be nothing but a calculus of my self-interest.

At McGregor Center I have tried to make my actual living-and-learning consistent with this health ideal: Everyone always *is* his own physician ever educating himself to the benefits of life affirmation as best he can. I have hoped and achieved some small success in observing my McGregor Center colleague, in the kitchen at the clinic and on the board, furthering his own appreciation of the *positive* life value of every health condition, however critical; working up his understanding of the never-failing goodness of his arduous living, however "bad" seeming.

Board of Governors, Wayne State University

Board of Governors of Wayne State University at the beginning of my University Professorship (inclusive dates indicate term of office):

Thomas B. Adams	1961–1968
Lynn Bartlett	1957–1963
Benjamin D. Burdick	1959–1963
DeWitt T. Burton, M.D.	1959–1961, 1962–1968
Michael Ference, Jr.	1959–1964
Jean McKee	1959–1966
Clair A. White	1959–1961
Leonard Woodcock	1959–1962, 1963–1970

Subsequent Board members and their terms of office:

Leon H. Atchison	1971–1978
Wilber M. Brucker, Jr.	1967–1972, 1973–1980
Augustus J. Calloway, Jr.	1969–1976
George C. Edwards, III	1969–1976, 1977–1984
Michael A. Einheuser	1975–1982
Charles H. Gershenson	1964
William B. Hall	1965–1967
Dauris Jackson	1977–1984
Mildred Jeffrey	1975–1982
Kurt R. Keydel	1969–1972, 1973–1980
Max J. Pincus	1971–1978
Benjamin M. Rose	1965–1969
Alfred H. Sokolowski, M.D.	1967–1974
Norman O. Stockmeyer	1964–1966, 1967–1974
Alfred H. Whittaker, M.D.	1964–1970

Council of Deans, Wayne State University, 1960–1961

Clarence B. Hilberry, president
Winfred A. Harbison, vice-president
Arthur Neef, chairman
Gordon H. Scott
Owen E. Thomas
Randall Whaley
James P. McCormick, assistant to the president, and secretary,
  Board of Governors

Deans:

J. Russell Bright
Charles B. Brink
Katharine E. Faville
Walter C. Folley
Harlan L. Hagman
J. Stuart Johnson
Victor A. Rapport
Francis C. Rosecrance
Woodburn O. Ross
Harold E. Stewart
Stephen Wilson

Associate Deans:

William N. Borgman, secretary
Henry H. Pixley

Letters

The following selected letters concern my University Professorship up to its receiving Emeritus status in 1971.

October 24, 1960, President Clarence Hilberry wrote to William J. Norton, President, McGregor Fund:

Last spring I addressed the following memorandum to the various Councils of the University and published it in full in *Inside Wayne,* our campus house organ. The response was enthusiastic and unanimously favorable. I received more letters from individual members of the faculties on this suggestion than on any I have ever made. The University Council after appropriate consideration took formal action in support of the plan.

Like every other University in America, Wayne State University faces a number of basic and urgent problems. All of them seem to require money. Some of them money alone will solve. Others also require new approaches to our fundamental educational task. Perhaps none is more urgent or more difficult than the job of wisely controlling the constantly increasing emphasis on specialization. This specialization in universities is a direct response to the needs of our complex society. And it tends to produce not only students who become more and more narrow in their interests as they advance through the upper division and graduate work, but also professors who become increasingly high specialists.

I believe it is clearly both impossible and undesirable to try to reverse this trend in higher education. What is necessary at all times is to lay particular emphasis upon the opposite approach to human life and knowledge and to do so in a wide variety of new ways. Our Liberal Arts College, for example, is trying with considerable success to work with other colleges in providing an unbroken sequence of liberal studies paralleling and "liberalizing" the professional specialization in these colleges. Monteith College is working in the same direction. A number of the colleges have given creative attention to providing lectures and to bringing individuals to the campus who represent the "generalist" approach to human experience.

Other universities, notably Harvard, are experimenting with giving sustained attention to this effort to integrate knowledge by carefully choosing a few men with the creative gift for seeing knowledge, not in pieces, but whole, or at least as nearly whole as it is permitted any of us to see it in these days. These men are named to University Professorships not to professorships in one of the departments. They teach a limited amount of regular credit work when one or more of the colleges and the individual agree on a course which would serve a wide usefulness to the student body. But at least as important, the University Professor is available for informal contacts with students and faculty, for bringing his wide reading and his own creative work to bear on the life of the campus. He should also be able to bring other men with similar intellectual concerns to the campus for short periods of time to share in this effort.

Until we find and try to use such a man we shall not know whether he can make a significant contribution to the intellectual climate of our campus. If we agree, however, that it is important to try to cultivate this wholeness of vision, we must pledge that he become neither the slave nor the victim of the requirements of our credit hour system. Since the primary mission of such a Professor would be to stimulate the thought of a wide variety of students rather than to develop one department he might be attached to the office of a Dean. Or since he would represent his own intellectual discipline in its University-wide significance we could make him responsible to a Vice President. The credit hour system is our park bench and we must insure that this elder statesman, this philosopher, can sit on it from time to time. For the remainder, let him be peripatetic.

I would like to try to interest a donor in supporting such a plan to stimulate the intellectual climate of this campus. This may not be easy. As you all know, I am sure, many donors have sharply defined objectives for their gifts. None the less, there are some who increasingly share our own desire to see the University and society steadily and whole rather than exclusively from the vantage points of high specialization. I hope, therefore, that we may find donors willing to help us.

If you think the University Professorship an appropriate matter for your consideration I shall welcome your comments and suggestions.

I am sure it is clear to all of us that the growing emphasis upon specialization which I have described in this memorandum means that very few men have the breadth of interest, the genuinely philosophical frame of mind and approach to human knowledge and human life which the University Professor must possess. I prepared the memorandum and sent it to the faculty when I did because I believed I had found a man who had the qualifications I was describing for the University Professor. The man was Dr. John Dorsey. The members of McGregor Fund Board know him so well and have known him over so many years that it would be absurd for me to attempt to state here his qualifications as University Professor. I believe that each of you will agree with me that he has the rare combination of personal qualities and intellectual and philosophical interests which the University seeks.

With Dean Scott's permission I talked with Dr. Dorsey about undertaking this new, untried, exciting, and critical responsibility of representing on the University campus these concerns not as a specialist but as a humanist generalist. Dr. Dorsey and I talked on two occasions at considerable length. On the one hand I think it is impossible to overstate the importance of the University Professor assignment on this campus and since few universities have experimented in any way with this kind of proposal the project can be of nationwide significance. But I also recognize how great a change this would seem to make in Dr. Dorsey's professional life. As I said to him, however, I know of no one else whom I believed could undertake this task with such assurance of success and I felt confident that he would find it deeply rewarding personally. This was also Dr. Dorsey's final conclusion. It gives me very great satisfaction to say to each of the members of the McGregor Board personally that Dr. Dorsey is willing to undertake this new and very significant University assignment. . . . I could speak in much greater detail of the discussions between Dr. Dorsey and me but I believe this is enough to

indicate both the general character of the proposed University Professorship and the absolutely fundamental role which the University
Professor would play in the life of the University. . . . As I have
indicated above, a few other universities have experimented with
this general concept freeing individuals to work in the broad fields
of concern to them but none, so far as I know, have named a man
with responsibility to *be* and to represent the "generalist" for the
whole academic community. I believe this venture will pay enormous
rewards and will be watched with keen interest across the nation. I
hope the Fund will be willing to support the project for five years.
The University will try to supplement the Fund contribution each
year and be ready at the end of five years to carry the project if it
proves successful. May I say that I believe this project may well
prove to be one of the most important if not the most important
single new proposal I have ever made for the University. I hope
your Board will find it possible to assist us. . . .

December 6, 1960, President Hilberry wrote to me:

I have just got off to the Board an informal note telling them all
about the negotiations with McGregor Fund and the results thereof,
and telling them that at the December 14 meeting I will announce
the McGregor Fund grant and recommend your appointment effective February 1 at a salary of $20,000 to the post of University
Professor. I am explaining to them that filling your Chairmanship at
Medicine will be a long and difficult assignment and that for the
period of this transition you will be devoting to the College whatever
time and energy is essential. I am sure everyone will understand that
these arrangements must remain flexible and that we do not need to
do more by way of trying to define them.

I announce this grant and recommend your assignment as University Professor with greater satisfaction than I have had in anything in a long time.

August 15, 1960 I wrote to President Hilberry:

The visit I had with you, Friday, August 5th, left me decidedly a
man realizing that he had just completed some most important living. Indeed I was startled by the fitness of your proposition, —and
that is the only way I can account for my not thanking you before
now for your speaking with me of your fine conception of your

central all-connecting study of studies. Yes, as an educator, I must heed that there are no wonders but my wonder; that there is nothing new but the new man I put on; that there is no Cinderella of the curriculum but my own ignored humanity.

Only with the greatest of difficulty have I been able to see that there is absolutely no possible meaning to the expression, "one's losing his mind," except the meaning to be found in his losing his appreciation that his mind is all his own. Therefore, I take special satisfaction in your fine intention to see to it personally, systematically, but only as soon as is compatible with being educational, that scholarly inexperience with this very root of education (learning is all and only personal living) is eliminated, —eliminated in a peacebringing way, without faultfinding.

For everyone's now disordered world, clarity as to the very *meaning* of education is an emergency need. It is quite as though nearly everyone is needing to be rescued from his not knowing that he does not know what his own learning process is and does. Thought about education itself, as being nothing but individual human development, is properly the *pivotal* in-service training discipline of every faculty member. Without its graduated exercise, it is an insight which inconspicuously becomes unavailable, not being understood. The idea of "the growth of acknowledged self-knowledge," has never been liked at first sight and, hence, has not been painstakingly minded as constituting the central essence of learning. Lucidity is impossible without it. It is natural for me to dislike what I cannot fully understand; it is impossible for me to dislike what I can fully understand. Literally, I have had to make myself see that I cannot transmute my own living into truth by imputing not-self to it.

As you requested, I am working on the question of my effectiveness in advancing this buried-alive educational issue, and it is an exciting mental exercise. My analysis is helpfully accompanied in my vision of your spirited comprehension of the opportunity.

The following letter from Dean Harlan L. Hagman to Vice President Winfred A. Harbison, December 19, 1960, embodies the conception of the University Professor when this special office was being considered.

This is the substance of a communication I prepared for the President some months ago, but did not send. If a University Professor is to be attached to the VPAA [Vice-President Academic Affairs] office, this paper may be more appropriate now than when it was originally drafted.

The University Professor

Selection of any person to serve as a University Professor might be based upon the following considerations: a) The person is distinguished for contributions to many fields or for eminence in a field communicating to all people. b) The person has ability to communicate in various media, i.e., speaking, writing, music, art, etc. c) The person has a deep interest in broad fields of knowledge. d) The person has an attitude conducive to communication to undergraduate and graduate students, faculty, and the general public.

Consideration of the effective employment of the University Professor in the general life of the campus might turn upon the following:

1. The University Professor should be housed in some central place open to the students and faculty who might wish to speak with him informally. Such a place is possibly the General Library where a comfortable office appropriately furnished might be provided. A good secretary is needed.

2. The University Professor might be expected to give lectures weekly and perhaps during the noon hour. These lectures should be encouraged to give as many students as possible contact with the University Professor. It is likely that they would be relatively short, given attractive titles, and be under the direction of student organizations with perhaps a different organization each week assuming the sponsorship and responsibility for promotion.

3. In addition to scheduled lectures, the University Professor might offer each semester a seminar for credit. Such seminars ought to be cross-listed in college catalogs and be treated as proper electives for any college. The seminar should be organized around some general subject to which a professor would bring special interest and competence. It is conceivable that a seminar for undergraduate students might be offered and that another seminar for graduate students might be provided.

4. It would seem important to have the University Professor available for conversations. Some of these conversations could be in

his office as students and faculty might wish. It is conceivable an old-fashioned custom could be reinstituted in the form of having the Professor at home for tea an hour each week. If his office were large enough to accommodate a dozen people, the Professor could have a pleasant pattern of intellectual conversations now almost lacking on the campus. It could be expected that as larger numbers of students are housed on the campus, dormitory groups would invite the University Professor to come for conversation in the dormitory lounge.

5. The University Professor should have a budget for receptions, teas, luncheons, dinners, etc., so that he could invite members of the faculty and others to join him.

6. There should be developed a practice of inviting the University Professor to participate in classes in the various colleges. On some occasions he might be the guest lecturer, on others he might be an interested visitor.

7. The University Professor should be welcome at faculty meetings of all colleges and at various times might be expected to lecture formally or informally to the college faculty. At meetings of the whole University faculty, the University Professor might be expected to make an address on a topic of general and intellectual interest. The University Professor might meet at a series of luncheons with various key faculty groups to discuss the enhancement of the intellectual life of the campus. With the exception of chance conversations, it does not appear that at the present time we devote intentionally time to discussing the intellectual life apart from curriculum considerations.

8. The University Professor could be the University host representing the faculty when distinguished visitors are on the campus.

9. To encourage students and faculty to explore the broad fields represented by the University Professor, the Library might be asked to develop a special library collection and display under his name.

10. The University Professor might be asked to prepare a series of lecture-essays which could be published in pamphlet or book form by the University Press.

11. The *Collegian* might carry a weekly three or four-inch comment by the University Professor under his picture.

12. The University Professor could in one sense be eyes and ears for

the President in appraising the encouragement to the intellectual life on the campus.
13. At least one presentation a year should be to the Board of Governors. This presentation might be only in the Professor's having lunch with members or in his having a few minutes in Board meeting to speak of the work he is doing.

The following letters to Dean Harlan L. Hagman describe my growing understanding for the privilege and responsibility of my University Professorship.

June 15, 1961

This letter is deliberately diffuse since its intention is mainly to open up deliberation. Also, it aims at a breadthwise view of the two large issues which are of most concern to me: education and health.

Following recent conferences with you I have found it useful to put down on paper this tentative proposal, that Wayne State University under the auspices of President Hilberry offer a five year series of conferences on education. On many counts it is desirable that the President appoint each member of a University Education Conference Planning Committee especially selected for his demonstrated ability to comprehend the meaning of the given year's conference. Members of the Planning Committee or their representatives can also function as recorders of views expressed during the sessions so that such offerings along with main contributions may be published as conference proceedings by the University Press.

To get to the root of the matter of greatest interest to me, right at the start, it is apparent to "everyone who knows me" that I wish to direct my own education to one end and aim, and that I do try to steer my mind's actions accordingly. As I see it my education is a product of my intuitive consciousness, not of any externally focused vision. It provides me with a continuing source of life affirmation. I would like to see each conference presented as a "One Man" conference, in the sense that it is conspicuously intended to be entirely the sole property of each one who experiences it. However, this wish is one which I can renounce and I must.

In my conversations with you I have expressed in various words my ways of looking at the learning event. According to my experience an individual's education has "taken" when he has taught himself to rely consciously upon his force of education for his solution of his life's difficulties. However, once any conference theme is selected I would be most in favor of revering each person's educational psychology alike, all the way from one's conception of learning as acquiring knowledge of subject matter to another's appreciation of study as the growth of his conscious self-knowledge. It is my enjoyable work to try to accommodate my peace of mind to whatever mode of perception my fellowman uses.

It seems to me that the 1961 Conference on Education might disclose the purpose of the whole series. Just as a starter, the first conference topic might be called "Education to Education." In accord with an idea expressed by you it would be a wonderful development if each of these proposed conferences might lead primarily to the formulation of a number of leading questions as to the nature of the human being as an educator.

Of greatest interest to me is what I distinguish to myself as *education consciousness*. My world is describable as a world of learning steering itself according to the prevailing winds of educational doctrine. I see with Tolstoy that the happiness of man consists in life, with Lincoln that most folks are about as happy as they make up their minds to be, and with Jefferson that "Health is no more than learning."

My experiences taught me the value of having the truth of myself consciously in mind as much as possible. Each of my students has discovered that his giving his own individuality a fresh breath of life by observing it, where possible, has been a most worthwhile exercise of his health. Nevertheless, whenever I live any other kind of view about my existence I discover that it also has true preciousness, which invariably lies in the very fact that I live it. I am reminded of T. S. Eliot's "The Rock":

> Where is the life we have lost in living?
> Where is the wisdom we have lost in knowledge?
> Where is the knowledge we have lost in information?
> The cycles of Heaven in twenty centuries
> Bring us farther from God and nearer to the Dust.[1]

---

[1] T. S. Eliot, *The Complete Poems and Plays 1909–1950* (New York: Harcourt Brace & Co., 1952), p. 96. Quoted with the permission of Harcourt Brace Jovanovich, Inc.

It would be a wonderful achievement if I were able to state the chief beliefs and assumptions about my human nature under which I operate. The so-called educated person takes upon himself great power and responsibility. If he can clarify for himself such concepts as "human individual," "education," "health," "awareness,"—the fruits of such labor would guarantee a continuation of the same.

Dean Hagman, kindly endure this rambling of mine. It is intended to express my wish to help myself in my new work as University Professor. With considerable right it has been claimed that the way to bring a point home is to say rather too much.

Enough to add that on all I have written I am open ended. Whether or not an exploratory or any other kind of educational conference is, or shall be, propitious, is an issue I am unable to decide. As University Professor I go on devoting my energies to the observation (study), definition (meaning), appreciation (clear recognition), evident immediate effectiveness (practicability), and discoverable human worth (virtue), of my own individual power (biological force) of my education (disciplined self-experience).

Once Thoreau was asked what food he liked best. Promptly he replied, "The nearest." This orientation somewhat describes my work as University Professor thus far. As one of my friends noted, I am University Professoring on the campus, in the hall, in the elevator, and in my office, as well as in the occasional organized sessions I have held. It seems to me that I have been functioning very much as a kind of sounding board, not only for the individual student, but also for the individual faculty member. And now and then, each one has functioned as my sounding board. Most of all I conceive my work as meaning unifying, integrating, peacemaking. Whenever I find myself otherwise engaged I am delighted if I can recall this one kindness of Socrates: He is not only idle who does nothing, but he is idle who might be better employed.

Each of my sessions with you has been so very much worthwhile that I trust that nothing will interfere with the continuation of such fine experience.

March 19, 1962

I use this occasion to record my appreciation of the highest level educational love and freedom I have enjoyed and profited from in my every contact with yourself, Vice President Harbison, and President Hilberry.

The first year of my University Professorship has tried and tested my manpower in many an unusual and unexpected direction. For instance, called upon to introduce a speaker on Detroit Adventure Series, the speaker being delayed by travel conditions, I found myself giving the speech on the philosophy of art. In Kalamazoo, as banquet speaker for the Michigan Association of Deans and Counselors of Women I had to forego my cherished functioning as an examiner for the American Board of Neurology and Psychiatry in Chicago. Enjoying the privilege of being on the University of Purdue Old Master's Program I had to get Professor [Herbert M.] Schueller, Head of our English Department, to introduce one of my visiting professors at an open university meeting here. Faced with the probability of radical restriction of student health services here, I was the banquet speaker at the Annual meeting of the American College Health Association held in Detroit. With my interest focused on my latest manuscript on health education, I found myself still editing the Franklin Lecture Series Essays (*The Growth of Self-Insight*).

During the first months of the year I was without secretarial help but exceedingly busy with continuing College of Medicine and related business, expectable during a transition period. Gradually I began to secure office supplies, telephone service, mailing facilities, and other bare working necessities, including finally a secretary. Practically all of my room furnishings are even now either borrowed or my own private possessions.

The shift from my own way of life which was tightly scheduled, organized and exacting to its opposite, challenged depths of self-reliance, capacity for renunciation of habits, insightful endurance, as well as any ability I might have for striking out fresh for myself. Everyone on campus, beginning with yourself, was wonderfully kind and left me free to fare for myself, naturally expecting me to be able to rise to my new occasions. I devoted much of my energy to sounding out university educators regarding their views of my work, and met consistently with friendly curiosity showing promise of growing into interest. My exalted academic position seemed to me to be one requiring my utmost in careful and caring interpretation. This estimate has firmed itself throughout the year.

Although my not using up the money budgeted to me for the year must raise the question, Why?, I am pleased to report that, by conservatively planning and studying and reviewing possibilities, I have been able to avoid certain costly commitments which I am glad I avoided. I refer specifically to selecting potential possible visitors to the campus. Thus far this aspect of my University Professorship has been very successful although limited, —waiting upon my development of myself so to speak as the entirely new University Professor.

Getting to know better the University Administration members, several deans, professors, instructors, non-academic university personnel, has been a great experience which has been a basic necessity. My work on the University Social Committee helped very much. I have become a member of the Editorial Board of the University Press, and a member of the Advisory Board of the Women of Wayne. I have been functioning on Examining Committees for Ph.D. candidates, conferring with authors on manuscripts, and helping prepare speeches. During my first weeks on the job I met with the Dean of the College of Education and later with the College faculty members. On both occasions I scored the need for understanding of the educative process. I am pleased to observe that a center for the specific study of the cognitive process has now been established on the campus, whether or not my urging its development counted.

I have spoken with student groups, and heads of student groups. I have given one of the four Adult Education Program Lectures this year. Most of my student and faculty contacts have been individual ones during the day, at lunch, at supper, or at night. The demand for my services as a speaker has been so heavy that I have had to limit it, in the interest of my health.

During the year I was consultant to the Division of Education of the Veteran's Administration in Washington. I am on the Medical Education Committee of the American Psychiatric Association (requiring out of state sessions). I continue as Chairman of the Michigan State Medical Society Mental Health Committee, Chairman of the Mayor's Committee for the Rehabilitation of Narcotic Addicts, Physician-in-Chief McGregor Center, Vice-President of Staff of Detroit Rehabilitation Center, Trustee of Luella Hannan Home, of John Scudder Foundation for Old People, and Detroit Receiving Hospital Research Corporation. I also continue as Head of Neurology and Psychiatry at the Children's Hospital of Michigan, Educational Staff of Harper Hospital, and other local hospital staffs. I am on the Advisory Committee of The Mayor's Youth Commission. I continue to function as a 24 hour health information center for students and physicians (particularly my former students).

Any spare time I have, has been going into the preparation of a book [*Illness or Allness*] descriptive of my theoretical and practical education views of my past 15 years as Professor and Chairman of the Department of Psychiatry.

There follows some account of my actual and potential campus visitors to-date, and of my present prospecting over my University Professorship. Having a visiting dignitary, or sage, here can require a considerable amount of groundwork with the dean and faculty members of the college most concerned.

The poet Wilbert Snow visited on the campus for two weeks endearing himself to faculty member and student alike. His helpfulness to me was, and continues to be, of the very finest. I intend to have him here next year, if possible. Personal friend of Robert Frost, he has contacted Frost, as I have, about coming to Wayne. Pneumonia, as you know, hospitalized Mr. Frost. Poet Snow has also written to his friend Archibald MacLeish about visiting Wayne, as I have, and that invitation is very much alive at present. I am also considering inviting Carl Sandburg, another of Mr. Snow's good friends.

Dr. William B. Bean, internationally renowned medic, brought to Wayne State and the Detroit Community the finest kind of health education orientation. His meaning for the College of Medicine student was indeed far reaching and profoundly humanizing. The results of his work here have been extensive in shaping student and faculty member devotion to health ideals. . . . It has been, as you know, a wish of mine to develop a Wayne State University Conference on Education from the standpoint of its only realistic significance (as self-development). That will be a costly but valuable conference.

Right now I am working with Hubert Locke, Assistant Counselor of Religious Affairs, and several others, on planning an Emancipation Proclamation Centennial celebration (January 1, 1963). . . .

June 13, 1963

Being now in my third year of my University Professorship it is satisfying to review with my colleagues of the Administration some of my very numerous and interesting University (including community) activities.

Quite as in the first recording of my experiences, again I wish to observe grateful appreciation for the extraordinarily fine educational spirit and effect I derive from my privilege of being close to you, as well as to Vice President Harbison and President Hilberry. I have continued to enjoy the wise and good life of American academic freedom and service, admiring the mature humaneness of each one of you. I am fully sure that your kind of sane expectation that everyone will do what he can to be alive to his educational opportunities and responsibilities, has served to bring out the best possibilities.

My office of University Professor continues to define itself, ever more broadly and deeply, often to my surprise. These shocks of life have never been overwhelming, but they have clearly demonstrated the keenly perceptive wisdom and love of President Hilberry for his Wayne in his conceiving the need for establishing this specific kind of freely unattached university structure in his academic community.

It is not possible to describe at all definitely certain very important aspects of my work with students, faculty members and community citizens. It is often difficult to avoid becoming mostly a health information resource on a local and state-wide basis.

Bearing in mind that up through recorded history the poet has been well ahead of his time in insight (the source of love wisdom and vision) I have taken special satisfaction in becoming a member of the Miles Modern Poetry Committee, extending myself to be useful in building up the meaningfulness of this most worthwhile organization. I have been able to be of practical service in this respect, encouraging and attending all meetings and contributing financially to forwarding the work of the committee. The last Poetry Week (May, 1963) was an outstanding University and community success.

I continue to work with students and faculty members on their papers, books, doctoral programs, and examinations.

I keep myself available for top-level and near top-level consultations on health, education, ethics, as well as other general subjects.

Right now I have been very much occupied in trying to do all possible to prevent the moving out of any part of Detroit Receiving Hospital's Department of Psychiatry, having worked with Vice President Scott, Mayor Cavanagh, and many others, in the effort to uphold the standard of modern medical emergency care.

I have continued as consultant to Kingswood School, and to the Veterans Administration. This June, 1963, I completed my trusteeship of the Detroit Receiving Hospital Research Corporation. I continue my trusteeship of the Luella Hannan Memorial Home and of the John Scudder Foundation For Old People.

With the Mayor's Committee for the Rehabilitation of Narcotic Addicts membership I have been able to make great progress towards establishing an in-patient and out-patient unit for the rehabilitation of narcotic addicts.

I continue on the Mental Health Committee of the Mayor's Commission on Children and Youth, and I am also active in the following committees: Michigan State Medical Society, Mental Health Committee; Wayne State University, Emancipation Proclamation Centennial Committee; Shakespeare Quadricentennial Committee; Miles Modern Poetry Committee; Editorial Board, Wayne State University Press; Counsellor's Committee of Wayne County Medical Society; Counselling Board of Metropolitan Y.M.C.A.; American Medical Writers Association; Education Committee of American Psychiatric Association; Detroit School-Community Behavior Project, Detroit Public Schools; Wayne County Medical Society, Library Committee.

I am on the staffs of the following institutions: McGregor Center, Detroit Rehabilitation Institute, Jennings Hospital, Harper Hospital, Children's Hospital of Michigan, Veterans Administration Hospital, Detroit Receiving Hospital, Alexander Blain Hospital (honorary).

The medical students made me an honorary member of their William Beaumont Society.

This year I received the Merrill-Palmer Institute Citation Award for my educational efforts.

Even though I have been unable to do so, for the past three years the College of Medicine graduating classes have voted that I deliver their graduation Oath, or Address.

I have given a great number of special lectures and speeches, the most outstanding of which I have tried to enumerate as follows: "Action for Mental Health," panel discussant, Eighth Annual Conference of American Medical Association, Mental Health Representatives, Chicago, February 2, and 3, 1962. "A Man's Woman," Detroit Association of Educational Secretaries, March 23, 1962. "Anxiety and the Creative Process," discussant of Henri M. Peyre's Detroit

Adventure address, April 27, 1962. Three-hour seminars on Mental Health with Michigan State administrators, Lansing, Michigan, May 11, and 18, 1962, and March 29, and April 5, 1963. All-day Clinical Seminar on Psychotherapy, East Lansing, Michigan, June 7, 1962. "The Growth of Self-Insight," for University Seminar in Public Speaking, Department of Speech, June 27, 1962. Address on "Education to Health" for the opening of schools, Board of Education, Wyandotte, Michigan, September 4, 1962. "Orientation-Ethics," Department of Pharmacy, October 24, 1962. "Mental Health and Religion," Jefferson Avenue Presbyterian Church, October 24, 1962. "Humaneness and Mental Health," American Humanist Association, November 2, 1962. "Poetry," Prismatic Club, November 17, 1962. "Religion and Mental Health," Wayne County chaplains, St. Paul's Cathedral, January 8, 1963. "Mental Hygiene," Wesley Foundation, January 24, 1963. "Dunglison and Beaumont," William Beaumont Society, January 24, 1963. "The Physician and Poetry," Nu Sigma Nu Annual Banquet speaker, March 1, 1963. "Medical Education is Self-Development," Nu Sigma Nu Faculty Assembly speaker, March 1, 1963. "Health and Education," Monteith Student Seminar, March 4, 1963. "Mental Health in Adolescent Years," St. Paul's Cathedral, Youth Convocation, March 24, 1963. "The Unmarried Adult and Mental Health," Augustana Evangelical Lutheran Church, March 31, 1963. "Cultural and Technical Education," Annual Meeting of the Michigan Academy of Pharmacy, Detroit, April 4, 1963. "Mary Baker Eddy and Psychiatry," panel discussant, American Medical Writers Association, May 15, 1963. Inauguration Address, Michigan Society of Neurology and Psychiatry, Detroit, June 8, 1963. "The Meaning of the Mural," unveiling of mural depicting insightful teaching of psychiatry, Wayne State University, College of Medicine, Class of 1962, June 9, 1963.

The center for my medical work continues to be in my functioning as Physician-in-Chief at McGregor Center. There has been a desirable change in emphasis at this institution resulting in the closing down of the in-patient service, the extension of the out-patient services for children and adults, and the beginning of a day-care program. . . .

I have arranged for the following guest lecturers to contribute insightfully to University events:

May 31, 1962	Dr. Norman Hilberry, College of Engineering, Argonne National Laboratories, Argonne, Illinois.
August 22, 1962	Professor Syuzo Naka, Medicine (Psychiatry), Osaka, Japan.
October 3, 1962	Mr. Adrian van der Veen, journalist, Netherlands.
October 9, 1962	Professor Melvin Calvin, atomic scientist, University of California, Berkeley, California.
October 16, 1962	Dr. Walter Harding, Thoreau student, State University Teacher's College, Geneseo, New York.
October 18, 1962	Professor Gordon Allport, psychology, Harvard University, Cambridge, Massachusetts.
November 1, 1962	Dr. William Birenbaum, Dean of New School for Social Research, New York.
November 15, 1962	Dr. Lee Edward Travis, speech specialist, Beverly Hills, California.
February 11, 1963	Mr. Jacob Glatstein, Hebrew poet, New York.
February 14, 1963	Dr. Harry F. Harlow, psychologist, University of Wisconsin, Madison, Wisconsin.
April 1, 1963	Dr. Caron Kent, psychoanalyst and author, Melbourne, Australia.
April 10, 1963	Dr. William B. Bean, editor, internist, medical administrator, University of Iowa, Iowa City, Iowa.
April 22, 1963	Mr. Henry R. Luce, publisher, New York.
April 29, 1963	Mr. Mark Van Doren, poet, Falls Village, Connecticut.
April 29, 1963	Professor C. Wilbert Snow, poet, Middletown, Connecticut.

April 29, 1963   Professor C. A. Hackett, literary critic, Brown University, Providence, Rhode Island.

April 29, 1963   Professor John Berryman, poet, Brown University, Providence, Rhode Island.

April 29, 1963   Professor William D. Snodgrass, poet, Wayne State University, Detroit, Michigan.

June 17, 1964

The past year of my University Professorship has been enriching. During it I cultivated directions of my work which might continue to promise rewarding developments. No doubt, a person who keeps himself very busy clearly upholding the principle of the dignity of the individual as being the only principle of sane humanity may be excused for wondering how his institution could get along without his evident contributions, much less without his "presence."

The finest kind of academic freedom has been mine. I have always felt administrative cooperation and collaboration accessible and available. I can ask for nothing further in this regard, and trust that my own workability with my administrative colleagues is equally ideal or that I shall have the opportunity to try to make it such.

As was my experience last year, again I find that the office of University Professor is one which fully justifies itself, even though one might continue to find it difficult to define the nature of its services for catalogue purpose. Although difficultly thus defined, I hold that the meaningfulness of that achievement would be well worth the effort.

My analysis of the nature of my job continues to be that of honoring, to the best of my ability, every integration of university *health* and *education*. Each year of my work I have observed clearly:

1. The importance of conceiving *all* medical work (including surgical) as an educational experience for the patient as well as for the physician.
2. The importance of conceiving *all* educational work only for its health significance: as a conscious self-development of the student, as well as of the teacher.

This orientation,—the student's careful disciplining his mind to see to it that all of his education will mean personal hygiene for him, and to see to it that all of his hygiene will mean his personal education for him,—appears to me to be, without question, the number one university issue everywhere. I have completed a book around this purview which will be published by Wayne State University Press by the end of the year. It is the same book [*Illness or Allness*] about which I wrote you in my last year's letter.

Insofar as I can find it possible to do so I make myself available for a specially needy faculty member or student with respect to his manuscripts, books, doctoral programs, and doctoral examinations. A considerable fraction of my living is devoted to administrative and near administrative level conferring on the subjects of health, education, ethics, curricular innovations, and even occasional courtesy consultations of strictly private nature. My exertions frequently extend from the campus into the community. Often I am called upon, on account of the fact that I am identified with the University rather than with any specific college. With each passing year I find increasing a certain identity of mine as a kind of one-man health and education information resource. Daily I am called upon for just about every kind of such direction imaginable. I extend professional courtesies to clergymen, physicians, and to individual members of their families, whenever possible.

In the interests of my health I have to be selective with regard to the number of speaking or conference assignments which I can accept.

My experimental work continues to be concentrated at McGregor Center, where I am Physician-In-Chief. Every Monday from 11:00 a.m. to 1:00 p.m., I hold an open lecture there devoted to the nature of healthful living. During the past year I have held two series of special presentations, 1) on the Healing Aspects of Poetry, and 2) on the Insightfulness of Shakespeare.

I teach a class at McGregor Center every Monday, with the exception of the month of August. Every quarter on Wednesday I teach a class for the Applied Management and Technology Center. Course title, *Psychology of Successful Living.*

I saw through to publication in *Diseases of the Nervous System,* May 1964, the lecture material given by Professor Syuzo Naka (assisted by Professor Yukio Kawakita), "Psychiatry in Japanese Culture." Dr. Naka was one of my University lecturers last year.

In the Christmas issue of the *Michigan State Medical Society Journal* I wrote an editorial, "The Spirit of Medicine."

I have given much time to assisting in the preparation of letters and articles for newspapers and journals.

My community activities are extensive.

I am Vice President of the Board of Trustees of the Luella Hannan Home and of the John Scudder Foundation for Old People. . . .

Each year the Miles Modern Poetry Week has enjoyed outstanding University and community success. It is my opinion, and that of each member of the committee, that poetry as a dynamic force is of university-wide importance and deserving of university financial support. From the start I have found the potential health significance of poetry to be fully worthy of cultivation as a university-wide resource for each student's appreciation of the dignity of his individuality. I am hoping that it will be possible in time to work up this potential area of resourcefulness for insightful humaneness.

I have been able to be of service in activating the Samuel and Louis Hamburger Foundation grant to the College of Medicine, and in contacting the Samuel and Louis Hamburger Foundation president, Mr. Samuel Hamburger, in the interest of the new Children's Hospital fund drive.

The listing of Visiting Lecturers under the auspices of my University Professorship follows. Associated with each of these lectures I have delivered brief talks on such topics as "Insightfulness," "The Allness of Individuality," "The Medical Consultation as an Educational Experience," "Poetry and Mental Health."

September 26, 1963	Mrs. P. C. Mahalanobis, Calcutta, India. Lectured to the psychology students.
October 24, 1963	Mr. Archibald MacLeish, poet, Uphill Farm, Conway, Masschusetts.
November 5, 1963	Mr. Louis Ginsberg, poet, Paterson, New Jersey.
November 13, 1963	Dr. John Hope Franklin, Emancipation Centennial Celebration, Brooklyn College, New York.
December 2, 1963	Professor Wilhelm Emrich, Visiting Professor, Northwestern University, Evanston, Illinois.

December 10, 1963	Dr. Urie Bronfenbrenner, Cornell University. Topic: "The Making of the New Soviet Man."
January 23, 1964	Dr. Harry F. Harlow, University of Wisconsin. Lectured to the psychology students.
January 28, 1964	Professor Roman Jakobson, Harvard University.
January 29, 1964	Mr. Charles E. Feinberg, Detroit, Michigan. Lectured at the Medical School. Topic: "Perspective on Whitman's Medical Problem."
February 27, 1964	Mr. Louis Untermeyer, Newtown, Connecticut. Topic: "The Writing and Reading of Poetry."
March 13, 1964	Poetry Reading. University of Michigan poets, Ann Arbor. Dorothy Donnelly, Konstantinos Lardas, and Earl Prahl.
April 3, 1964	Professor C. Wilbert Snow, Middletown, Connecticut, poetry readings and lectures on poetry, on the main campus, at the College of Medicine, and at Merrill-Palmer Institute.
April 8, 1964	Dr. Richard W. Hamming, Murray Hill, New Jersey. Topic: "The Impact of Computers."
April 5–11, 1964	Miles Modern Poetry Week poets: Philip Levine, William Stafford, and Muriel Rukeyser participated.
	Stephen Spender, London, England. Topic: "The Image of the Poet and the Idea of Poetry." A dinner was given in his honor.
April 16, 1964	Camilla Jose Cela, Spanish author (lecture in Spanish). Topic: "The Spain

	Mystery: What Is Spain: What Are Spaniards? and What Is Spanish?"
April 24, 1964	Dr. John Edelman, Washington, D.C. Topic: "The Labor Lobby and Its Role in the Changing Political Scene."
April 24, 1964	Dr. Francis Horn, president of the University of Rhode Island. Phi Beta Kappa. Lecture on campus.
April 30, 1964	Professor J. Erik Jorpes, Stockholm, Sweden. Visiting Professor at the University of Buffalo. Topic: "Alfred Nobel and his Work."
May 11, 1964	Younghill Kang, internationally distinguished author and lecturer from New York. Topic: "Oriental Influence on Western Art and Literature."
May 17, 1964	I introduced Douglas Campbell, Shakespearian actor, who completed the Presidential Lecture Series.
June 10, 1964	Dr. Francis J. Gerty, McGregor Memorial Conference Center. Lecture on psychiatry.

There follows an outlined running account referring to most of my lectures and functions during the past year.

June 13, 1963	Tea honoring Dean Charles Brink.
June 17, 1963	Conference on Management of Emotional Problems in Comprehensive Medical Care, in Metropolitan Hospital.
June 18, 1963	Participant in Section III (Mental Health) Department of Gerontology, University of Michigan.
June 24, 1963	Torch Program, Committee for the year 1963–64, First Unitarian Universalist Church.

June 28, 1963	Tea and reception honoring Dr. Douglas A. Sargent's departure.
July 9–September 1, 1963	Mrs. Otto Fisher, art objects.
July 16, 1963	WXYZ taped lecture, "Contributions of Women to the Community."
July 24, 1963	Dr. Dorsey and Dr. [Harold] Basilius, discussion on Goethe at the University Broadcasting Station.
August 12, 1963	Lecture, McGregor Center, Reverend Malcolm Ballinger and 12 chaplains who attended from Ann Arbor.
September 12, 1963	Lecture, College of Medicine. Topic: "Death and the Dying Patient"—100 medical students.
September 24, 1963	"Psychology of Successful Living" begins fall classes—4801 Third, Room 102.
October 10, 1963	Commissioner's Ball honoring Mayor and Mrs. Jerome Cavanagh.
October 10, 1963	Welcome to Wayne, McGregor Memorial Center.
October 13, 14, 15, 1963	Assistant Examiner, Chicago, Illinois, American Board of Psychiatry and Neurology, Inc.
October 21, 1963	Lafayette Clinic Lecture, "The Development of Psychotherapy."
October 30, 1963	Sereck Fox, class lecture on Ethics.
November 1, 1963	School Community Behavior Project Meeting.
November 8, 1963	Mayor Cavanagh, Mental Health Meetings.
November 18, 1963	Oral Examination, Gary Golkenberg, Emancipation Centennial Committee.

November 22, 1963	Mental Health Committee, Robert E. Forbes, Chairman.
November 22, 23, 1963	University Composer's Exchange, Roy T. Will, Chairman, Music Department—Meeting.
November 30, 1963	Pharmacy lecture, State Hall, "Ethics in Pharmacy."
December 6, 1963	Charles Burton Marshall, Phi Beta Kappa.
December 7, 1963	Dr. Herbert M. Schueller, N.C.A.-M.C.A., High School-College Engineering Conference.
December 12, 1963	Mayor's Mental Health Committee—Charles F. Wagg.
December 13, 1963	Merrill-Palmer, Examination of our center for prospective National Institute of Mental Health Grant.
December 16, 1963	Dr. Icie Macy-Hoobler, Dr. Frank Sladen, Dr. John Dorsey, Mark Beach, Dr. Paul Rankin—Engineering Society of Detroit.
December 26, 1963	Department of Psychiatry, Receiving Hospital.
January 10, 1964	Motion picture project, "From the Ends of the Earth," Mr. Shelby Newhouse, WWJ. [A reading and discussion of the script.]
January 15, 1964	Miss Erma Bley, Suicide Prevention Center.
January 30, 1964	Addressed staff, Department of Psychiatry, Receiving Hospital.
February 9, 1964	Attended "An Evening with Langston Hughes," Negro History Week.

February 14, 1964	Attended Second WSU Workshop on the Late Sequelae of Massive Psychic Traumatization. Lectured.
February 16, 1964	Interviewed by Anthony Ripley. Title: "Spare Part Surgery—a Frankenstein."
February 18, 1964	Hilberry Classic Theatre.
February 20, 1964	Open House for administrative officers of WSU at Charles Feinberg's home.
February 21, 1964	Dr. Dorsey spoke before 50 doctors from all over the country at McGregor Center.
February 24, 1964	Lecture to the Sophomore Medical Class at McGregor Health Foundation.
February 27, 1964	Mayor's Prayer Breakfast, Ballroom, Cobo Hall.
March 2, 1964	Open House for administrative officers of WSU at Charles Feinberg's home.
March 18, 1964	Dr. Franco Ferracuti, Acting Chief, Bureau of Social Defense, United Nations, luncheon.
March 20, 1964	Interviewed by W. Paul Neal, Jr., of the *Detroit News*. Topic: "Give Drivers Mental Test, Says Doctor."
April 6, 1964	Wayne County Medical Society lectureship, Historical Committee subscription breakfast for Dr. [Albert I.] Lansing.
April 6, 1964	Dinner and participation for the conferring of an honorary degree to Associate Justice of the Supreme Court of the United States, William O. Douglas.
April 11, 1964	Detroit Council of United Presbyterian Men, Littlefield Presbyterian Church, Dearborn, Michigan.

April 10, 17, 1964	Lecture to the Michigan Civil Service Commission, Executive Development Program. Topic: "Understanding Ourselves."
April 22, 1964	President and Mrs. Clarence B. Hilberry's tea for McGregor Fund Trustees for their participation in the Emancipation Proclamation Centennial.
April 23, 1964	Dr. Sereck Fox—Class in pharmacy. Topic: "Ethics."
April 25, 1964	Lectured on "Shakespeare, the Poet," Prismatic Club.
May 26, 1964	Birmingham Community House. Topic: "The Individual's Mental Health."
June 4, 1964	Professor J. Frank Campbell's class lecture. Topic: "The Meaning of the Self."
June 5, 1964	Michigan State Medical Society, Mental Health Committee. "The Dangers of Wild Hypnosis."
June 19, 1964	Pontiac, Pediatrics Residents' Annual Dinner. "Parental Insight."

Throughout the year, through the cooperation of Mr. and Mrs. Charles E. Feinberg, I have organized faculty groups to study the valuable literary resources in Mr. Feinberg's library.

Through the introduction of Mr. Charles E. Feinberg, I have been able to be of service in bringing together University officials with Mrs. Otto Fisher. Mrs. Fisher has made free gifts of most helpful texts for the College of Medicine through the offices of Mr. Flint Purdy and Vice President Gordon Scott.

December 15, 1964

To paraphrase Bacon, I can remain a happy well man to the extent that my nature sorts with my vocation. About to begin the fifth year of my University Professorship, I wish to offer certain views about that rare experience, particularly with the idea of prognosticating its future course. How might I more wisely steer my life has been a guiding interest I have used steadily. Why keep up this exceedingly difficult, however honorable application, is another lively view which tests the value of the effort most thoroughly. Always I end up realizing my sense of power and my need to exert it.

Writing you of my past and present all-university activities introduces a note of forecast of their future course. Although I have not used up the funds at my disposal in one sense, my maturing program calls for my using all of them and more. Unless actually engaged in the development of a new and vitally important educational program, such as this one of mine, you can hardly be expected to understand the indispensable role that accessible financial resource must play in it. Originally the spending idea discussed was that of starting it out in full strength, then possibly tapering it off later. My experience has forced me to see the practicality in doing a lot of looking before leaping in respect to my expenditures, for the most part. However, as you know, even though you and I have repeatedly tried to buy new furniture (not new equipment) suitable for my purposes, *nothing* has come of that effort, thus far, on account of the tremendous building program going on. I was never informed that I *must* use my funds up within a special period, so that I presume these monies will continue accessible to me whenever I may need them. If I am mistaken, please correct me as soon as you can, or advise me. But now let me continue with my describing my ongoing educational orientation.

So-called democratic veneration for mere schooling which is not conscious *self-development,* is the open secret of the life-cheapening effect of formal schooling throughout my world. I can find no more valuable use for my life than that of seeing my fellow educator confide this secret to himself. To wit, my privileged opportunity to write this truth to the chairman of the committee searching for a new dean of the College of Education is a cherished emolument to my office. May a student live his university for the avowed purpose of learning how to live, himself,—and not how to "get an education" in some self-belittling sense. Unqualified "study" is no cure for human wretchedness; study, in its only possible true sense, namely, self-study, reveals a student's glorious human being to him. Unqualified "work" is not the answer to life dissatisfaction; work, in its only possible true sense, namely observing how one's self can work, discovers the student's marvelous human nature for him. Whoever seeks an "object in living" is really crying out his need to see himself as his only life subject. To retain his conscious integrity he must learn he is not "in the University"; his university is in him. For successful living the life student needs only one talent,—learning from conscious self-experience to steer clear of use of his life forces that conceal from him his own personal identity. Precious salvation lies in his avoiding experiences leading to his misprision of his priceless *conscious* self-hood. For lack of this vision, the joy of living perishes.

Purposefully identifying myself with whole university living has spurred the growth of my mind particularly to extend the range and enrich the liveliness of my imagination for my formal educational institutions and their provident communities. I have had extraordinary opportunity to cultivate practical realization of the innumerable concerns of a university administrator, along with a sense of the sincerity of his devotion to his responsible office.

As I observe my directions, and especially as I indulge the "looking ahead" attitude, I am critically aware of my necessity to see my university's good as my own. On that head, from all I have been able to learn thus far, my work has been deemed uniquely useful, both on and off the campus, reaching into every college, extending over the state, across and beyond the nation.

On every occasion, public or private (even as in this letter to you), I use my mind to verbalize appreciation for my marvelous human powers and to study and practice myself in the acknowledgements of my comprehensiveness (my *allness, wholeness, oneness*). Thus, my choice mental position observes: Whatever is, individually is. This one insight, instead of dividing continents, or sects, or faiths, or colors, is capable of revealing all in a single allegiance to each human individual for whom they stand, by whom they were created, and through whom they continue their being. On every occasion I speak my mind upon what a different world everyone's would be if he could learn the one lesson of life upheld by his religious and secular educator alike: Whatever is, justly is. War will pass only with this just view.

To further my effectiveness, I have kept up and extended my personal and professional interest in cultivating my self-insight. My all-campus community experiences have enriched me I am sure more than I can know fully at once. Monies entrusted to my sense of their value have been wisely and economically spent to greatest benefit of the members of the faculty and students.

There is every indication that the office of the University Professor has enjoyed fortunate beginnings, solid academic growth, and is now getting into full swing. University and college administrative officers and faculty members are taking to the idea of a colleague of theirs officially representing disciplined appreciation for "the examined life" for each individual. At first feeling little more than a symbol of my ideal (education is only self-development), with each passing year I find myself more and more in the situation of being expected to stand up for this real academic freedom, to witness the fact that peace is the product only of appreciated wholeness of human being. I have received letters, notes and calls only of most encouraging and reassuring kind. Rumors of similar nature only have come to me. I can only assume that this kind of a *working* university professor takes care of a vital campus-community need. However, my university colleagues are in fine position to criticize my years with them, and to make up their own minds as to whether or not my special kind of university effort is well worth supporting.

Main factors consciously favored and operative today in my life and thought are my necessity to do all and only my own living; my observance of my spirit of free inquiry and general free mindedness; my recognition of the peace and prosperity provided by my learning the unobstructed uses of my mind, particularly the free functioning of my imagination; and my self-reliant self-orientation of self-helpfulness. I see my continuing duty to be that of creating life-revering, self-cherishing, mind-appreciating, soul-stirring campus opportunities for *conscious* self-fulfillment by way of special private and public demonstrations,—lectures, seminars, conferences and even larger congresses, audio-visual recordings, and publications of various kinds. As Blake put it, "we become what we behold." The peacemaking truth is: eternal self-vigilance is the price of whatever free freedom there is. "Unbridled selfishness" is the protecting misnomer for *bridled self-recognition.*

This kind of meaning of my office is now already functioning. I have worked up its effectiveness with great care. Even as I often wonder at all I have been able to accomplish (by collaborating with whomever I find "just ready" for the great work opportunity he requests) I also feel strengthened to proceed with this exceptional program, this most remarkable new academic dimension providing for each faculty member's and student's growth of his appreciated ideality. It is gladdening to my heart to be able to know that President Hilberry's foresight, in seeing to it that everyone of his beloved Wayne State University give himself experience about *conscious* self-fulfillment, is its own just reward.

Thus far, apart from a few publications, my writing has focused upon what might be called an exhaustive account of the way my mind has been working. For illustration, I have presented my insights with regard to the several subjects constituting my learning about my world. This record of my mental conditions and situations is to be available in book form [*Psychology of Emotion*] as I enter upon the fifth year of my office.

On the university campus, I have been observing three immense streams of humane experiences coverging; health powers, educational forces and religious interests. Recognition of the basic identity (namely, concern for the individual's good) underlying each of these seemingly disparate disciplines is a continuing need. I have been feeling this need and have been doing all possible to meet it. Any unifying of these worthy concerns is a benefit to everyone.

My further years of my imaginatively conceived and potentially creative office will continue to be devoted to advancing realization concerning the inviolable integration of man's self-helpful nature, an already existing integration despite his appearance of being at cross-purposes with himself,—a distressing appearance which can and does distract him from securing the benefits of observing and cherishing his true greatness and excellence. Greatness and excellence at their best, are the individual's seeing each in himself. There is no aspect of this reality which is not most practical. Regularly exercising such awareness for self-responsibility eventually makes it relatively effortless. Nothing but one's own practice of self-accounting can make him a practitioner of it. Little wonder Aristole listed contemplation as the greatest help for the conduct of one's life.

During recent years the issue "wild hypnosis" has concerned the medical profession. In response to a request of my medical colleagues, I worked up and published my views on the subject in *Michigan Medicine,* the Michigan State Medical Society journal issue of July, 1965. You also have a copy of this work. Similar invitations to prepare publications I am postponing until time will permit me to accept such opportunity.

Right now there is a new head of the College of Education, good friend Dean Joseph W. Menge. President Keast most kindly allowed me to forward to himself my experienced considerations with regard to that office. Seldom does a university president have the opportunity to place in the academic heavens that most important (health) educational north star, *the Dean of the College of Education.* Just knowing that I could write to President Keast, to Vice President Harbison, and to you on that all-important fact, has been a source of tremendous relief for me. Hence I take every chance I can to sharpen this point: How soon in life an individual's fascination for that which he can do begins to preempt his awe for that which he *is!* This process of enjoying functioning without appreciating who is creating it all, undergoes great acceleration with the building up of vocabulary. One's every word is quickly endowed with the meaning of reality whether or not its entire meaning as self-expression is at all clear. Thus, even the most thoroughly verbalized person may appear the least self-conscious. Indeed he may complain that self-consciousness blocks his free flow of words. Little wonder that mediaeval and modern philosophers seem to put most of their energy into trying to clear up verbal questions.

September 23, 1965.

As I wrote to you December 15, 1964, I have given particularly earnest attention to evaluating the worthwhileness of the kinds of activities I carry on in overall terms of the University's best interest. After studying this due concern it seems to me that I can "present my case" to myself no more effectively than I have in past letters to you on this subject, by attempting to list major projects I have undertaken so far this year.

Perhaps, first of all I might mention the publication of the book *Illness or Allness,* April, 1965, by Wayne State University Press. This publication represents 15 years of teaching psychiatry at Wayne State University prior to my becoming University Professor. I am highly pleased that the positive reception of this work by my colleagues thus far warrants its wide distribution.

A new and notable direction of my university work was that of teaching 18 classes in the Police Department on the general topic of American police authority and community health. I wrote up the general nature of the orientation of my lectures, and you have a copy of this prepared material. Education of this kind is urgently needed and it is deeply gratifying to me to be able to bring my health education orientation to bear upon it. There are grave civic dangers in treating the citizen's criminality only as "undesirable" and thus refusing to learn the public health lesson implicit in it. A word's work is not clarified by its dictionary sense. In brief its work is what one's own *living* immediately puts into it.

Before and since Plato (in Phaedo) contended that false words are not only evil but also infest the soul with evil, the scholarly mind has concerned itself with the power and glory of the word. By "scholarly mind" I mean specifically the mind-conscious student. John Locke observed that the far greatest number of words, in every language, consists of general terms for particulars, the particular being the only possible existent. Each such "general" word, or term, properly serves the only demonstrably valid end of language, man's naming of an element of his very own mental power. But who is there who does not learn such names and practice using them only that they may be understood as foreign bodies in his mind. May not the official one to hold himself responsible for bringing the full force of education to bear upon the healthfulness in the pupil's *recognized* mind-working be the teacher of the college of education! A required and continued specific part of language study—well understood insightfully by each language teacher—can prove as helpful as fog signals in calling attention to the life danger in one's using his words to make himself dense to himself, and the lifesaving in one's using his words to make himself clear to himself.

Proof positive of the educator's *sustained perseverance* exclusively in understanding education as only and entirely the student's mental growth, may well be his one absolute job prerequisite. Whoever has worked up that kind of active self-knowledge for himself may be readily forgiven other ignorance, for he knows precisely how best to develop his learning in whatever direction of his living. Otherwise the name "educator" presupposes what it denies. He who has the immediate and intense sense of urgent demand that the attention of man, of every man, be drawn back to his exclusive reality, his own mind, away from his habit-forced illusions of not-his-own-mind,—

that one can be appreciated by everyone whose driving conviction it is that only admitted self-culture is hygienic. Ignored self-culture is suppressive and mind weakening in that it leads to atrophy of the function of purposive self-fulfillment.

The remainder of this description of my interests I devote to recording my one certain present educational ideal and aim as they have taken their directions out of my University Professorship thus far.

June 15, 1961, I wrote to you in some detail of the potential value in a series of university conferences devoted specifically and merely to finding and revealing the education in education. Since then I have steadily directed my efforts towards having each of my University Professorship's special events assume as much as possible the significance of an educational conference for faculty personnel, students, and members of the metropolitan community.

It seems to me that the name "Wayne State University" could only gather honor and glory in everyone's life through having its professional educators take the lead in this direction, the only one, of soul learning. First of all there must be careful planning for such an adventure. Statements of noted educators might be helpful, such as this one of Grayson Kirk, "The most important function of education at any level is to develop the personality of the individual and the significance of his life to himself" even if President Kirk did go on to add, "and to others," thus diluting the heady idea of absolute individuality. But most helpful of all would be the clear statement of the vital issue, the frank confrontation of the professional educator with his official responsibility, the willingness of the faculty member to study the importance of undertaking such an all-out educational program, the consent of the administrator about such heretical undertaking.

Only *how* a pupil studies the *what* of his own living, can provide answer for his all-important question: Why live? His whole so-called "view of life" can be nothing but his acknowledged or unacknowledged view of his very own life. However, the university instructor as a rule is prejudiced heavily in favor of teaching knowledge "about" something rather than of experiencing all of his teaching as self-realization. I need a language of self-respect which constantly elucidates the truth that I am always all that can be, for me; that I can never have anything to complain about but my own wonderful self.

Certainly the educator who qualifies as this kind of lover of learning, as a lover of living (his own), will feel keenly the need for a language capable of expressing for the pupil his realization of the life-giving value of his self-insight, the life-surrendering value of his self-blindness. He will see that man's, every-man's, language reflects his method of mind use. He will see that the realistic grammar of language must be one which respects fully comprehensive unique individuality of the linguist. He will see that language habituated to distract attention from the all-inclusive truth of its user, inevitably disrespects human life by contributing to its user's addiction of self-neglect. He will see also that freedom of speech is impossible where his very words imprison the speaker in the straightjacket of self-rejection in the guise of not-self acceptance. This educator has probably already been busy sanifying his own language usage, realizing that health education must be erudition created by, of, and about the very mind enjoying the functioning of its own power,—not "information" acquired through any so-called external linguistic reforms.

The identifying characteristic of *hygienic* learning is consciousness for the variety in the unity of one's own points of view. This most desirable experience of language, which cannot be taught except self-taught, is the only important consideration in any education for mental health. Only his recognized systematic self-experience can save the student from the "stamp of education." All learning is observing one's own human nature. It poses a large self-lesson, and without ordering it for himself, the so-called "traditional" common-sense "educator" can and must keep up his provisional scheme of authoritarian schooling based upon limited imagination of that world of man, his human individuality.

It has been claimed that knowledge of more than one language is desirable education, for instance, that Aristotle himself suffered the limitation of knowing only his mother tongue. All of the evidence of every great mind attests the truth that one language only can enlighten man with due appreciation for his greatness, namely, the language naming his personal identity in its every word. To enjoy one's own meaning rather than that of words or terms is the only method of observation which contains and compels humaneness by revealing all cold abstraction as ever one's own living being. Not-self is non-entity. Education to quickness in recognizing one's identity in one's own living can become Wayne's sane educational goal.

It were but too easy for me to prolong the list of benefits in self-insight, or the list of shortcomings in self-blindness. I know full well that each could not generate any reliance on self-observation to the neglect of self-rejection. Renunciation of a mental attitude, of an habitual posture of mind, cannot occur without the suffering of abstinence symptoms, quite as those endured in withdrawal from a drug.

However, the person who refuses to renounce an addiction must pay dear life for his *status quo*. Only the educator who does not realize the cost in human life of indulging a language of human folly *can* feel the urgency for the construction of a language of human wisdom. With the present constant stream of national and international public address systems, this age has been fitly named the Verbal Era. Is it not the insightful educator's responsibility to recognize the urgency for talking sense! If a teacher can begin to see any practical advantage to himself in disciplining his mind to appreciate that his life, including every word of it, is all and only about himself, —then this can be his pupil's greatest educational opportunity, namely, beholding his teacher who considers it most worthwhile to renounce the clichés of illusional communication in favor of building up his biologically adequate self-respect.

My entire possibility of language is to use meanings in my own mind. Every child first learns to speak by talking to himself. Only later does he succumb to his overpowering illusion "communication." He will cling to this illusion for dear life for it is just that, entirely of his own making. His fear of claiming the unity and integrity of his individuality is too terrifying to consider.

Rare indeed is the person who, as Plato put it, can see himself as the sole creator of his mind's meanings, as the obstetrician of his own ego, as identical with his own mind's deliverances. My language specializing in terms for not-self supports my frantic need to deny that my world is my own, to deny that my all is my soul. The educator seeing the irresponsibility in any not-self psychology will readily see its responsibility for so-called crime, war and every such disregard for human welfare. That kind of vision is necessary to produce the will to find the way to use the *kind* force of education in the interest of revering human individuality.

If the construction of a language of self-respect were easy to imagine, it would have become the conscious goal of the professional educator ages ago. He would consider it his gravest interest not to allow himself to see his pupil study in a way specifically sure to increase his blindness for his essential unity and integrity. I have had to satisfy myself by spelling out all of this selection of self for attention in my current book [*Psychology of Language*] and circulating it as best I can. As in all else, every individual must master the principle of the action involved in looking out for his welfare. Each of us has supplied himself with motives unknown to everyone who has not lived similar experience. I feel keenly the need for a revival of education. If it would be desirable I would gladly welcome the opportunity to bring practical answers to practical objections to any of these expressed views about providing literally liberal education for the present and future generations specifically in the direction of self-helpfulness.

My local, state, and national work goes on as before. Part of it concerns medicine. For example, I am scheduled to teach psychiatric residents at Detroit General (Receiving) Hospital; lectures for medical students; William Beaumont Society; introductory lecture for medical students just beginning their clinical experience; seminar for psychology department, Lafayette Clinic; and the like. I have lectured on mental health for College of Education classes, and on ethics for College of Pharmacy classes. I continue to assist in board examinations for the American Board of Neurology and Psychiatry. University Press Board functions provide unusually fine experiences. Trusteeships in charitable funds have been excellent investments. Right now my board members of one of these funds, the Luella Hannan Memorial, are working with our university administration (primarily through President Keast, Vice President Scott, and Dean Ernest Gardner) towards developing a gerontological center in the medical corridor. This development begun by former President Hilberry is already a prime interest of President Keast. The Hamburger Chair of Psychiatry in Pediatrics is now filled by an able psychiatrist, Dr. Joseph Fischhoff, and I am greatly pleased with the functioning of this greatly needed innovation. A further grant has already been planned by the same foundation towards the building of new Children's Hospital.

June 2, 1971, President William Rea Keast wrote to me:
Dear John:

You do not need the enclosed Emeritus Identification Card to remind you that you are welcome at any time to return to the campus which has been a part of your life for so many years. We are most grateful to you for your devoted service to Wayne. We join in sending our thanks and all good wishes for the years ahead.

Rea

University Professor Programs and Lectures, 1962–1966

1962

May 31	Dr. Norman Hilberry
August 22	Professor Syuzo Naka
October 3	Adrian van der Veen
October 9	Professor Melvin Calvin
October 16	Dr. Walter Harding
October 18	Professor Gordon Allport
November 1	Dr. William Birenbaum
November 15	Dr. Lee Edward Travis

1963

February 11	Jacob Glatstein
February 14	Dr. Harry F. Harlow
April 1	Dr. Caron Kent
April 10	Dr. William B. Bean
April 22	Henry R. Luce
April 29	Mark Van Doren
April 29	Wilbert Snow
April 29	Professor C. A. Hackett
April 29	John Berryman
April 29	William D. Snodgrass
September 2	Mrs. P. C. Mahalanobis
October 24	Archibald MacLeish
November 5	Louis Ginsberg
November 13	Professor John Hope Franklin
December 2	Professor Wilhelm Emrich
December 10	Dr. Urie Bronfenbrenner

1964

January 23	Dr. Harry F. Harlow
January 28	Professor Roman Jakobson
January 29	Charles E. Feinberg
February 27	Louis Untermeyer
March 13	Poetry Reading:—Dorothy Donnelly, Konstantinos Lardas, and Earl Prahl
April 3	Wilbert Snow
April 8	Dr. Richard W. Hamming
April 5–11	Stephen Spender, Philip Levine, William Stafford, and Muriel Rukeyser
April 16	Camilla Jose Cela
April 24	Dr. John W. Edelman
April 24	President Francis Henry Horn, Providence College
April 30	Professor J. Erik Jorpes
May 11	Younghill Kang
May 17	Douglas Campbell
June 10	Dr. Francis J. Gerty
October 12	Robert Bassil
October 14	Anna Trzecialkowska
October 16	Marquis Childs
November 4	Hilde Domin
November 12	Louis Ginsberg
November 17	Professor William Arrowsmith
November 18	Professor Klaus P. Wachsmann
November 19–20	Professor Robert Agger
November 23	Arthur S. Adams

1965

January 13	Professor Roman Jakobson
February 5	Professor Max Hayward
February 22	Senator Frank Church
February 23	Isaac Bashevis Singer
March 29	Wilbert Snow
April 6	Dr. William B. Bean
April 8	Elmer Rice
April 30	Anthony Hecht

May 7	Cyril Greenland
May 11	Rosey Pool
May 17	John Ciardi
May 18	Professor S. Chandrasekhar
May 25	Judge George Edwards
June 1	Professor Harry Johnson
June 11	Professor Jean Charlot
June 25	Dr. Lee Edward Travis
September 19	Dr. William C. Menninger
September 30	Robert St. John
October 15	John S. Coppin
October 15	Professor Svatava Jakobson
November 7–9	Louis Ginsberg
November 19	Professor Dvora Elon

1966

January 13	James Foreman
January 20	Professor Frank C. Jennings
January 27	Professor W. B. Stanford
February 3	James McGarrell
February 10	Colonel John P. Stapp
February 23	Dr. Uriel Simon
February 28	Theodore Bikel
March 7	Dr. Jacques Lacan
March 11	John Ciardi
April 4	Reverend Arthur Seegers
April 12	Wilbert Snow
April 13	Professor Johannes Urzidil
April 16	Polish Millennium Conference
April 18	Professor Israel Efros
April 22	Professor Jack Tworkov
May 10	Professor Roman Jakobson
May 19	Professor Arnold M. Rose
May 22–24	Professor L. G. A. Schlichting

Epilogue

George E. Gullen, Jr., President Emeritus,
Wayne State University

John Dorsey was a man of boundless energy, of boundless wisdom, of boundless compassion, and to treat him as a biographical subject is not at all revealing of the warmth and depth of feeling that each of us experiences in thinking of him. There is really no other way of thinking about John Dorsey than of his being very much alive—thinking, participating, contributing to the betterment of each one of us.

I remember as though it was yesterday my first meeting with John Dorsey twenty-five years ago. I immediately came under his influence, which has never ceased. My pastor, the Reverend Walton Cole, declared his church [First Congregational of Detroit] at the corner of Forest and Woodward avenues as the place "where religion and psychology meet." He invited Dr. Dorsey to lead a series of discussions on Sunday evenings for those of his congregation who were seeking to "discover themselves" and to adapt more adequately to their life circumstances. Of course Dr. Dorsey was exactly the right man for that job.

My mind overflows with the vivid pictures of those first meetings with John Dorsey—he was so impressive in both words and manner. When we applauded *him,* he applauded *with* us. In fact, when we responded in any way to him, he responded *with* us. We were instantly "at one" with him. The feeling that enveloped me at that first meeting never left me.

It was the beginning of my own understanding that he was in a real sense "my John Dorsey."

It is of great interest to me that Dr. Dorsey wrote so much about religion and psychiatry. He seemed to summarize his thinking in his essay "Religion and Medical Psychiatry," where he said, "My kingdom of God is within *me*. The view of consciously religious man is that *his* kingdom of God (his all) is within *him;* that he actively creates his own environment."

John Dorsey was born in Clinton, Iowa, November 19, 1900, and prepared for his medical career at the University of Iowa, receiving the M.D. degree in 1925. He completed there, too, the demanding years as intern and resident in psychiatry. And it was in Iowa, he told us, that he learned his greatest lesson— at his mother's knee—"to love his neighbor as himself." I hardly need to mention how well he learned *that* lesson. His whole life revealed it.

In later years came his period of study with the great Dr. Sigmund Freud in Vienna. He devoted a recent volume to that important part of his development, calling it *An American Psychiatrist in Vienna, 1935–1937, and His Sigmund Freud.* He also punctuated his writings with reminiscences, quotations, and lessons learned from his Professor Freud. Freud was the most powerful influence in John's philosophical life, with the possible exception of his Ralph Waldo Emerson. In *The Psychic Nature of Physiology,* Dr. Dorsey wrote, "Only my own systematically conscious self-analysis undertaken with my Professor Sigmund Freud provided me with the experience of self-consciousness enabling me to construct my consciously psychic psychogenesis."

Certainly, however, Ralph Waldo Emerson was the star to which John Dorsey hitched his wagon. All of Dorsey's writings, as well as his conversations, were beautifully lighted up by quotations from Emerson. He gave Emerson such glorious titles as "the Scholar's Scholar," "America's All-Time Great Scholar," and always referred to him as "my Emerson," taking unto himself those very qualities of thought which he most admired in his Emerson. One of his oft-quoted Emerson admonitions is that "he who would gather immortal palms must not be hindered by the name of goodness but must explore if it be goodness. Nothing is at last sacred but the integrity of your own mind."

In the foreword of his *American Government* (John Dorsey really put himself into the forewords and prefaces of his writings) he described his complex but motivating philosophy in these words:

Ever since discovering the sole place of all my truth as being entirely and only in myself, I have been interested in applying this realization to my study of my personal experience.

I have spared myself enormous expenditure of energy by taking the trouble to awaken to the fact that my living is wholly and solely internal, subjective, self-contained.

To my immense relief this insight enables me to "do something" about my life's complaints, dissatisfactions or disappointments of any and every kind and degree.

I see there is only one way for me to change my world, namely, by growing myself in the direction of the desired modification.

John Dorsey's writings are not always easy for me to understand. I am not alone in this. In the University archives I find a wonderful letter written by a Dorsey admirer, gently taking to task a reviewer of Dorsey's *Psychology of Emotion*. The reviewer had sincerely expressed concern about the difficult language of the book, and the writer of the letter assured the reviewer that it was "a problem she shares with a number of his admirers," explaining that "this situation is common [in] reading the works of an original mind."

The occasional opportunity of discussing with Dr. Dorsey the meaning of his words was a rare treat. Many of his explanations came in sentences that were not only revealing but quotable. He said to us once, "After all, I am all there is to my world." I like that statement very much. I've quoted it a thousand times (more or less), along with a story to which Dr. Dorsey called my attention—one that had been put into circulation by Charles E. Wilson, former president of General Motors.

The scene of the story was a small-town general store complete with pot-bellied stove, around which sat the town cronies eating from the cracker barrel and swapping yarns. The one with the beard had fallen asleep, and the practical joker of the crowd had carefully worked limburger cheese into his beard. On waking, the bearded one sniffed with obvious displeasure, walked about the store and then went outside, still smelling the limburger cheese and not knowing whence the odor came. He returned to the group and observed, "It's no use, fellows, the whole world stinks." Now, if I am all there is to my world, explained John Dorsey, and something becomes malevolent about it, it may well be something about myself that makes it so.

All this is an attempt to express something of a dear and remarkable man, who gave of himself fully to aspects of our society which both interested him and needed him greatly and which he consciously took into his own world as an integral part of his living. You certainly wouldn't call John Dorsey a "volunteer worker" in the usual sense for the organizations he served. He wrapped both subject and the people deeply into his personal life and "lived" his colleagues and his contributions. The diversity alone of this partial list of his activities shows something of his eclectic nature:

> Mayor's Committee for the Rehabilitation of Narcotics
> Addicts
> Mental Health Committee, Detroit Commission on
> Children and Youth
> Wayne County Medical Society (five major committees)
> State Committee on Multiple Sclerosis
> American Medical Writers Association
> Research for the State Board of Alchoholism
> Governor's Committee on Sex Deviates

Editorial Board, Wayne State University Press
Board of Education, Highland Park (fifteen years)
Board of Trustees, Luella Hannan Memorial Home
Whitney M. Young, Jr., Memorial Lecture Series
Committee

The list could literally go on and on. It is small wonder then that dozens of organizations vied to give him ever more distinguished recognition for his significant help to them. I have selected a few to suggest something of his remarkable record of achievement, appreciation, and respect:

Merrill-Palmer Institute Citation Award
Probus Club Award
Old Master's Citation Award, Purdue University
Leo M. Franklin Memorial Chair in Human Relations
John M. Dorsey Day: Proclamation, City of Detroit
John M. Dorsey Day: Celebration, Michigan Society of
Psychiatry and Neurology
Thomas Jefferson University Bicentennial Address
Lecturer

This recollection of John Dorsey's life would be most incomplete without a special word about the McGregor Center (a hospital founded for health education and rehabilitation), of which Dr. Dorsey was both director and physician-in-chief, and its successor, the Center for Health Education. Each of these organizations was designed "to put into practical use understandings about ministering to the health needs of the whole person." Dr. Dorsey attributed to the Center a contribution to his own growth and understanding, which he described as "using my mind to study my mental functioning with specific reference to my bodily activity." He often quoted from Dr. S. Weir Mitchell's poem "The Physician" to illustrate his view:

There are among us those who haply please
To think our business is to treat disease;
And all unknowingly lack this lesson still,
'Tis not the body but the man is ill.

John Dorsey came to Wayne University as psychiatrist and head of Wayne University Mental Hygiene Services thirty-eight years ago, in 1940. In 1946 Dean Hardy A. Kemp of the Medical School, seeking to strengthen full-time teaching as well as several of the school's major departments, named Dr. Dorsey Chairman of Psychiatry. It is a matter of interest that Dr. Walter Seegers was at the same time named Chairman of Physiology. The two men became friends as well as colleagues and together wrote the most significant volume *Living Consciously: The Science of Self,* which was published by the Wayne State University Press in 1959. Dr. Clarence Hilberry, President of the University from 1953 to 1965, said of Dr. Dorsey's years as Chairman of Psychiatry:

Fourteen years ago when John Dorsey first joined the faculty of the University and thus became more closely and happily into my circle of friends, it was most important that we get absolutely the right man to do the job which had to be done in the Department of Psychiatry. We have never had reason to do more than reaffirm the correctness of that appointment. His broad gauge philosophy and teaching in Psychiatry, his personal and professional impact on four-teen generations of medical students speaks more loudly than words.

It may seem ungracious of me to dismiss in a single paragraph fifteen years of such unparalleled service, but in retrospect—important as that major contribution was—his chairmanship was but one of many contributions made to his university by this amazing man.

So I turn, finally, to Dr. Dorsey's years as University Professor and, of course, as University Professor Emeritus. It is impossible to distinguish between the two periods, for he was continuously engaged in living his responsibility from the time of his appointment in 1961 until his death in 1978. He was in the process of completing a book on his University Professorship at the time of his death.

In explaining the nature of the University Professorship, President Hilberry said that, in his view, our way of life and our way of education tend to produce not only students who become more and more narrow in their interests but also professors who become increasingly high specialists. He said that it therefore becomes important to "try to cultivate by some new means a wholeness of vision . . . about the human experience." President Hilberry and Dr. Dorsey were obviously singing from the same hymnbook on that theme, and it was natural for Dorsey to be appointed the first University Professor.

In addressing the Board of Governors to recommend and designate Dr. Dorsey for that post, President Hilberry said:

I think you will agree with me that very few men have the breadth of interest, the genuinely philosophical frame of mind and approach to human knowledge and human life which the University Professor must possess. . . . It is our great good fortune that we *have* such a man on our *own* faculty. That man is John Dorsey.

With this accolade ringing in his ears, Dr. Dorsey began his eighteen years as University Professor, never failing in the zeal and enthusiasm that he brought to this unique educational service.

In his account of his University Professorship, John Dorsey speaks with great admiration of and appreciation for the support provided by the McGregor Fund throughout his years in Detroit. This most insightful group subsidized Dr. Dorsey's salary and the beginnings of his department at the time he became chairman of the Department of Psychiatry at Wayne University; provided for him the use of McGregor Center of the McGregor Health Foundation for his teaching program; became the trustees of the Center for Health Education to support his *university-wide* health education activities; provided a significant five-year grant to support the University Professor program; and continued financial help during his tenure as chairman of psychiatry and as University Professor. The Center for Health Education sponsored the publication of several of his books, contributing thereby to the permanence of the record of the science of health as Dr. Dorsey propounded it: *American Government: Conscious Self Sovereignty* (1969); *Psychology of Emotion* (1971); *Psychology of Language* (1971); *Psychology of Political Science* (1973); and *The Psychic Nature of Physiology* (1977).

Acting with great wisdom, the trustees of the McGregor Fund and the Center for Health Education were careful to leave all of Dr. Dorsey's decisions up to him—in his own words, "letting nothing but the facts speak for themselves."

The full story of John Dorsey's University Professorship will be difficult to relate. Even his own book about it does not reveal the full impact of that unique and very personal service. What I tell of it will match what hundreds of persons *in* this University and *out* of it experienced as a result of John Dorsey's concern as University Professor.

When I returned to the University as an administrator in 1966, a brief and friendly note welcomed me to that post with an offer of any assistance. This was followed at intervals with references from him about books that might be useful and helpful to me in my function. I learned to expect and began eagerly to await notes from John following a University function—notes with helpful comments and encouragement. Books old and new arrived periodically—some of John's own to be sure—but others which he thought would be useful and helpful to his University President.

I always opened my office early in the morning and John was always right there behind me for an early start, which in his case began by using the Mackenzie Hall stairs for seven floors—no elevator for John, who loved even that taxing climb. He was vibrant. He was physical—he still played a good game of tennis.

I had many precious personal conversations with John Dorsey. There were many small committee meetings, none too unimportant for his personal attention. There were contributions in the form of checks to be used in any way I thought best for the University. There were countless dinners, meetings, lectures, and community affairs that were graced by his presence.

Now this seems routine enough until you stop to think that this busy professional man's other activities were all taking place at the same time without let-up, and that what he was doing for me he was likewise doing for many others. He had the special gift of making whatever he did very personal. He was my John Dorsey, and he was Mike's John Dorsey—and Harlan's, and Ed's, and Mary's, and Louise's, and Walter's, and Bill's, and Emilie's and so on, and so on, and so on. It is as Edwin Markham said in these lines from "Outwitted," a poem that John often recited:

> But Love and I had the wit to win:
> We drew a circle that took [them] in![1]

---

[1]Dr. Dorsey referred to the following lines as his "favorite quatrain":
> He drew a circle that shut me out—
> Heretic, rebel, a thing to flout.
> But Love and I had the wit to win:
> We drew a circle that took him in!

See especially *Illness or Allness*, p. 185. Ed.

Index

Adams, Arthur S., 265
Adams, Thomas B., 225
Adult Education Program Lectures, 238
Afro-American Museum of Detroit, 96
Agassiz, Jean Louis Rodolphe, 191
Agger, Robert, 265
Aiuto, James J., 157
Alexander Blain Hospital, 241
Allport, Gordon H., 243, 264
American Board of Neurology and Psy-
    chiatry, 237, 249, 262
American College Health Association,
    237
American Humanist Association, 242
American Medical Association, 241
American Medical Writers Association,
    241, 242
American Psychiatric Association, 17,
    238, 241
Antaeus, 149
Applied Management and Technology
    Center, 245
Argonne National Laboratories, 243
Aristotle, 24, 103, 137, 256, 260
Arnold, Matthew, 191
Atchison, Leon H., 225
Augustana Evangelical Lutheran
    Church, 242

Bacon, Francis, 252
Ballinger, Malcolm, 220, 249
Bando, H. Walter, 95, 220
Bartemeier, Leo H., 219, 220
Bartlett, Lynn, 225
Basilius, Harold A., 49
Bassil, Robert, 265
Beach, Mark N., 250
Bean, William B., 239, 243, 264, 265
Becker, Carl, 27
Beluffi, Max, 94
Berman, Robert H., 157

Berryman, John, 244, 264
Bias of Priene, 74
Bikel, Theodore, 266
Bingham, Mrs. Jackson, 220
Birenbaum, William M., 243
Birmingham Community House, 252
Bley, Erma, 250
Board of Governors, 234
Boon, Julia V., 154
Borgman, William N., 226
Bowen, Edgar W., 222
Bowen, Lem W., 222
Bright, J. Russell, 226
Brink, Charles B., 226, 248
Brock, Donald R., 157
Bronfenbrenner, Urie, 247, 264
Brooklyn College, 246
Browne, Sir Thomas, 11
Brown University, 244
Brucker, Wilber M., Jr., 225
Bryant, Mrs. William Robert, 220
Buffalo, University of, 248
Burdick, Benjamin D., 225
Burroughs, Charles, 96
Burroughs, Margaret, 96
Burton, DeWitt T., 225
Burton, Ralph J., 41
Butler, Broadus N., 36
Butzel, Mrs. Martin L., 220

California, University of (Berkeley), 243
Calloway, Augustus J., Jr., 225
Calvin, Melvin, 243, 264
Campbell, Douglas, 248, 265
Campbell, J. Frank, 252
Canfield, George L., 222
Cavanagh, Jerome P., 240, 249
Cela, Camilla Jose, 247, 265
Center for Health Education, 31, 33, 56,
    64, 95, 161, 172, 220
Chandrasekhar, Subrahmanyan, 266

Charcot, Jean-Martin, 115
Charlot, Jean, 266
Children's Center of Detroit, 18, 219
Children's Fund of Michigan, 219
Children's Hospital of Michigan, 238, 241, 246, 262
Childs, Marquis William, 42, 265
Church, Frank (Idaho), 43, 265
Ciardi, John, 48, 266
Clarence B. Hilberry University Professor. See Cushman, Edward L.
Cobo Hall (Detroit), 251
Cohen, Wilbur J., 192
Coleridge, Samuel Taylor, 65
Collegian, 11
Columbus, Christopher, 11
Conway, Moncure Daniel, 17
Cooksey, Warren B., 220
Cooper, Ralph R., 157
Coppin, John S., 266
Cousins, James, 219
Cranefield, Eleanor, 220
Crim, Mrs. William D. (Suzanne Copland), 220
Cushman, Edward L., 25, 30, 99, 154

Danhof, John J., 41
Day, William M., 222
Detroit, City of, 219; Police Department, 258; Public Schools, 241
Detroit Adventure Series, 237, 241
Detroit Association of Educational Secretaries, 241
Detroit Council of United Presbyterian Men, 251
Detroit Economic Club, 24
Detroit Psychoanalytic Society, 219
Detroit Receiving Hospital Research Corp. (Detroit General), 238, 240, 241, 250, 262
Detroit Rehabilitation Institute, 238, 241
Detroit Urban League, 195, 196, 198
DeWitt, Robert L., 199, 220
Diogenes, 117
Domin, Hilde, 265
Donnelly, Dorothy, 247, 265
Dorsey, Edward C., 150
Dorsey, John M., Jr., 150
Dorsey, Mary Louise Carson, 30, 150, 153
Douglas, William O., 251

Dow, Douglas, 31, 200, 222
Dunglison, Robley, 57
Du Sable Museum of African American Art (Chicago), 96

Eddy, Mary Baker, 242
Edelman, John W., 248, 265
Edgar, Norris H., 219
Edman, Irwin, 89
Education to Education, 235
Edwards, George, 196, 266
Edwards, George C., III, 225
Edwards, Margaret (Mrs. George), 220
Efros, Israel, 266
Einheuser, Michael A., 225
Einstein, Albert, 87, 139
Eliot, T. S., 235
Elon, Dvora, 266
Emancipation Proclamation Centennial, 239, 241, 246, 249, 252
Emerson, Ralph Waldo, 11, 17, 23, 50, 81, 85, 87, 88, 104, 119, 122, 133, 142, 145, 158, 169, 174, 188, 191
Empedocles, 101
Emrich, Wilhelm, 246, 264
Engineering Society of Detroit, 250
Ensign, Dwight C., 95, 220
Epictetus, 101
Epicurus, 101
Esperanto, 175
Ezekiel, 159

Faville, Katharine E., 226
Feinberg, Charles E., 22, 93, 247, 251, 252, 265
Feinberg, Lenore (Mrs. Charles E.), 23
Ference, Michael, Jr., 225
Ferracuti, Franco, 251
First Unitarian Universalist Church, 248
Fischhoff, Joseph, 262
Fisher, Josephine H. (Mrs. Otto), 249, 252
Fite, Warner, 27
Fleischaker, Margo Franklin (Mrs. Stanley), 202
Folley, Walter C., 226
Forbes, Robert E., 250
Foreman, James, 266
Forncrook, Elva M., 220
Fox, Sereck, 249, 252
France, C. Jackson, 157

Franklin, Benjamin, 31
Franklin, John, 31
Franklin, John Hope, 193, 246, 264
Franklin, Leo M., 202
Freud, Anna, 133
Freud, Sigmund, 80, 114–16, 133, 159, 168, 186, 205
Freund, Hugo A., 219
Frost, Robert, 239

Galen, 12
Gardner, Ernest, 262
Geneva, Declaration of, 35
Genung, John Franklin, 81
Gershenson, Charles H., 225
Gerty, Francis J., 248, 265
Gilbert, Sylvester, Jr., 35
Ginsberg, Louis, 98, 246, 264, 266
Glatstein, Jacob, 243, 264
Goethe, Johann Wolfgang von, 85, 142, 169, 249
Goldsmith, Oliver, 61
Golightly, Cornelius L., 192
Golkenberg, Gary, 249
Grawn, Gertrude (Mrs. Carl B.), 95, 220
Greenland, Cyril, 266
Greenough, Horatio, 103
Gribbs, Roman S., 97
Grindley, Robert F., 95
Gullen, George E., Jr., 30, 195, 196, 198, 220
Gullen, Ruth (Mrs. George E.), 195, 196

Hackett, C. A., 244, 264
Hagman, Harlan L., 25, 26, 29, 30, 37, 226, 231, 234
Hall, William B., 225
Hamburger, Louis, 246
Hamburger, Samuel, 246
Hamburger Chair of Psychiatry in Pediatrics, 262
Hamming, Richard W., 247, 265
Harbach, Sheldon, 220
Harbison, Winfred A., 29, 30, 155, 226, 231, 237, 240, 257
Harding, Walter, 243, 264
Hargrave, Colleen Moore, 156
Harlow, Harry F., 243, 247, 264
Harper Hospital, 239, 241
Harris, Julie, 195
Harris, William Torrey, 24, 147, 177

Hartmann, Eduard von, 207
Harvard University, 228, 243, 247
Harvey, William, 11, 12
Hayward, Max, 265
Hecht, Anthony, 265
Heenan, Mrs. Earl I., 220
Henry, David D., 29
Heraclitus, 101
Hercules, 149
Herrold, Rose E., 157
Higbie, Carlton M., Jr., 222
Hilberry, Clarence B., 17, 20, 25, 26, 29, 30, 36, 41, 226, 227, 230, 234, 237, 240, 252, 256, 262
Hilberry, Norman, 243, 264
Hilberry, Ruth (Mrs. Clarence B.), 152, 252
Hilberry Classic Theatre, 251
Hippocrates, 12, 101, 148
Holden, James S., 41
Horn, Francis Henry, 248, 265
Hughes, Langston, 250
Hughlings-Jackson, John, 80
Hulbert, Henry S., 222
Hutchins, Robert Maynard, 24

Ikeda, Daisaku, 187
Iowa, University of, 243
Isaiah, 159

Jackson, Dauris, 225
Jakobson, Roman, 247, 265, 266
Jakobson, Svatava, 266
James, Thelma G., 49
James, William, 88, 174
Jefferson, Thomas, 57, 103, 171, 203, 235
Jefferson Avenue Presbyterian Church, 242
Jeffrey, Mildred, 225
Jehovah, 102
Jellema, William W., 112
Jennings, Charles G., 220
Jennings, Frank C., 266
Jennings Hospital, 241
Jesus, 159
John Scudder Foundation for Old People, 239, 241, 246
Johns Hopkins University, 67
Johnson, Arthur L., 200
Johnson, Harry, 266

Johnson, J. Stuart, 226
Johnson, Lyndon Baines, 36
Jordan, Vernon E., Jr., 198
Jorpes, J. Erik, 248, 265

Kang, Younghill, 248, 265
Kapustin, Max, 44
Kawakita, Yukio, 245
Keast, Mary (Mrs. William R.), 153
Keast, William R., 29, 96, 150, 153, 240,
    262, 263
Kelly, William H., 17
Kemp, Hardy A., 219
Kent, Caron, 243, 264
Keydel, Kurt R., 192, 225
Kierkegaard, Søren, 11, 123, 206
Kingswood School, 241
Kinney, Richard R., Jr., 154
Kirk, Grayson, 259
Kornegay, Francis A., 193, 194, 198

Lacan, Jacques, 266
Lafayette Clinic, 249, 262
Lansing, Albert I., 251
Lardas, Konstantinos, 247, 265
Lauriola, Luigi, 94
Leibniz, Gottfried Wilhelm, 27
Leidecker, Kurt F., 24, 57, 147
Leo M. Franklin Memorial Lectureship
    in Human Relations, 19, 45, 237
Leone, Leonard, 195
Levine, Philip, 247, 265
Lincoln, Abraham, 235
Linnaeus, Carolus, 124
Linnaeus, Nils Ingemarsson, 124
Lippman, Walter, 147
Littlefield Presbyterian Church, 251
Locke, Hubert, 239
Locke, John, 125, 258
Luce, Henry R., 243, 264
Luella Hannan Memorial Home, 238,
    241, 246, 262

Mabley, Mrs. T. Hollister, 220
McCormick, James P., 226
McGarrell, James, 266
McGregor Center, 22, 31, 220, 221, 223,
    239, 241, 242, 245, 249, 251
McGregor Fund, 22, 26, 31, 219, 220,
    221, 222, 227, 229, 252
McGregor Health Foundation, 220

McGregor Memorial Conference Center,
    248, 249
McGregor, Tracy W., 222
McKee, Jean, 225
McLean, Don W., 157
MacLeish, Archibald, 38
McMath, Francis C., 222
McMath, Neil C., 220, 222
Macy-Hoobler, Icie, 250
Mahalanobis, Mrs. P. C., 246, 264
Maire, Edward D., 157
Mann, Horace, 158
Mark, Saint, 159
Marshall, Charles Burton, 250
Matthews, Mrs. William E., 220
Mayor's Commission of Children and
    Youth, 239, 241, 242
Mayor's Committee for the Rehabilita-
    tion of Narcotic Addicts, 238, 241,
    242
Menge, Joseph W., 240
Menninger, Karl A., 194
Menninger, William C., 266
Merrill-Palmer Institute, 241, 247, 250
Metropolitan Hospital, 248
Michigan Academy of Pharmacy, 242
Michigan Civil Service Commission, 252
Michigan Medicine, 256
Michigan Society of Neurology and Psy-
    chiatry, 17, 242
Michigan State Medical Society, Mental
    Health Committee, 238, 241, 252
Michigan, University of, 219, 247, 248
Milan, University of. See Beluffi, Max
Miles Modern Poetry Committee, 38, 39,
    241, 246, 247
Monteith College, 228, 242
Moore, Kenneth L., 222

Naka, Syuzo, 243, 245, 264
National Institute of Mental Health, 250
Neal, W. Paul, Jr., 251
Neef, Arthur, 30, 226
Newhouse, Shelby, 250
Newman, John Henry, 23
Newnan, William L., 220
New School for Social Research (New
    York), 243
Newton, Isaac, 190
Nicol, Frank D., 220
Nobel, Alfred, 248

Norton, William J., 26, 31, 34, 219, 220, 222, 227
Norwood, George M., Jr., 199
Novalis, 168
Nu Sigma Nu, 242

Old Masters Program. See Purdue University
Osler, Sir William, 12, 191
Owen, Richard, 191

Paul, Saint, 165
Paynter, John W., 222
Penn, William, 64
Perring, Raymond T., 222
Pestalozzi, Johann Heinrich, 117
Petrini, Mario A., 220
Petty, Thomas A., 220
Peyre, Henri M., 241
Phi Beta Kappa, 248, 250
Phillips, Elliott H., 222
Pincus, Max J., 225
Pixley, Henry H., 226
Plato, 144, 159, 258, 261
Polish Millennium Conference, 266
Pool, Rosey E., 266
Prahl, Earl, 247, 265
Prismatic Club, 41, 242, 252
Purdue University, 237
Purdy, Flint, 252
Pythagoras, 101

Radbill, Samuel X., 199
Rankin, Paul T., 222, 250
Rapport, Victor A., 49, 226
Raskin, Herbert A., 97
Ravitz, Mel, 151
Rhode Island, University of, 248
Rice, Elmer, 265
Ripley, Anthony, 251
Romney, George W., 200
Romney, Lenore (Mrs. George W.), 200
Rose, Arnold M., 266
Rose, Benjamin M., 225
Rosecrance, Francis C., 226
Ross, Woodburn O., 226
Rousseau, Jean Jacques, 120
Rukeyser, Muriel, 247, 265
Rumble, Thomas C., 154

Sadler, H. Harrison, 220

St. John, Robert, 47, 266
Saint Paul's Cathedral, 242
Salchow, Paul T., 220
Samuel and Louis Hamburger Foundation, 246
Sandburg, Carl, 239
Sargent, Douglas A., 249
Sargent, Emilie G., 95, 220
Schelling, Friedrich Wilhelm Joseph von, 169
Schlichting, L. G. A., 266
Schueller, Herbert M., 237, 250
Schwartz, Louis A., 220
Scott, Gordon H., 35, 220, 226, 240, 252, 262
Seegers, Arthur, 266
Seegers, Walter H., 31, 93, 95, 98, 220
Seneca, Lucius Annaeus, 87
Sexton, James H., 220
Shakespeare, William, 73, 85, 245, 248, 252
Shakespeare Quadricentennial Committee, 241
Shelden, W. Warren, 222
Sibille, Michael R., 153
Simon, Uriel, 266
Singer, Isaac Bashevis, 44, 265
Sladen, Frank J., 220, 222, 250
Smith, John (Cambridge Platonist), 142
Smith, Lauren H., 199
Smuts, Jan Christian, 138
Snodgrass, William D., 38, 264
Snow, Gregory, 45
Snow, Wilbert, 45, 239, 243, 247, 265
Socrates, 236
Sokolowski, Alfred H., 225
Spender, Stephen, 247, 265
Spinoza, Baruch, 58, 127
Stafford, William, 247, 265
Stagner, Ross, 46
Staley, John W., 222
Stanford, W. B., 266
Stapleton Reading Room, dedication of, 157
Stapp, John P., 266
State University Teachers College (New York), 243
Stearns, Martin, 49
Sterba, Editha, 220
Stewart, Harold E., 226
Stockmeyer, Norman O., 99, 193, 225

Strong, Homer D., 92
Stumpf, Carl, 174
Sweeney, Donald N., Jr., 222

Thomas Jefferson University, 57, 199
Thomas, Owen E., 226
Thoreau, Henry David, 236
Thurber, Cleveland, 31, 222
Tilley, George C., 220
Tilley, Thomas C., 220
Tolstoy, Lev Nikolayevich, 235
Torch Program, 248
Travis, Lee Edward, 46, 243, 264, 266
Trzecialkowska, Anna, 265
Tufford, Norman, 219
Tworkov, Jack, 266

United Nations, 251
United States Supreme Court, 251
Untermeyer, Louis, 40, 247, 265
Urzidil, Johannes, 266

Van der Veen, Adrian, 243, 264
Van Doren, Mark, 37, 38, 243, 264
Veterans Administration Hospital, 238, 241
Vidor, King, 77, 93, 156
Virgil, 29
Virginia, University of, 203

Wachsmann, Klaus P., 265
Wagg, Charles F., 250
Walker, Alice H., 220
Watson, John B., 67

Watson, Maud E., 219
Wayne County Medical Society, 241, 251
Wayne State University, 17–26, 56, 74, 228, 234, 239, 241, 247, 256, 259; Education Conference, Planning Committee, 234, 235, 239; Press, 233, 234, 238, 241, 242, 245, 257, 262; School of Medicine, 219, 230, 237, 239, 241, 242, 246, 247, 249, 252; Social Committee, 238; Women of Wayne, 238
Wertheimer, Max, 29
Wesley Foundation, 242
Whaley, Randall, 226
Wharton, Clifton R., Jr., 201
Wheat, Renville, 222
White, Clair A., 225
White, Kirby B., 222
White, William Alanson, 56
Whitney M. Young, Jr. Memorial Lecture Series, 192, 193, 194, 197, 198
Whittaker, Alfred H., 99, 157, 225
Will, Roy T., 250
William Beaumont Society, 241, 242, 262
Wilson, Stephen, 226
Wisconsin, University of, 243, 247
Woodcock, Leonard, 197, 225
Wright, Charles H., 96
Wyandotte, City of, 242

Yajnavalkya, 61
Young Men's Christian Association of Metropolitan Detroit, 241

Zabriskie, Mrs. Charles C., 220

COLOPHON

John M. Dorsey (1900–1978) received his M.D. degree from the University
of Iowa in 1925 and became chairman of the Department of Psychiatry at
Wayne University in 1946. He was appointed Wayne's first University Professor in 1961, and University Professor Emeritus in 1971, continuing active in his post until the time of his death, August 6, 1978.

The manuscript was prepared for publication by Barbara Woodward. The
book was designed by Gary Gore. The typeface for the text is VIP's Baskerville, based on an original design by John Baskerville in the eighteenth
century, and the display face is Goudy Old Style, designed by Frederic W.
Goudy about 1915.

The text is printed on Edwards Brothers' Arbor text paper. The book is
bound in Joanna Mills' Arrestox B over binder's boards. Manufactured in
the United States of America.